The Bedside
'GUARDIAN'
33

'Haven't I seen you on television?'

29 March, 1984

The Bedside 'GUARDIAN' 33

A selection from The 'Guardian' 1983–84

Edited by
W. L. WEBB

With an Introduction by
Peter Ustinov

Cartoons by

Gibbard
Bryan McAllister
Peter Clarke

COLLINS
8 Grafton Street, London W1
1984

William Collins Sons & Co. Ltd
London · Glasgow · Sydney · Auckland
Toronto · Johannesburg

British Library Cataloguing in Publication Data

The Bedside Guardian. – 33
I. English essays – Periodicals
082'.05   PR1361

ISBN 0–00–217365–4

First published 1984
© Guardian Newspapers 1984

Photoset in Linotron Plantin by
Rowland Phototypesetting Ltd, Bury St Edmunds, Suffolk
Made and printed in Great Britain by
Robert Hartnoll Ltd, Bodmin

Introduction

Foolishly, I decided that a trip on my ancient ketch, 1929 with no mod cons, would be the ideal place to contemplate the Introduction of the 1984 *Bedside Guardian*. Even in steadier times I have never had recourse to bedside books, since insomnia is not one of my pleasures, but within earshot of the terrible pulse of the sea, as raucous, wheezing and irregular as that of an ageing giant, the contemplation of anything but survival was clearly and miserably impossible.

Now that I am on dry land, I ask myself with a kind of urgent insistence what masochistic folly in human nature it is which makes us expose ourselves to such intense discomfort under the guise of indefinable delight. The adventure has not yet receded, since the panting of the diesel engine is still throbbing in my ear, and the cool tiles of the hotel floor sway playfully from side to side, changing their dimensions. Perhaps the necessity to clear the mind of everything but fundamentals lies at the base of such mock-heroics, for which we must dress up with comic hats and slippery yellow coats much as crusaders and other historic trouble-makers dressed up to perform their mischief. Perhaps the illusion of risk-taking is much like a cure, a period of fasting as a needed self-denial before the exquisite rediscovery of food. And food includes, of course, food for thought.

I was told by my father, who was a journalist, that the *Guardian* was the best of British papers. At least, that was its reputation among foreign correspondents in the twenties. It is one of the few things I was told as a boy which I still believe. The reasons for this are not a desire for base flattery, nor yet a hot-headed wish to antagonize all the others, but merely a recognition that, like a good conversationalist, the *Guardian* gives a real impression of at least having listened before it talks. There is a pertinent and powerful piece about just such an obligation towards free speech, and its dependence on accurate

5

assessment of opposing views, by Jill Tweedie in the pages of this volume.

The past editions of these *Bedside Guardians* are redolent of the years in which they were compiled. In other words they have dated, as news itself dates, but they supply an instant nostalgia for moments and concerns which are still within very recent memory. It is therefore more than natural that the contents of this volume are to a certain extent dominated by the personality of Mrs Thatcher. Nobody who has met her can fail to detect a very evident personal charm, and even, dare I say it, a considerable vulnerability. At times, it seems, she is a victim of her own reputation for ironness, a quality which had already betrayed the Duke of Wellington as a politician. However, things have changed since then. The Americans, with all that is advantageous and disreputable in a free society, have set a cracking pace in technical innovation. There are thousands of different methods of instant communication. All that has not improved is the quality of what we say to one another. And every now and then an event occurs which reminds us that only an inch beneath the surface of the streamline lie prejudices of an epoch we might have wished long past.

Under normal circumstances, Mrs Thatcher's expressed desire for a return to Victorian values appears no more than a conservative desire for order, although all the anomalies of *Nicholas Nickleby* and the Industrial Revolution were also intrinsic elements in such values. She is no doubt unaware, and would scoff incredulously if told, that the most militant harbinger of Victorian values in this day and age is the Soviet Union. There is discipline on a grand scale, obedience, an insistence on high standards of personal morality (as difficult to divorce from hypocrisy as is the tawdry from indiscriminate freedom), and an immobility as dangerous as is, at times, American mobility.

Perhaps it could be said that the great danger today is the fact that whereas the means for destruction at our disposal increase by the hour, these means are almost exclusively in the hands of governments which are essentially conservative by nature, such as those of the United States and the Soviet Union.

And it is at moments of local crisis that the hideous possibilities of real crisis are revealed in all their sickening insanity. The incident of the Falkland Islands set us momentarily far further into history than the Victorians and their gunboats; Raleigh and Drake set sail once again to singe what was left of the King of Spain's sparse beard. Certainly such a reaction was essential on the part of Britain in response to an absurdly reckless initiative by Argentina, but the effect it had on the victor was as regrettable as humiliation on the enemy. When a certain newspaper was able to report the sinking of an obsolete warship with a huge headline, 'GOTCHA', then it could be thought that war was merely an extension of the World Cup, and that conflict was still a question of winning and losing, and, if the worst came to the worst, of the return match. In the flush of victory, it appeared that Britain had rediscovered some ancient vitality, and that the future confrontation with the Soviet Union would be merely an extension of the Falklands incident, on, admittedly, a slightly larger scale.

Even the United States, streaking into the future with its wonderful capacity for controlled negligence, was suddenly reined in full gallop by the atrocious massacre in Beirut, and rediscovered its confidence by a totally disproportionate invasion of Grenada at the urgent invitation of other Caribbean countries (where have we heard this before?). Certainly, if the world were as simple a place as President Reagan imagines it to be, he would be a very great President indeed. Unfortunately the script of reality can be neither approved nor understood by the Front Office.

I, for one, will never forget the *Guardian* leader on this subject. I cut it out, and kept it in my pocket as an anchor of sanity. I was in the United States at the time, and it seemed to me that this massive nation had suddenly become nothing but a vast safety-valve, in which everybody talked and nobody listened. All through the night, the airwaves throbbed with phoned-in opinion, cranks without a moderating or civilizing influence on their bedside tables choking with righteous anger and expressing their nonsense with the eloquence of superannuated sergeants. Happily there were others, but not many, for not everyone has the patience or inclination to vent their views at four o'clock in the morning.

All this was depressing enough, but if the listener happened to know Grenada, referred to by George Schultz on a casual fact-finding mission as a piece of real estate, then the pomp applied to these particular circumstances became nothing less than grotesque. The final grace-notes of this silliest and saddest of symphonies was supplied by the cause of original Grenadan revolution, Sir Eric Gairy, now back in his fiefdom, who smilingly suggested that the airport, almost completed by the Cubans, should be named the Ronald Reagan International Airport. Prosaic justice.

It would be churlish to pick out favourites among the contributors to what now read as a rich series of informed essays. The quality which pervades them all is a degree of irony and often a scathing detachment, which is a very English way with demolition. They presuppose a degree of intelligence in the reader, which is far safer these days than to presume that the degree of stupidity is average. If I must pick (and pick I must) a voice from among the general brilliance, then it has to be that of James Cameron, who combines the self-confidence of a major prophet with the self-deprecation of a minor one, and who has the added, irritating habit of expressing the opinions of a lucid and exasperated person more eloquently, more succinctly and even, more beautifully, than this or any other reader is capable of doing. He discourages by his mastery of his chosen art-form, and exhilarates by proving the impossible, that the liberal spirit can be militant and that tolerance and equanimity can be sharper weapons than mere rhetoric of left or right.

Now that I have been introduced to the highly concentrated pleasures of this book, especially after my spiritual purification by rough waters, I realise that my future as an insomniac is assured, for there is nothing less calculated to induce sleep than the *Bedside Guardian*.

PETER USTINOV

Corn this happy morning

'And a Very Good Morning to you! It is Monday, June 25, and you are reading the *Guardian*.' (God, look at that lot out there, half asleep in their singlets. Give them a quick flash of the Heartbreak Budgie. Where's the Heartbreak Budgie . . . who's got the . . . for chrissake who put the Heartbreak Budgie beside the Tug-Of-Love Pussy?)

Breakfast television leans rather heavily on animals and none was leaned on more heavily than a snail on TV-am. You had to get up pretty early on a Sunday to catch him. When, in fact, the snail was on the thorn. He had been sitting on a thorn when Jon Miller took him to TV-am on the specious excuse of getting him into show business. 'Look, he's climbing out to see what it's like being in a studio.' The studio was evidently a nasty shock. 'Oh dear, he's fallen off my finger. I promise you that hasn't hurt him,' lied Miller (the plucky gastropod waved a dazed antenna). Miller then put him beside a monstrous tropical snail. 'Look at the size of that one! He's having a feel. He's going right over him! It's as though he's swallowed him! He's got right on top of him! It's as though he's swallowed him! He's got right on top of him! He LIKES him,' cried Miller, wrenching the combatants apart with difficulty. 'Big Snail says "Goodbye! Have a good breakfast everybody!"'

The presenters of *Good Morning Britain* are kept pretty busy assuring viewers that various vermin have not died in the night. Roland Rat was, apparently, whacked to death over breakfast and when I arrived *Good Morning Britain* was getting it in the neck from Britain's mothers: 'I have just spent half an hour explaining to my 2½-year-old that Roland Rat is alive and well.'

He is? Oh well, never mind.

What, we must ask, was it that the snail saw in the TV-am studio which made him lose hold and hurtle to the floor with a hoarse cry. Blood probably. I have not watched *Good Morning Britain* for a year or so and it's as if something that *eats* people

9

had been through there. Anna, Angela, Michael, Robert, Greg have all departed in dudgeon. The dudgeon, you might say, was ever at the door with its engine running.

Back at *Breakfast Time* the same old BBC bottoms are on the burgundy sofas. Many a purple cow must have laid down its hide for those sofas. Frank Bough is still playing that virtually discontinued role, the BBC Uncle. Selina Scott, I was concerned to see, was palely puffy, like Krystle Carrington discovering that money cannot buy happiness. This comes of cavorting around on Normandy beaches in a cape, looking like the Winged Victory of SW1, instead of wearing, as Dame Vera Lynn wisely advised, winter woollies. By mid-week ('Selina's throat has caught up with her') she had vanished, a victim of the reckless habit of going out before the streets are aired.

You became quite caught up in the welfare of this bronchial dawn chorus. Russell Grant's Mum's feet *burst* on us on Monday: 'They've come up like a barrel!' On Tuesday they were worse: 'She can't get out! They're feeding her through the window with a hosepipe.' By Wednesday, thank God, all was well: 'She's so pleased she can go to Sainsbury's.' In my view she would be safer at home.

On *Good Morning Britain* Benny Green, jogging as part of 'A campaign to make the nation fitter', demonstrated how a middle-aged media man can imitate the action of the impala when about to be run over by a car.

During the D-day anniversary coverage a nurse said mistily that *Good Morning Britain* reminded her of the dark days of the war. She may have been referring to the high mortality or the almost hysterically high spirits. There is a suggestion of people running round with hats on sticks to give the impression of a cast of thousands. When the famous five disintegrated in the Big Bang (thought to be caused by sexual chemistry) Lord Mars said, as I remember, that it had been like hiring the RSC to do *Blue Peter*. Now it is like watching *Blue Peter* tackle *Timon of Athens*.

Hardly anyone looks old enough to vote. They face each frightful day with fits of giggles and cheerful insults. It sounds, if you shut your eyes, a little like *Rowan and Martin's Laugh-In*. Guests often seem inclined to shut their eyes.

'I'd rather,' said Spike Milligan during a particular chaotic edition, 'be in a phone box in Reading.' Rustie Lee, who has the fattest laugh on television, was busily burning spaghetti. 'Have we,' asked Milligan, white lipped, 'got to *eat* this?' The next day, in 'A historic record-breaking attempt here on TV-am', Donne Maiello tried to eat 100 yards of spaghetti in 21.7 secs. There seemed eerily more spaghetti around at the end than at the beginning. Gerard Kenny's wife clung horrified to her husband. Roger Vadim, who takes the stomach seriously, was sympathetique: 'I imagine the stomach was *stretched*.' Worse things happen in Japan. Nick Hayward said he ate a live fish on Japanese television. 'It was wriggling about on the plate.'

But not much worse. Of the awfulness of Saturdays with poor Commander Philpott doing the weather dressed as Superman in crimson knickers, Bob Carolgees giving his impression of a ferret down the trousers and a sudden influx of tranvestites in tutus I Shall Not Speak.

James Fox, actor and lay missionary, who was only there to plug his book, looked incapable of speech. Breakfast TV is infested with authors. Leslie Thomas, Virginia Wade, Bryan Forbes, Richie Benaud, Roger Vadim, Jonathan Gathorne-Hardy (who arrived windswept at *Breakfast Time* having legged it lithely from *Good Morning Britain*), Norris McWhirter, Sammy Kahn, Sharron Davies, former Chief Constable John Alderson and 'Sixties trouser-splitting sensation P. J. Proby' all tore off their whiskers in the course of the week and revealed themselves as authors. That their audience would, in the case of *Good Morning Britain*, have some difficulty spraying its own name did not seem to discourage them.

The TV critic of *Good Morning Britain* has not, of course, read *King Lear*. 'I understand it's one of Shakespeare's most celebrated tragedies. Murder, madness, common-or-garden family life really. 'Ere's Lord Olivier 'aving a pretty torrid time under the Shah.' ('Blow wind and crack your cheeks!' cried Lord Olivier under the shower). 'Act 4 Scene I,' said Greaves triumphantly: 'I looked it up. Leeds United 3,' he added. He looked it up wrong, but I had to prise myself away from the notion of Shakespeare played as soccer.

'Our show is Pumpernickel Raisin,' said James Sikking, referring to *Hill Street Blues* (and demonstrating both the charm of a lazy, laid-back manner and the sea-change English suffers crossing the Atlantic). 'It has texture and density.' On the Pumpernickel scale, breakfast television is Popcorn. Palatable, professional popcorn at the BBC. Cheap corn at TV-am which Lynne Faulds Wood, their excellent consumer guide, would expose if it came in plastic bags.

I make certain allowances for the summer. Both programmes assumed their audience was going if not gone. Don't soak your dentures in the local water, watch out for tropical snails, and buy a Drive Alert. You hook this over your ear and, if your head drops forward, it rings. Invaluable also while watching breakfast TV.

And now can anyone tell me how to stop waking up at 6.30 a.m.?

25 June, 1984   **Nancy Banks-Smith**

Rejoice again – or at least buck up

The 1983 Conservative Party conference convened in Blackpool yesterday and loyally rallied round the politician in the controversial breach of promise case. Yes, they cheered Mrs Margaret Thatcher, even though millions of voters are claiming that she has left them in the lurch. At times like this you know who your friends are.

The only other topics which caught the conference's imagination on anything like the same scale were capital punishment and the Trade and Industry Secretary, Mr Cecil Parkinson – the mention of whose very name was enough to start a spontaneous surge of applause. In its way it is very encouraging. Hanging is an old favourite here, but trade and industry are all too often neglected.

What Mrs Thatcher, the rope and Mr Parkinson had in common was that they were not on yesterday's agenda; not even in town in Mr Parkinson's case. This gave them a great advantage over more lack-lustre colleagues and topics which were.

A succession of ministerial bigwigs, including the Home Secretary, Mr Leon Brittan, and the new boy chairman of the party, Mr John Selwyn Gummer, tried to sweep the conference off its feet. But the conference remained earthbound. This year it is unexpectedly overshadowed by falling popularity, infiltration by the Militarist Tendency and the terrifying burden of now having nearly 400 MPs, all of them with private lives and secretaries.

One could tell by the way they started the proceedings with such a dispirited rendering of the South Georgia Hymn – 'Rejoice again, I say Rejoice' – that it will take an injection of Heseltine straight into the veins to buck them up later this morning.

Meanwhile we had Mr Peter Rees of the Treasury making his first – and possibly last – cabinet speech about taxation. After Mr Rees – and possibly after his cabinet seat – came Mr Ian Gow, confidently winding up a housing debate which included the quintessential Tory line: 'Speaking as a person who started married life in a tent. . . .'

And so it went on . . . indignant, reasonable, complacent. Representatives here who dare to oppose motions generally do so because 'it does not go far enough'. Occasionally it goes too far, but Tory conferences do not take what Mr Brittan later called 'detailed words' too literally – unlike Labour. The whingeing here is also more polite, though no less penetrating.

True, in the general tedium the conference did give a standing ovation to Mr Gummer for his competent but unremarkable first chairman's speech. But this was out of kindness of heart. Whatever doubts the activists have about the Youth Training Scheme it is party policy and up to now Mr Gummer has only had odd dead end jobs writing speeches for Prime Ministers. He has never had a job with real security. This one may only last six months but it is work experience and could lead to a real job.

On yesterday's evidence Mr Gummer would make a good vicar.

Strangely enough it was Canon Gummer himself who kept drawing our attention to his most striking disparity. Mr Gummer is 43, but he looks and sounds about 17 and what comes out suggests that he has been 52 since he was eight.

He began a shade defensively by recalling that he joined Gravesend YCs 26 years ago, a precociously middle aged thing to do. Next he claimed to have remembered at the time Mr Attlee's ill-fated ground nut scheme, when he must have been about nine, the little creep. Finally, he reminisced about his Mum's reaction to the Tory election victory of 1951. 'Well, I feel much freer today,' Mrs Gummer had told her infant son. Exactly. And look where it led to: the permissive society, or trade and industry as it is known here this week.

'You can see how easily it could happen – staying late at the office typing out all those speeches about the family unit and a return to Victorian values.'

7 October, 1983

With no sense of irony the law and order debate subsequently decided that this permissiveness, this lack of respect for family life and traditional values was one of the causes of the crime wave. Menacing references to the ultimate deterrent went down extremely well, but the hangers did not have it all their own way. Several speakers attempted to smuggle liberal penal notions into the debate disguised as something else – like files in fruit cakes going into Wormwood Scrubs. The idea was that they would not be noticed among the other fruit cakes.

Mr Brittan himself attempted this technique, only a pale imitation of the ratlike cunning of the late Lord Whitelaw, but certainly better than his speech in the Commons debate on hanging. Unfortunately he gave them the good news, about interfering with the judiciary, first (the judges may yet need Ken Livingstone to save them), and the bad news about emptying the prisons of minor offenders later.

For once, the conference cottoned on and heard him out in rather cool silence. But at least they did not lynch him. There was a standing ovation at the end, not for Mr Brittan but for the tea room.

12 October, 1983   **Michael White**

Great day for a media spectacle

'Great day for you,' said the chief inspector, very friendly, looking up at the blue sky and then addressing a group of striking miners who were about to lead a protest march through Nottingham, 'so let's see a smile on your faces, not hatred in your eyes. Don't look as though you've crawled out from under stones.' This was taken, I think the expression is, in good part. It was a scene from an archaic British film, probably in black and white – Jack Warner bobby sharing a joke with British workmen.

And yet later, when the 2,000 or so demonstrators reached their mass rally in the city centre, they roared their applause on being told this was full frontal class war, and that if the police went on using strangleholds on pickets, then we should see a murder committed by police in broad daylight.

Later, too, miners fought bitterly among themselves, but at the start, as they assembled at Forest Park, where Goose Fair is held, all was peace. The banner of Houghton main colliery bore a portrait of Clement Attlee. The banner of Bolsover called for progress and welfare and showed white flannelled miners playing bowls, tennis, and cricket.

The 31 miners from Kent, who, having been stopped by police at the Dartford tunnel, had left their cars behind and walked, taking 10 days, said they had not been harassed on the way, though they thought this was because the Tories wanted to

'Me too, we were going to picket in Nottinghamshire, took a wrong turning trying to evade the police, found ourselves in the middle of a demonstration in Liverpool, finally headed south again, got stopped on the M4 because they thought we were protesting against cruise, tried to avoid the GLC protest in the centre of London and have ended up here.'

30 March, 1984

keep them out of the media. Only one had been arrested, Mr Stan Matthew Garnett, and he showed around the charge sheet on which the Herts Constabulary had booked him for wilfully obstructing the Queen's highway. He said all the others had been on the pavement at the time.

Many miners had been put up by local families the night before. Mr John Higgins, of Doncaster, wanted me to write that Chris and Janice Knight, of 268 The Wells Road, Nottingham, had given him new shoes, jeans, underpants and socks. As the procession formed up, two men, shaking hands, greeted each other as 'Comrade!' which it struck me was the first time I had heard the word used in that way, off a public platform. Members of the Workers' Revolutionary Party sold copies of their paper, *News Line*, which called Mrs Thatcher Bonaparte and ended with this appeal: 'Smash Thatcher's Bonapartist dictatorship: Build the *News Line* circulation!'

The union's own literature was not so imaginative. A leaflet from the Sheffield Miners' Support Group simply asked for money for strikers' families, and made what sounded like a Tourist Board invitation to 'visit Nottinghamshire and experience the police state.' There was also in this pamphlet, a cartoon which showed a policeman, handcuffs in hand, telling a pregnant woman, 'I am arresting you because I have reason to believe that you intend giving birth to a son who will grow up to be a Kent miner, who will then proceed to go picketing in the North of England.'

A copy of this was given to one of the policemen standing by, who said thank you, carefully folded it, and put it in his pocket.

The miners took off for their two-mile walk, led by the men of Kent, who told the population of Nottingham, through loudhailers, to get up off their knees and bite. Any able bodied men encountered on the way, who declined an invitation to join the march, were called scabs, a photographer was told, again over the loudhailer, that he would be lynched, but was not, and every now and again a policeman was greeted with cries of Sieg Heil. The amiable chief inspector kept on walking in front of the leaders, and kept smiling.

The indifferent people in the streets were then told that it didn't matter whether they were company directors or miners,

Mrs Thatcher was out to smash them all, and on the dole they would all be socialists. And had they noticed how there were fewer buses these days? Soon there wouldn't be any buses any more.

Having reached the Old Market square, the marchers listened to speeches for an hour. This in the middle of a busy shopping centre, and it was extraordinary that hardly anyone stopped to listen, even out of curiosity. Prosperous Nottingham wanted to be seen to have nothing to do with it all. The local afternoon paper bore the headline 'Siege City', but that was evident nonsense.

Then the demonstrators moved off to the Albert Hall, which belongs to the Methodist Mission, and as soon as they got there the mood changed. There were some older men, but the marchers were mostly young, and they began to look like a football crowd. They ran through the open doors of the hall, scrambled for seats, then changed their minds and scrambled for other seats in other parts of the hall. Two men just jumped from the balcony into the stalls.

A TV camera was spotted, and at once there was a chant of 'Get out, you bums, get out,' and 'Press out, Press out.' This was a ritual chant. The miners turned on a TV crew and ran them out. Arthur Scargill himself was very nearly shouted down when he intervened.

Mr Scargill and Mr Benn were to be the principal speakers, but four others spoke first, though they were barely given a hearing.

Their speeches were denunciations. The Attorney-General was called infamous; Lord Gormley was hissed; the Leader of the Labour Party (not named) was scornfully said to be answering the Tory call; Nottinghamshire miners still working were swine, Judases, and renegades; and Mr MacGregor, chairman of the Coal Board, was said never to have dissociated himself from the shooting of some American miners a few years ago. This was full frontal class war. (Cheers.) If this went on police would commit a murder.

A voice was raised to defend Nottinghamshire miners, at which scuffles broke out, and then scattered fights, and amid the pandemonium a man on the platform, having noticed a camera recording this, hurled himself off the platform and down the aisle to get at the cameraman. Mr Scargill again tried to restore some order, this time shouting through a loudhailer, but even with that it was three minutes before he could be heard.

'We are,' he said, 'providing a spectacle for the media.' This placated no one. The miners, both in the hall and on the march beforehand, expressed without exception, so far as I heard, a deep conviction that the Press and television are manipulated by the Tory government. It took all of Mr Scargill's popularity, strength of will and strength of voice, amplified by the loud-hailer, to produce anything like order, and still sporadic scuffles continued.

There was not quiet even when Mr Benn rose to speak. He is the most eloquent and reasoned of speakers, but even he did not get an attentive hearing. The audience was by then just picking up a phrase now and then and cheering it.

In all, Mr Benn spoke more briefly than I can remember him doing and ended with these words: 'If you stop struggling, they'll take it all from you.' (Cheers.)

To put together an account consisting of phrases from speeches, with a running commentary of disturbances, looks most unfair. But to present any coherent account of the speeches made would be much more misleading, because such an account would have to be made coherent. The speeches I have so far reported were not, with the exception of Mr Benn's, coherent at all. This is partly because the audience would not let the speakers be heard. Only bits here and there were audible. Even then, groups round the hall hardly listened at all, but engaged in their own conversations, arguments, and skirmishes.

This was a rally of mainly young men, who had been on the picket lines most of the week, who feel a sense of bitter injustice, who want a social revolution, who really believe this is a police state, and who, having been on strike for five weeks, are also broke. They feel betrayed by everybody – by a Tory government whose good faith they could not possibly concede or consider, by Mr Kinnock because he wants a ballot, by other miners who are not on strike, and by Joe Gormley, who spent his life working for them.

In this contempt of Lord Gormley, always scornfully referred to by his title, they are encouraged by Mr Scargill, who asserts that the incentive scheme accepted by Gormley divided man from man and pit from pit. Equality is everything. Anyway, the young miners in the Albert Hall had come to hear Mr Scargill, and most skilfully he spoke.

He had, he said, been asked on television whether the young miners were not different from the old ones. Well, he had replied, yes they were. The young miners of this country (he told the young miners in the Albert Hall) represented the finest in trade unionism. (Applause.) Having praised, he then asked for help. Loyalty worked two ways: at the end of the day, when the Coal Board told him he was getting nothing, he had a right to come and ask his members for their support. (Cheers.)

And here Mr Scargill told the story he has told before, how, after the historic struggle of 1972, a miner in his 80s had come up to him in the street, in a Yorkshire town, and said, with tears in his eyes, 'I want to thank you for wiping out the memory of 1926.'

There was a hesitation in the applause. Mr Scargill's allusion had not been taken by everyone, and he briefly explained about the General Strike of 1926. Then he went to the future. In a year's time, he said, they would look back and see how they won their fight to preserve their loyalty, dignity, and self respect.

Those words got the loudest applause of the day, and then the audience took up the chant of 'Arthur Scargill, Arthur Scargill, we'll support you evermore, evermore,' which is sung to the tune which usually goes, on football grounds, to the words of the hymn 'Bread of Heaven'.

16 April, 1984   **Terry Coleman**

All together now

While I can still bring myself to write the accursed numerals, let me denounce the year, the book, the image, the cliché 1984.

In my opinion, if after all this I can still claim to have one, 1984 has already dragged on rather too long. Three days can be an eternity of saying exactly the same things to the same people, when the convivial smile on the weary face becomes a sort of paralysis, like a TV comedian's.

Why can we not abolish January for ever? Can we be allowed to forget George Orwell for a minute or two? We all know that Orwell chose 1984 as his apocalyptic date by the merest chance, simply juggling the figures of the year in which he wrote it, 1948. George Orwell was a great and good man, and also shrewd enough to die soon thereafter, so that 1984 would haunt us, not him.

I always thought that his prophecy was rather mild anyway. Big Brother was more daunting but less boring than Small Sister, and I believe I would rather be bullied by a brute than patronised by a prig. Lord forgive me, but I would almost rather have the bang than the whimper.

By now the serious prophets have had their serious say, the analysts have defined their terms of reasoning, the moralists have moralised and the pessimists have pessimised; the optimists have understandably kept their mouths shut, for fear of ridicule.

I am none of those things, or rather I try to be all at once, thus obviously succeeding in none. Even as a prophet of woe I am beginning to slip, since just as in the kingdom of the blind the one-eyed man is king, so in a world of Cassandras you have to be merry to be noticed, and right now I feel as sanguine as a dinosaur contemplating the future of his grandchildren.

This is not, I hope, to be taken too seriously, except indirectly. I am regretting nothing, except perhaps the evident disappearance of my trade. I distinctly recognise 1984 as the year when people stopped learning how to read and write.

The prospect is not new, and indeed is a great bore for those who do not write for a living. But it saddens me to imagine the ghost of the late William Caxton turning in his grave when he sees the craft he gave us five centuries ago surrendering to horrible little machines that take education back to the images of the cave-men.

Ask any child or teenager almost anything now and he reaches into his *pocket*, not his memory, for the little machine with the appropriate button that will have the answer. He will not look for a book, for that will be as tiresome as hunting for a quill pen. For his leisure he will take up one of the abominable machines that play his games for him on a screen.

Obviously 1984 will not see the end of the written word, but the writing trade is on a life-support machine. Writers are now with the flint-knappers, architects, and owners of dancing bears, a species hastening to extinction. George Orwell's sinister Newspeak will soon give way to Nospeak.

I can hardly be sentimental about this: I was educated up to about the five-times-table level, and for anything more complex I go to my grandchildren—or perhaps one day to my computer.

I have the illusion that I read better than I hear. To this day I would far rather read a page of Shakespeare than hear him spoken even by Olivier. Even he sometimes gives the wrong values to phrases that I feel belong to me. I don't want to *hear* the words, I want to *see* them. So when everything is on cassette I shall give up, until the books wear out.

I have a cassette of some readings I did for a TV programme long ago. I play it once a year when I want to humble myself. The scripts were not at all bad, and the recording sounds like Robin Day or someone. The shoe-maker should stick to his last, and the scribbler to his pencil.

I cannot end this first column of a brave new year on a note of such makeshift modesty. Yesterday I got a letter from a stranger in San Cristobal, Venezuela, of all places—mysteriously to my home address (I must watch the street for Venezuelan spies):

'Dear Mister. I am a writer and a poet, and very soon the world will know my name and I will be a celebrity. Mister C., I am very interested to become your friend and the possible meeting with your person. Sincerely and truly, Eduardo Mendez Uzcategui.'

Well, Senor Mendez, my person is at your disposal any time, with or without your celebrity. I am honoured. Don't ring us, we'll ring you. Next time I'm in Venezuela.

Meanwhile, a good New Year to one and all—or almost all.

3 January, 1984   **James Cameron**

Mother Courage and the council

This is a brief summary of one year in the life of a woman I shall call Mrs London.

At the beginning of the year Mr London takes himself off, leaving his wife and two small boys in the squat where they were living. Unable to cope on her own there, Mrs London moves herself and children into her mother's small flat and goes onto supplementary benefit. Over-crowding soon leads to quarrels and homelessness again. The council put Mrs London and the boys into a small hotel.

Two months later, the family is moved into temporary accommodation. The roof leaks, there is no heating, there are rats. Under constant pressure from Mrs London, the council offer her two flats on their list. She refuses both. Eventually, reluctantly, she accepts a third, which the council decorate for her. They ask her frequently if she knows where her husband is so that they may extract maintenance from him but Mrs London says she has no idea of his whereabouts.

After three months, Mrs London applies to move again. The flat is too far from the children's school and she is lonely, she has no friends nearby. The council say she must change the children's school and she refuses – they are happy there. Mrs London starts working four days a week washing up in a restaurant but she does not tell the council. At last, they find her a garden maisonette in the district she wants.

Everything pleases Mrs London but she does not care for the wallpaper. She tears it off before the council visit and they agree to redecorate. She is also given a new cooker and a new refrigerator. The London family is settled now. The year's bill for settling them (hotel costs, three furniture removals and two house decorations) comes to approximately £2,500. This does not, of course, include Mrs London's benefits or any of the costs of the bureaucratic process involved.

The bald facts of this true-life case are of the kind that enrage many people. Furiously, they fire off letters to local councillors, MPs and assorted newspapers about scroungers and parasites before they gallop into the arms of Mrs Thatcher. When I first became involved in Mrs London's life, the facts didn't do my blood pressure a lot of good either. The Blimpish part of me began to snort with indignation.

Secret voices in my head harangued me along the lines of 'Who's paying for all this, then? Us, that's who.' I became even more vexed when Mrs London confided her hearty dislike of the council and all its works. The council! Her benefactor, her sole support! The very people who looked after her so infinitely better than the man who had solemnly vowed to keep her till death did them part! And then, to cap it all, Mrs London informed me on election day that she had voted Conservative. One in the eye, she said, for that lot. The Labour council. The Blimps reared up and charged.

However, further talks with Mrs London revealed the web of tangled motives, emotions and fears that now seems to me to lie at the heart of many of the problems of the Welfare State and socialism itself. It soon became clear that no one had ever thought to explain to Mrs London, as a schoolgirl, how her society worked. Therefore, she has no idea of how anything is financed or where she fits in the scheme of things. She absorbed the message that patriotism was the Queen and England versus the world, not how England manages her internal affairs. In her view, she has one overwhelming duty in life – to provide her children with the most of whatever was going. And that meant wresting it from the council. Tirelessly she nagged them, staunchly she harassed them, doggedly she exploited every loophole in the system. She is Mother Courage doing battle with the Enemy that tries to deny her babies what they need. Each deception practised, she sees as a survival tactic. The idea of honesty vis-à-vis this Enemy is obviously absurd.

It turns out that, though she certainly quarrelled with her mother, they agreed on her eviction, since in what other way could she begin the struggle for a home of her own? It also turns out that she knows where her husband is but will not tell the council because he sometimes gives her money. If she told, they would cut off her benefits, and she cannot rely on him. Best not rock the boat. Also, she doesn't declare her earnings because she needs the money and, again, dare not risk a cut in benefits when she could lose her job at any time.

Ironically, every deception tightens the web. When the children badly needed winter clothes she tried to make her husband pay for them by threatening to tell the council where he lived. He, in his turn, threatened to tell the council that she was working. The same threats now operate in her dealings with most of her relatives, neighbours and employers. If you do this or you do that, I'll tell the council. The potential for blackmail has become a way of life.

The State and its functionaries are forced into the role of a policing force. They are seen, not as the alleviators of life's problems but as their cause. And the 'welfare', the nosey-parkers who come knocking on your door, are all (Mrs London believes) Labourites because Labour *is* the Welfare State. Mrs Thatcher wouldn't have it and neither would Mrs London, if she had her way.

Even the word 'privatisation' means, to her, 'privacy', the sort that Labourites won't let her have. Added to this, Mrs London has her pride. She doesn't like living on handouts. It lowers her estimation of herself and for that she again blames Labour.

She did not vote for them *because* they look after her – like Groucho Marx, she won't join any club that will have her as a member. Using a curious but understandable mental juggling act, the more she takes from the 'welfare' (and, therefore, the more they intrude), the more she is in favour of anything that will get them off her back. She cannot be independent but she wants to be and so she sees those who talk in terms of independence as superior and right. Logic plays no part in this process. Simply, the 'welfare' is her prison and she wants to break out.

Some of us will be tempted to feel that Mrs London must be taught a lesson. They reason that as the Thatcherite cuts bite deeper, she will begin to understand which side butters her bread. That may be so but it will not solve the long-term dilemma. A government dedicated actively to helping those who cannot always help themselves must also work out ways to heal the inevitably wounded egos or that help will boomerang. A passive recipient of benefits is no ally of the benefactor – it becomes a matter of pride to bite the hand that feeds you.

What, then, is to be done?

25 October, 1983   **Jill Tweedie**

A talent to abuse

You must bear with me. What follows is a rather lengthy description of a single painting, a portrait of Margaret Thatcher by Hans Haacke, which has just been unveiled at the Tate Gallery.

The Prime Minister is shown in her drawing room, perched on the edge of a chair in that alert pose which royalty invariably adopt when they know an artist is watching. Back straight, head up, chin out, she would not have looked out of place on the prow of one of Drake's galleons.

The Rt. Hon. Member for Finchley East wears a very regal dress of powdered blue chiffon. The artist has given her a splendidly ornate frame to sit in, flanked her with fluted ionic pilasters, thus establishing the picture in the tradition of grand royal portraiture which stretches from Marcus Gheeraerts to the appalling Bryan Organ. So far the painting is wickedly funny, no more.

But then you begin to inspect its details, all those signs and symbols with which it is cluttered. An allegorical portraitist of the past, of the kind Haacke is so consciously imitating, would have included a statue of Venus in the background with which to compare the sitter's beauty, placed volumes of Virgil on the bookshelves to suggest her erudition, given her a white lily to play with in celebration of her purity.

Haacke shows two cracked plates on the top of the bookshelf decorated with portraits of the Saatchi brothers. The books on the shelves give the names of all the companies and institutions which employ Saatchi & Saatchi to advertise for them: the Conservative Party, of course, the South African Nationalist Party, the *Daily Mail*, Tottenham Hotspur, Walt Disney, Wimpey, as well as the Tate Gallery, the National Gallery, the

26

Arts Council, the V&A, the British Museum. . . . When it comes to image-building our public galleries are currently keeping strange company.

Everywhere you look in this painting some detail or other is drawing your attention to the complexity of the relationships that link big business, art and politics. The depth of the Saatchis' involvement with the Tate as collectors, patrons, advertisers, advisers and lenders is recorded in fragments of Roman script on the base of the column behind the Prime Minister's back.

The news, revealed by *Private Eye*, that the director of the Tate had himself asked Haacke not to include the work in the show should surprise no one. After all, two years ago when the Tate held its Julian Schnabel exhibition, all the paintings came from the Charles Saatchi collection. Privately and publicly, the Tate Gallery has long recognised the importance of the Saatchi collection and expressed its willingness to profit from Saatchi generosity.

This is not the first time that Haacke has gone out of his way to bite the hand that feeds him and annoy the very gallery which is giving him floor space. He tried to do it at the Guggenheim in New York in 1971 and had his exhibition cancelled. Galleries have been putting pressure on him ever since. Haacke's response is to research long and hard into the reasons for their nervousness and then to make his discoveries the main exhibits in his case against them.

He has set himself up as a painter/gladiator thrown into the corrupt arena of art. One of the strong emotions you sense in his work is a childish glee in annoying the Establishment. It is a very simple, very direct joy. It was the same spirit which could often be felt moving Hogarth and Goya or, 150 years later, the pre-war German satirists.

Very skilfully, Haacke is exploiting the exciting atmospheres of subversion. The galleries find themselves out-manoeuvred. No matter how hard he bites their hand they cannot take it away without making him into a martyr and casting themselves as reactionaries. Most of the thrills at a Hans Haacke exhibition are psychological. The current Tate show is a perfect example. By suggesting that the gallery indulges in favouritism, Haacke is

27

challenging the Tate's central exhibition policy. By revealing all the links in the Tate/Saatchi connection he implies strange goings-on in high places. At the very least he undermines the gallery director's personal authority. Yet not only is the gallery prepared to grin and bear it but they've paid for the pleasure, given him a catalogue in which to continue his accusations and turned over prime exhibition space to his art. By any standards it is a piquant situation, a dramatic piece of theatre.

'Remember never to take your eye off the ball if you're to have any chance of smoking for England.'

13 March, 1984

The other works in the show are invariably overshadowed by the Thatcher portrait. Haacke's art has a short, disposable life-span. It needs an appropriate social history around it to complete the picture. His vicious attack on Dr Peter Ludwig,

28

the German chocolate king and art baron, makes much less sense outside Cologne away from the German political situation.

In the Ludwig piece, and indeed in most of the work before the Thatcher portrait, Haacke had used the stern format of photographs and texts to make his points, exploiting the power of the plain-speaking image. The facts fill his exhibitions with their chilling, irrefutable presence. The facts become his works of art.

There are those who question the validity of such an approach and challenge Haacke's right to be seen as an artist rather than a political agitator. As someone very high up at the Tate said to me at the opening, 'It doesn't seem to me to be so different from cartoons. The sort of thing Jak does in the *Evening Standard*.'

The main difference between Jak and Hans Haacke is that Jak deals in the minutiae of politics, the difference between right and left, where Haacke deals in the gigantic issues of human morality, the difference between right and wrong. As the distinguished American critic, Lucy Lippard, wrote: 'He spotlights aspects of society we have taken for granted, thereby performing the classic artist's function of teaching people how to see.'

What Haacke teaches people to see is that art and commerce and politics are as entangled today as they ever were under the Medici. Art is still being used by those in power as a means of self-glorification. Money is still doing all the talking. And being kind to an artist is still one of society's favourite ways of laundering its own reputation.

25 January, 1984   **Waldemar Januszczak**

Blessed release

A rare redbreast bird has arrived at Slimbridge which Sir Peter Scott, who doesn't watch a lot of television and is totally out of touch, has identified as a Bulgarian Goose. This was obviously the exceptionally rare and probably insane Thorn Bird which, according to Richard Chamberlain, impales its breast on a thorn and dies singing while the whole world stills to listen and God in his heaven smiles.

Why God in his heaven smiles is a matter of conjecture unless He has already seen the script, but it is a fact that the whole world stills (or as we would say, stops) to listen to *The Thorn Birds* (BBC1). At 9.10 last night you could have felt the earth give a sudden lurch to the left as everybody got up to put the kettle on.

After the penultimate episode the Central Electricity Generating Board reported an increase of 2,200 megawatts more than after the royal wedding. Evidently the Archbishop of Canterbury should have had a more starring role, worn a sensitive look and, possibly, jodphurs like Cardinal de Bricassart. The last episode of this turbulent saga of love, ambition and desire (*Radio Times*) was—you must bear with me while I compose my self—extremely emotional.

Richard Chamberlain has been pipped at the post as Pope, having failed, I assume, the mental arithmetic. Due to an inability to count to nine on his fingers, he does not realize that he is the father of Meggie's son, Dane. Dane, a striking instance of heredity, is like his father a priest and much pursued by women ('Cute.' 'I wonder how we can meet him?') As he is a good chap but only a so-so swimmer, the last we see of him is a pair of soles disappearing under the sea.

Well, I can't begin to tell you. It is as though the torrid heat of the story had set off a sprinkler system. Meggie, all set and cold like a blancmange, says: 'Dane was your son!' And Richard Chamberlain breaks down. Meggie's mum who has worn a series of depressing hats with great stoicism for half a century, finally breaks down too and so does Meggie and her daughter Justine. 'Meggie, it's not too late!' 'Oh Mom, oh Jussie, I've made you pay so dearly!' 'Oh Mom, I did love Dane!' 'Oh Jussie, I do love you.' Justine is a great tragic actress who has played Phaedre to a rather cool critical reception, but Richard Chamberlain is the star so he gets to sob the most.

Meanwhile back at the ranch, Richard Chamberlain who has just returned from burying Dane, dies himself among a tremendous upsurge of roses and the theme song from the series and sheep baa-ing in the background and Justine taking off in an aeroplane, flying fearless into the future and another lot of dreadful notices for her Cordelia. In the circumstances it was hardly worth Richard Chamberlain coming back from the cemetery at all. Just made a lot more work for everybody.

Emmys have been scattered on *The Thorn Birds* like birdseed but, in my opinion, nothing like enough. I would like to present my own award, the Bulgarian Goose:

To Barbara Stanwyck's agent, who kept her name up there in the credits 50 years after she was supposed to die. a striking proof of life after death.

To Judy, the maid at the Ranch, who when Drogheda was ringed with bushfires was abruptly ordered to 'Make stew for a hundred.'

To the dialogue coach who worked so selflessly on the cast that they seemed to get more Irish as time went on, as if they were practising. Though their insistence on calling the Ranch Drawheeda would purse the lips of Irish purists, the ideal being a more throat-clearing sort of sound.

To Father Terence Sweeny, the religious consultant to the series, for spiritual guidance. The Catholic Information Service keeping, unlike God, a perfectly straight face, said it was delighted at the sudden interest in the priesthood.

To the Central Electricity Generating Board without which none of this would have been possible.

23 January, 1984   **Nancy Banks-Smith**

All the Raj

Salman Rushdie, Fid. Def., derided *The Jewel in the Crown* in an *Observer* article last Sunday as a literary version of mulliga- tawny soup. 'It tries to taste Indian but ends up being ultra- parochially British, only with too much pepper,' he wrote. Fair enough; fairer than Mr Rushdie intended. The British Raj, not just the Scott Raj, *was* like mulligatawny soup.

The British in India remained an alien breed; one of Scott's earlier Indian novels is actually called *The Alien Sky*. It too is set in the summer months of 1947 and in it, when Indian workers disappear quietly, sinisterly, and suddenly from an estate, the two English sahibs don't comprehend why, though they have worked with the Indians and think they understand them.

The subsequent tension is a dramatic device, but it says something deeper about the British relationship to India, and it is the same statement that underlies the *Raj Quartet* (or *The Jewel in the Crown* as it must now be called in deference to the nearly eight million viewers Granada attracted every Tuesday evening).

The British camped in India; literally, sometimes, in tents as big as houses pitched around real brick chimney stacks (built against the Punjab winter evenings). Queen Mary herself camped under canvas with George V on the plain before Delhi and fell forever in love with India; half a century later, on the night before she died, she called for a book about India to be read to her. But there never was a British Akbar, the Mughal emperor who tried to obliterate the boundaries between the religions and cultures of invader and invaded.

Akbar failed, the failures of Gandhi and of Mountbatten followed, and those trains passed in the Punjab night between Amritsar and Lahore with their freights of slaughtered corpses – Muslim in one direction, Hindu the other. It was one such train that Scott adapted to his fictional Premanagar.

Where Akbar failed, no European conqueror could have succeeded, not coming to make money and staying to rule as the British did: to rule with 'eminent prudence, integrity, and benevolence', in the words on the memorial to the first of the modern pro-consuls, Lord William Bentinck, who set a pattern of British cultural and racial superiority that persisted until the coming of Midnight's Children, Nehru's 'tryst with destiny' on the night of August 14/15, 1947.

Paul Scott's (and marvellous Judy Parfitt's) joyless, bitter Mildred Layton, anaesthetised with alcohol, contemptuous of her servants, seeing India reflected in the silver of the officers' mess, is the very archetype of a prevailing style of memsahib. So is stupid, well-meaning Aunt Fenny. And Mrs Layton's lover, the narrow, bigoted, regimental Captain Coley will stand for the kind of officer who saw all Indians only as potential criminals.

Curiously for a novelist, Rushdie chides Scott for having failed to write a panoramic history of India in the twilight years of the Raj, with Indians in more than walk-on parts. But in the India Paul Scott knew, Indians did only have walk-on parts, as ayahs and bearers and sweepers and malis (the British don't even get walk-on parts in *Midnight's Children*, which is about the India Rushdie knew).

To Mildred Layton and her uneasy daughter, Sarah, to Kevin Coley, even to Jimmy Clark and Guy Perron who knew how to 'cross the bridge', Indian nationalist leaders were no more than the flitting shadows of the cinema newsreels used to anchor the Granada serialisation in time.

The rape in the Bibighar Bagh that Rushdie finds a pale echo of *A Passage to India* is nothing of the sort: the rape is not central, Kumar's love-making is. Merrick knows Kumar to be guilty, because for an Indian to make love to an Englishwoman is tantamount to rape, a rape of the superior race, a defilement. That is why the British kept Anglo-Indians at arm's length – Anglo-Indians officially, 'chee-chees' in the vernacular of contempt.

An Indian makes love to an Englishwoman, the Japanese take Singapore and march on Assam, Indian PoWs join the Japanese, Quit India turns violent and trains are derailed and attacked, the American allies arrive. In the regimental messes life goes on, wives summer in Kashmir and Simla and Naini Tal. Still, the dream is dissolving and at war's end English headmasters appeal to English pupils, stay on, your life is here.

But all through 1946 and 1947 trains converge on Deolali, British families disembark and wander distracted for a few days inspecting the show prefabs erected as a foretaste of just how good life is back in post-war Blighty. Then they embark on the troopships in Bombay harbour, the *Georgic*, the *Franconia*, the *Mauretania*, and sail home, the home that some have never seen and never wanted to see.

After that there was a missing generation in Britain. The hippies sought dharma in India, the old remembered the India of chota hazri and barra pegs. But the millions who watched *The Jewel in the Crown*, who are they? Was it just the high drama and romance that pulled them in? Are they the frustrated post-imperial British who cheered the 1966 World Cup victory and rejoiced at Falkland exploits? Or are they the middle class, middle income, middle aged parents beginning now to look further afield than Corfu for their holidays?

One tourist operator at least is betting on the third option: it has set up a cheap (under £600) Raj Quartet culture tour. In 1979 there were 15 tour firms dealing in holidays in India. Two years ago there were 25. This year there are 70. In 1982 there were 120,000 British tourists to India, in 1983 135,000. This year, with party packages on offer, there will be thousands more.

'I arrest you for not being at home watching the final episode of Jewel in the Crown.'

4 April, 1984

And in a way *The Jewel in the Crown* is a Granada tourist package even more than it is an exotic and compelling *Coronation Street*. There is a scene of Susan Layton recumbent beneath

34

a mosquito net, but otherwise no suggestion of heat, insects, disease, poverty.

The bazaar where Perron looks for Kumar in the last episode is a sanitised approximation. Calcutta is a series of studio interiors. But Kashmir plays herself, Simla stands in for Pankot, and Udaipur simulates Mirat with the Lake Palace as the Nawab's residence and the hinterland of Lake Pichola the terrain for Sarah's and Ahmed's early morning rides and falconing. Thus the magic of television unites the outer Himalayas with central India, just as jet packages unite them in fact.

But India is unlikely to become a holiday haven for seekers of sun and cheap booze (though it could cope even with that). And there is another symbol in the *Raj Quartet* than in the picture of the Jewel in the Crown showing the old Queen in an imaginary durbar receiving the Koh-I-Noor. It is the Urdu verse of Gaffur.

Gaffur was an ancestor of the Nawab of Mirat and it is Lady Manners who remembers this and recommends to Sarah Layton that a volume of Gaffur will make a suitable present for the Nawab. The quartet of novels, though not the television serial, ends with Perron in turn opening a book that Count Bronowski has given him and finding, not the expected Pushkin, but the verses of Gaffur.

7 April, 1984 **Michael McNay**

Problems of the inner city

Those of us whose hours of work preclude watching *Coronation Street* will not perhaps feel the loss of Albert Tatlock as deeply as others. We are left merely with the vague impression of a run-down inner-city street, rapidly and dismally depopulated, beset by inner-city crime. It is a year since the court case of Len Fairclough/Peter Adamson; since when Pat Phoenix has left, Peter Dudley has died, Geoffrey Hughes has left, Violet Carson has died, Bernard Youens has had a stroke, Deirdre Barlow has been busted, Fred Feast has had a nervous breakdown, Christobel Finch has allegedly gone missing . . . and now poor old

35

Albert Tatlock. All this, for those with even vaguer impressions, is the off-screen action.

It is a false impression, according to Mr Norman Frisby,
Granada's estimable press officer. 'The trouble is that, like you,
Fleet Street reporters never watch it because they're working at
the time,' he says. 'They just presume that, because it has 16
million viewers, it must sell newspapers. In fact, there are still
20-odd members of the cast. There's no suggestion we're going
to kill it off. That's balls.'

3 April, 1984   **Alan Rusbridger**

The Museum of Horrifying Example

There is no rush hour in Liverpool, at least no rush hour anyone
would recognise in London or any other proper city. Liverpool
is no longer a proper city. It is a museum. The Museum of the
Horrifying Example.

That is Liverpool's future, and it should do very well out of it.
People will flock to Liverpool from Japan and Australia, Korea
and the People's Republic of China, from Bulgaria, Zimbabwe
and Albania, and all other places of the future, to see this
Museum of the Horrifying Example – to be warned of the dire
things that happen to an industrial city when it is industrial no
more.

And what a romantic port it once was. A pre-Raphaelite city
left out in the rain, someone poetic said. The whole city leans
down to the river, tilts towards the river, and the river leads to
the sea. Walking down to the river I look and there is nothing to
see there anymore. I remember the big Cunards and the gleaming white Empresses of the Canadian Pacific waiting on the
tide right down below me where I am standing now in Castle
Street.

What a wonderful sight that was of a morning, particularly of
a Saturday pub-crawling morning of which there were many and
for which, please God, there is always room for one more.

Well, anyway, I went back to Liverpool to see what I could see the other day. It was the first time back in my English home of 20 years since I left almost five years ago.

'Ah but don't you just miss Liverpool?' fellows were always saying to me. Then, before ever I could get a word out, they'd start telling me fine fantasies of Liverpool themselves: 'where you walk out in the evening and know JUST EVERYBODY!!'

'But do you like them?'

'Who cares? What does it matter! I'll tell you what we'll do. We'll get a party up and go to Liverpool for the Grand National! Why we'll stay at the Adelphi. You ever stay at the Adelphi?'

'No.'

'No, of course not. Neither have I. But we'll stay at the Adelphi this time. You and me and Ivo and Henry and Phil the Glass Morgan, and we'll have a time.'

Nobody ever goes back to Liverpool in a party. They sneak back in with a canvas bag on an inconvenient train with no dinner on just another night in November.

People are always telling you about Liverpool's two cathedrals. But actually it has three cathedrals. The third one is the Adelphi Hotel, looming up on Lime Street like a beached white whale, like some old Cunarder herself which somehow ploughed her way up Church Street from the Pier Head. Liverpool has many empty or half-used buildings, great acres of run-down docks and warehouses, but nothing, I think, is a sadder sight than the Adelphi Hotel. It is not closed. It is opened for business, under new management since British Rail started selling its hotels, but of all the sad sights in Liverpool it seemed to me the saddest.

The Adelphi was the cathedral in which the outside world came to worship Liverpool. It was the hotel where the stars and millionaires and the other glamorous people of this world stayed when they came to Liverpool to take a liner to New York or to see the Grand National. We were all very proud of these stars and millionaires staying up there in the Adelphi and that pride was a curious sort of Liverpool thing because as every fool knows Liverpool is a bolshy place, home of the wildcat strike, city of back-biters, full of envy and inverted snobbery, constantly alternating between drunken boasting and morning-after whingeing.

But there was not a Communist shop steward or a Trotskyite shite-stirrer who did not have a soft spot for the Adelphi Hotel; especially on Grand National Night when the toffs were inside guzzling themselves to death and destruction, the bastards, and the champagne flowed down the very steps.

'And the champagne flowed down the steps of the Adelphi Hotel': It was one of the clichés of old Liverpool. Another cliché was the one about there being Manchester men and Liverpool gentlemen. These Liverpool gentlemen were the men you saw walking into the Adelphi Hotel smoking big cigars. They were the haute bourgeoisie of Liverpool, as stuffy a lot as you'd find anywhere in the British Isles, except for a touch of the sporting blood. And this sporting blood made them all right with Liverpool. Liverpool never seemed to mind them being rich and walking into the Adelphi Hotel smoking big cigars. Could it have been really true then that Liverpool was a place full of spite and envy?

And where will you find the Liverpool gentlemen nowadays, what with the Athenaeum closed and the Racquets Club burned down in the Toxteth riots and the Adelphi Hotel's French restaurant closed?

The world no longer comes to Liverpool. The Prince of Wales in Southport is the place now for the Grand National. The Adelphi is yet another piece in the Museum of the Horrifying Example. There were plenty of rooms all right, but no hot water and with a room service that never did arrive. I seem to be the only person in the place. Me and the waiter and the porter and the upstairs maid.

But, you know, the world will be beating a path to Liverpool's door again come next spring. Everybody here is talking about the biggest festival in Britain since, well, since the Festival of Britain. The famous International Garden Festival will open here on May 2 and will run for six months until October 14.

'They're fobbin' us off wid a few flowers,' I heard a fellow say. It is the authentic note of the new whining Liverpool, something we hear reported about in Parliament where all the new Merseyside MPs seem to whinge and whine in bipartisan orchestration, Labour and Liberal together. It seems something new to me, all this whingeing and whining. It seems out of character with the Liverpool I knew as a jolly sort of place, a hand-me-down Dublin, but with talk second only to Dublin, and not this snivelling, snot-nosed sort of place I find all round me now.

Here was the Government lending £13 million so the International Garden Festival could be held in Liverpool. Here they were carrying out the largest land reclamation scheme in Europe, 125 acres, from the old Cast Iron Shore down to the Albert Dock, turning that tired, old dockland on the Mersey into a vast, wonderful parkland, and here were the Liverpudlians whining about how they were being fobbed off with a few flowers. And these whingers include the city council.

It is a red council, red as the Red Soviet of Islington, and they do not like the idea of the Garden Festival because the money is coming from a Tory government. It was Britain's turn to have the festival and, certainly as a sop to the destitution of the city and surely as an aftermath of the Toxteth riots, they decided to have it in Liverpool rather than in some sensible place. An estimated 3,500,000 people will come to Liverpool for the festival, but the city council is washing its hands of the whole idea.

'But when it's all over,' my friend the divi said, 'what we going to be left with?'

They will have a wonderful park running along the banks of the Mersey. In the end, the 125 acres of the festival will link up with the land reclamation that is being done by the Merseyside Development Corporation. This will be 250 acres in all. It will be the biggest land reclamation job in Europe. It will be the most imaginative use of a riverfront in the country, in all of Western Europe perhaps.

'What are we supposed to do wid dat?' my friend the divi asked.

'We'll bulldoze the whole fuckin' thing back into the Mersey for them if they don't watch out,' my friend the divi's divi friend said, and all the pub burst into laughter because that is the sort of stuff they really like. These fellows will be the curators of the Museum of the Horrifying Example. When the world and his brother comes to Liverpool in the springtime, these divis can whine them through a whingeing tour of the city and then grizzle about the tips they won't receive.

How wonderful the Museum of the Horrifying Example is! There is nothing like it in the world. It is unique. Listen to these prime exhibits:

'Trees,' a woman on the top of the bus said, 'all them trees. They gone an' planted all them trees. If you ever want to see a tree you can go to the park for that.'

'An' they create litter,' her friend said, mystifying me for a moment until I realised she meant that in the autumn the trees lose their leaves. I had never thought of falling leaves as litter before, nor had any songwriter or poet who ever lived.

Mr Michael Heseltine, the dreaded Tarzan of the political cartoons, when he was Minister of the Environment, in the wake of the Toxteth riots decided the thing to do was attempt to get the charred remains of Liverpool looking pretty again. So, true man of the Shires that he is, he planted trees. Hence the old ladies' displeasure on the top of the bus, but they soon forgot about the litterbug trees and went to work on the bus service.

Without any of the trumpet blowing that Ken Livingstone went in for over his fair fares in London a few years ago, Liverpool introduced a similar system of low-priced bus fares; and it works. People can now ride into Liverpool from those Godforsaken new developments on the outskirts for a mere 25p. This, of course, has not stopped the whining. It seems, in fact, to have increased it, not that very many people ride the buses. Only schoolchildren and old people go on the buses – everybody else in Liverpool takes a taxi.

What a wonderful sight for London eyes are the taxis of Liverpool. They are everywhere. The streets are full of them. Not radio cabs, but proper black taxis. Only they are not proper. They are in terrible states of disrepair. The tyres on one taxi I took were hanging in ribbons. Not a quarter or a half-inch long, but in long, dangling ribbons like a dray horse's. I gave the driver the address, glancing down at the tyres as I do, and saying, 'Do you think we'll get there?' And he laughs, a merry old Liverpool laugh without a whinge in it. A touch of old-fashioned Liverpool spirit, and very rare.

What a wonderful place, you think, Liverpool would be to live in if you had a little money. Why, you could live like a little lord, taking taxis everywhere. And have a fine house, too, in Sefton Park or up in Menlove Avenue, or down on the river in one of the new inner city places they are gentryfying. Six months ago, out of step with the entire rest of the country, house prices in Liverpool actually fell.

Ah, I could hire a valet – a Liverpool Jeeves – and take a taxi out to eat every night in one of all these new, little restaurants that seem to have opened everywhere, and wouldn't life be just grand *whining* and dining out every night!

They are eking out a modest living in Liverpool eating at each other's restaurants.

All the little restaurants are a sign of enterprise in hard times. But why is it that they all seem to be run by foreigners? Or all of them to have at least one partner who is not from Liverpool?

The restaurants are run by and for the new trendy riff-raff, the young of Liverpool who seem untouched by the fickle times, although surely most of them must be on the dole.

'You can tell the doleïtes,' a fellow tells me, 'because they are all rigged out. They sit at home all day on their tod and then they decide to go out and they can spend all day getting all dressed up for it.'

That was always true. I can remember that from before and a German girl who came on a visit to Liverpool and asked, 'Who are all these beautiful people?'

The little restaurants and the trendy riff-raff who fill them give certain parts of the city the look of the Weimar Republic, of Herr Issyvoo's Berlin. But there is no bustle.

How strange it is to be in a city with too many taxis, with four times the number of taxis of Birmingham, and how strange to be in a city in the Western world which is in no kind of a hurry at all. Liverpool is in slow motion, action replay. It is like a banana republic.

These are very much the notes of a fellow only passing through, staying at a hotel, taking a look at the Pier Head, going to pubs and restaurants. But I have never known anything very much about industry and business. The biggest business in Liverpool that I could see was heroin. There is so much heroin around in Liverpool right now that it is cheaper than any other drug.

Heroin is so cheap in Liverpool that they are not injecting it, they are smoking it, just as if it were grass. A lot of my friends in the trendy riff-raff seem to be killing themselves with drugs, and with booze, too, of course.

Drink is the big killer, though. And everyone in Liverpool seems half cut all the time. Then, of course, I remember they were always a little half cut in Liverpool all the time, and me along with them. Suddenly I realise that something has changed in Liverpool – I have come back sober and all my friends look like suicides to me.

'It's true,' my son Ambrose, a musician who lives in Liverpool, says. 'They are all sort of killing themselves.'

They will figure as just more industrial waste, Banzai McQuirk and the rest of them, in the Museum of the Horrifying Example. But along about evening, walking along by the Anglican cathedral I saw the forgotten Liverpool, the Liverpool which I forgot about after I left and went to live in London, where I thought it was only the people I was lonesome for.

It wasn't the people at all. It was this beautiful city with the sandstone of the cathedral and the buildings all around changing colours as the sky turned a hungry sort of pink over the river. There was a sight to see and to put under glass in any museum anywhere. A beautiful sight. Much too good for the Museum of the Horrifying Example.

7 January, 1984   **Stanley Reynolds**

Trucking with routiers

'All we have to do now is take this lot into Paris, sit round the Elysée and wait,' said Maurice Ossart yesterday – his second day blockading the outskirts of the capital. 'This lot' was his and nearly 2,000 other lorries in a straggling triple line between Le Bourget and Charles de Gaulle airports.

Ossart's plan was the logical conclusion of the lorry drivers' revolution that had astonished the French and pushed the Government into apologetic retreat. The plan was no longer practicable because the gendarmes had sealed off the inner city, keeping the dreaded lorries out of the ring roads and inner approaches.

But just outside, the routiers laid down the law while the gendarmes, who on normal days persecute them with endless checks, fines, and prohibitions, just smoothed down the motorists, directing them peacefully away from the trouble.

I felt their uncanny power on Tuesday night, driving north, avoiding or filtering through their barricades until I got back on to the deserted Autoroute du Nord at Senlis. And then, suddenly, at the Compiègne exit, there they were, coming down the southbound lane – a serried armada of light. A phalanx of articulated lorries, three abreast, headlights blazing, moving at a stately 15 mph with hundreds of awed motorists crawling in their wake.

It was science-fiction war, with mutant lorries invading, ruthlessly coordinated by their CB radios which the gendarmes had been unable to jam. John Wyndham might indeed have set last Saturday's scene when the Government called in the army. The soldiers hauled away a lorry or two, its tyres screaming because the brakes were locked, making no impact on a blockade manned by 2,000 lorries. And then a driver said: 'You're going to ruin the chassis with that hook. Who's going to pay?' And the soldier withdrew.

On Saturday the Minister said he would not negotiate until the roads were cleared. By Tuesday the blockades had doubled and the Minister was negotiating. By Wednesday the Government had conceded most of the drivers' immediate demands, promising more talks on the rest. The union leaders were powerless without the men on the ground – and they refused the deal, moving nearer to Paris.

And yet, talking yesterday in and around the routiers' restaurant in the middle of the giant Le Bourget blockade, a different story emerged. 'We are here because we are fed up with being messed around,' they said.

Serge Dupuis, owner-driver who is losing £100 a day in the blockade, explained that the routiers' macho image was misleading. Lorrymen in fact were pushed around all day long. He meant by customs men, gendarmes, tax inspectors, Communists, Ministers, and everyone else who got in the way of their lorries.

Most of the talk at the transport café (though the food was better than in its British equivalent, and everyone seemed to be able to afford the three-course menu with wine) was abuse – directed against the unions' leaders (in cahoots with the Government, pretending to be our leaders but it's us who are in the lead), the Communist Minister of Transport (what he cares about is the railways and his high-speed TGV train, not us). And the gendarmes: 'With these new 10-hour driving restrictions, they catch us 10 miles from home after a week away from our family and that's it: we have to wait there for the night.' This and other grievances were remedied by the Minister in Tuesday's concessions. 'But now we want it in black and white,' said Dupuis, 'promises will no longer do.'

Ossart is an employee driver, unconcerned with diesel costs and VAT on insurance premiums. But he and other employee drivers backed the blockade with enthusiasm, proving wrong the Communist and Socialist unions who say the action is politically motivated.

The endless customs delays are also blamed not just on Italy, whose procrastinating officials sparked off the protest. 'Dover is just as bad,' said Ossart. 'The place is too small for a start to handle the traffic it does. They tell us we'll have to wait four hours and it turns out to be 24. Nobody cares.'

The routiers' revolution began as a spontaneous local protest about a chronic and intolerable situation on the Italian border. The men surprised themselves by the sheer immovability of their vehicles, and spread the protest.

'Les Routiers Sont Sympas,' says the catchy slogan of a popular radio programme beamed especially at them. This week, with their juggernauts on the march, they have seemed less *sympa* than usual, but they offer a convincing case of victimisation and neglect by authority.

Ossart said he earned £106 a week for an average of 12 hours work a day, with Mondays to Fridays away from home, and much more time spent loading, unloading, and waiting, than driving. Many of the self-employed, small-time owner-operators work even longer hours and earn scarcely more after paying even higher fuel and insurance costs, not to speak of the cost of the delays and the fines.

'Can you imagine this happening on the M-1?' asked Charles Jackson, whose Pickford van was stuck in the middle of the blockade. A TGWU shop steward, he was shocked by the ruthlessness of the action. Other Britons – all victims rather than actors in the drama – said they saw its point.

'I've never been over in France without getting fined,' said Jock Halliday. 'It's always ridiculous little things that show they want to get you whatever you do. Once it was a dash instead of a dot on a trailer numberplate. Another time, warning signs were the wrong colour. Every time it's 600 francs (£50) on the spot. You can pay half as a bribe, but then you get no receipt.'

Perhaps in the end the weak point will be money. 'There's billions of francs standing idle out there,' said Dupuis. The revolution is costing the hauliers more than the Government in money terms. The moment may come when they feel they have won enough and had better get back on the road. But ever after, the terrible power of the juggernauts will remain in reserve.

23 February, 1984   **Walter Schwarz**

How Le Pen grows mightier

Mr Pierre Poujade may be distracted these days by his doubtless onerous duties as president of the French national federation of Jerusalem artichoke producers' cooperatives; but a spirit similar to that which made him a political sensation a generation ago seems to be abroad in his native land. The man who incorporates it is Mr Jean-Marie Le Pen, president of the Front National and once a Poujadist deputy when that movement won 53 seats in the National Assembly in its fifties heyday. Like the Poujade movement, the Front favours such things as less tax and government, more law and order and draws its support in the main from the petty bourgeoisie. The principal difference between

45

Poujadism and the Front lies in what has become the principal plank in the latter's platform: xenophobia against the 4.5 million resident foreigners.

Under the rule of three subscribed to by Damon Runyon and others, whereby once is happenstance, twice is coincidence and three times is enemy action, the French National Front now demands to be taken seriously. It won 17 per cent of the vote in the recent municipal by-election at Dreux, a town with a very high immigrant population. In a similar poll at Aulnay-sous-Bois, which also houses many aliens, its score of 9 per cent was hardly less significant because its candidates were completely unknown before the election campaign there. Now Mr Le Pen himself has scored more than 12 per cent this week at a parliamentary by-election in a part of Britanny where there are rather more menhirs than Muslims.

Whether this is a real breakthrough, whether a bandwagon has begun to roll or whether France is witnessing a mid-term wave of disaffection will probably not become clear until the nationwide European parliamentary elections in June. Mr Le Pen has considerable personal pulling power and was standing on his home ground (in the town of his birth which is part of the relevant constituency, he polled 51 per cent), in a traditionally conservative and disgruntled part of the country. It remains to be seen whether these isolated patches of racialist and neo-fascist sentiment will expand and join up into the 'one sixth of the national vote' Mr Le Pen confidently predicts the Front will get, on the basis of its claim to be the only real opposition of the Right. Like the Nazis in their early days, the Front is taking more votes from the Left than from the Right, but no true French democrat can now pretend that it is not a threat to both. If the orthodox Right, which is as divided as the ruling Left, is tempted to mop up the growing National Front support, there could be a new and ugly polarisation in France on the explosive issue of immigrants. In this context the recent and well-supported 'rally against racism' was heartening, but government and opposition parties have an equal duty to frustrate the odious aspirations of Mr Le Pen.

14 December, 1983   **Leader**

Canal du mayday

With a flourish I put the wheel of *Blue Calypso* over to starboard, to set course for the Phare des Onglous and the entrance of the Canal du Midi, and in so doing broke the third finger of my left hand. I don't know that I could do it again if I tried, but I suppose it was the flourish that did it. There's not a lot of room between the wheel and the bulkhead. I may very well be the only person ever to have broken a finger in this way.

The sun shone down with all its might on Marseillan and the people sitting out on the quay with their drinks – the temperature was 92 degrees F. Misinterpreting my risus sardonicus happy holidaymakers on other cruisers smiled and waved as the finger puffed up like a sausage, and *Calypso* entered the Canal with her skipper cursing. Before she reached Castelnaudary, 125 km and 67 locks away, the finger was well down the list of causes for a blue line in language.

When all goes well on your voyage on the canal, you doff your yachting cap to Pierre Riquet, who built it (with 15,000 labourers) 300 years ago, as you pass by his home town, Béziers. You admire the engineering elegance of his locks, with their olive-shaped chamber and the wide waist designed to withstand the pressure of the stone platforms.

You're glad to find that a pig could manage the boat between the locks, that your piglet crew is getting lots of fun and action scurrying up the steps to work on the ropes and lend a hand to the lock-keepers, and you feel after some practice of negotiating locks that you could probably thread a camel through the eye of a needle. The lock-keepers, you decide, are the most obliging of all civil servants. It becomes a laughing matter even to ascend the daunting stairway of seven locks at Fonserannes.

As the level rises over the parched hills of Occitaine, you have time to moor and scramble up the embankment for glimpses of Cézanne houses among the heat-hazed vineyards. Time to slither back down for the al fresco meal on the towpath in the shade of the blessed colonnade of planes. Time to toast Riquet for following the natural contours of the land, though he wasn't after an aesthetic of sinuousness, but saving money on embankments. Time to potter off down to a nice little old estaminet in a nice little old Languedoc village.

There isn't a lot of wildlife, but gradually the sightings accumulate: a hoopoe, just yards away, a purple heron, five magpies on a bridge, some moorhens nesting, cicadas clattering away, a watersnake, myriad caddis-flies in ecstasies of mating.

There's a pleasing mix about the human traffic too: yachts motoring through all the way from Bordeaux, teararse Swiss and Germans in smart cruisers all wanting to be first, a weird craft like a prototype for Captain Nemo's *Nautilus*, and the huge steel barges, 100-footers, carrying wines and cereals, hung about with pot plants, last survivors of the commercial heyday of the canal, which are just about able to squeeze into some of the locks, and have priority.

But when the foul-ups come, you register some contrary impressions. You suspect the lock-keepers of paranoia – could that have been deliberate when they suddenly launched the full weight of the sluice down the throat of that leading German cruiser? Are they trying to fluster you by making out you're in a hurry when you're not? You notice that whatever merits there may be in buying tomatoes and wine and perfume at the locks, economy isn't one of them.

You perceive with a pang that the canal is dying. That it's too shallow to take the larger vessels which alone could sustain its commercial life. That it was a mistake to replace the oaks with planes – they don't suit birds, and the leaves won't rot, so they give problems of disposal as they do to the London parks, choking the lock gates.

In the opaque, still waters, greasy as the grey Limpopo, you see Germans and Swiss and British swimming, but not the French. There is nowhere for the effluent of hundreds of pleasure cruisers to go. 'It's no worse than the sea,' says someone, but that's no answer. 'Anyway, we have a doctor with us,' says someone else. A bloated rat drifts by, riding high above the Plimsoll line. But the Swiss are always scrubbing and polishing their boats – it makes you hot just watching them.

48

Calypso was nine years old, a knot or two slower than younger Blue Line cruisers, and evinced a disquietening thirst for oil, but the first serious failure came one evening as we reached Homps, about half way. Water was coming up through the floorboards and oozing around our luggage. The bilge pump wasn't working. Turning it over to manual blew the fuses.

The routine drill is to phone HQ for a mechanic. This presupposes a phone to ring from, but Homps would surely provide. At the quayside restaurant I drank an ingratiating beer but le patron rebuffed me brusquely: 'It's not practical to use ours. We have our customers to serve. Use the public call-box.'

I found it, under the bridge. But I couldn't make it work. Perhaps there was another, secret Languedocian way? I appealed to a knot of idlers on the bridge who'd been watching me appreciatively. No, they reassured me, I'd done everything right. But the line was cut. Where then, was another *cabine*? They waved into the dusk: 'A few kilometres up the road.'

Instead, I plunged down into secretive, dilapidated Homps, in search of a bar, and found one at last called Le Treize. It was empty, but as I went in through the bead curtains, the group that was sitting out on the steps rose and followed me in. They watched me drink an ingratiating Pernod and joined in the talk about Rugby League triumphs – portraits of the best players in the world, who'd used his bar, hung above le patron's head. Could I use his phone? He was desolated – he hadn't got one. Madame came downstairs to have the situation explained. She was desolated too, and scandalised by thoughts of universal vandalisation. 'It's no use mending them. Young men use wires to get the money out. Everything gets broken.' After another Pernod le patron escorted me to the door. 'It's a bad town for telephones,' he confided.

In the morning we got through, from the Post Office. Two hours later Bruno arrived in a van, very charming, made light of our cares, dismissed the oil niggle – the dipstick reading was always on the safe side – installed 'thug' fuses, and told us about the house he was building with his wife and children. No danger now – just a petit problème of faulty connections. Would he, all the same, just check over the engine? Shrug, but of course.

'Ah!' he exclaimed. 'Ah-ah-ah-ah! Petit problème.' The main

pipe was severed. Water was coming straight into the boat from the canal. He bound it up. Petits problèmes all solved now. Bilges sweet and clear. It was much graver when they had to change the whole engine. Bon voyage. He drove off.

Between Homps and the next lock, Jouarres, there was a loud bang in the stern. Smoke rose. Gratuitously the alarm buzzer sounded. Gratuitously, passing cruisers pointed to the smoke. Limping on, even at low revs, we were overheating madly. It was clear no water was circulating round the cooling system.

The Jouarres lock-keeper said I was welcome to use his phone – but it was only connected to the next lock. We could pass through, with the other boats now, or wait a couple of hours after lunch. He couldn't take us through on our own. We pressed on. There was said to be a restaurant with a phone a couple of kilometres further up. But the overheating persuaded us to moor. I walked.

I walked three kilometres. No restaurant – only fishermen, a ruined house, an obsolete lock, an aqueduct over a river. Then a bridge, carrying a main road. Across the dusty landscape a town quivered in the heat stripes – 8 kms away? No buses. I tried to hitch, but I must have looked far too villainous.

In mid-afternoon I came on a scrapyard of smashed vehicles. It was deserted, and so was the shed in the midst of grotesque heaps of tortured metal. But I could see a tantalising phone in there among spare parts and salvage. The owner, a stout man in vest and striped underpants, emerged from sleep in his caravan. He said, kind fellow, that I could use his phone – if he could make it work. After half an hour of fiddling with wires and plugs, he connected it.

Bruno said he couldn't come to that spot, but it could only be the water filter. I should take out the steps and forage into the engine, for a copper instrument with butterfly screws: clean and replace. If that didn't work – but it would – stagger on as far as we could and phone again. I trudged back 6 kms.

I did everything he said, but it made no difference. To the relentless tune of the buzzer, travelling in 5-minute bursts we finally got into Laredorte. We had a cheeringly good meal in the Rivassel restaurant, with South Sea island decor, and phoned to say we had broken down altogether.

50

At 9.30 am Georges arrived, very efficient. He diagnosed the trouble as a broken turbine. He changed it. Would he kindly check further? But of course.

'Ah!' he exclaimed. 'Ah-ah-ah-ah! But you are losing too much oil!' Yes. 'But the oil filter is completely kaput!' He changed it, shaking oil all over everything, including the ropes. No more problems. Bon voyage.

Calypso was now in the condition she should have been in if she had been properly serviced at the outset. But we were way behind schedule for picking up our car, garaged in Marseillan for the second leg of our holiday. From Carcassonne we resolved to take the train back, and asked Blue Line to pick up *Calypso* from the basin there.

But Castelnaudary was adamant that we must deliver *Calypso* on time, or suffer sundry penalties – cost of crew, loss of holiday for the next customers, etc. The afternoon train would do our business for us.

Our outraged crew responded magnificently. In 24 hours, sharp as an outfit in a military tattoo, we whistled up the remaining 24 locks, travelling in the twilight, beating even Germans to the locks, and mooring tight by a lock for dawn departure. At La Criminelle, Pierre Riquet's motto is on the wall of the keeper's house: '*Il faut finir l'ouvrage, ou mourir à la peine*' – loosely, one must finish the job, at the cost of dying of it. We were praised by a surprised base for making it, but there wasn't in fact an afternoon train.

The last we saw of *Calypso*, a German family was taking charge. Father and son were wrangling over the correct way of tying a rope, when the bollard was close and the rope was long. A mysterious affection for *Calypso* invaded us: we hoped they'd treat her gently. They would have to!

7 January, 1984   **Alex Hamilton**

Fry's French delights

Roger Fry called Britain Bird's Custard Land and its inhabitants the Custard Islanders. His famous essay on Art and Socialism begins in a railway refreshment room where the Custard Islanders wait for their train to Blackpool or Skegness or wherever Fry in his best patronising manner imagined they spent their holiday.

He of course went to Tuscany, or the South of France. It was there that he acquired his own cheap taste for flashy brush-strokes and gaudy colours which he claimed was so preferable to the Custard Islanders' affection for pseudo-classicism and the appearance of old age.

Fry's dismay at the decor in the railway refreshment room moved him to write one of his best, his most bilious put-downs of Great British taste. He complains of the lace curtains with patterns 'taken from at least four centuries and as many countries'. The false classical mouldings, the fake effect of shimmering brocade on the wallpaper, the 'artistic way in which the table cloth has been laid at an angle', filled him with disgust. How commendable it would have been if he had started the Omega Workshops to set all this to rights.

But if there was one place that Omega Workshops' produce would not be found it was in the common railway refreshment room. Indeed, it is difficult to imagine any place in Britain for it apart from the living rooms of Bloomsbury where the blue nudes, the flowers, the vases, supplied a suitably colourful background for all those amusing anecdotes.

When Omega closed in 1919 Fry wrote to Arnold Bennett that 'people have the world the average man likes. I don't understand the animal and can't hope to imagine him.' The truth was that Fry never bothered to try. It wasn't custard which killed the Omega Workshops, but the poor diet of gentlemen's relish.

The Omega exhibits currently in London for a mass celebration are divided up in two shows. The one at the Crafts Council Gallery studiously charts Omega's progress from a twinkle in Fry's eye to the all-consuming force which appears to have overrun the house at Charleston in which Duncan Grant and Vanessa Bell lived. Every available surface is covered in swirling flowers or reclining nudes: every cupboard door, every wastepaper bin has been painted. The Omega Workshops have gone out of control like vegetation in a horror story.

Luckily the Crafts Council keeps it locked behind glass doors. Their exhibition leads you through a series of glass corridors in and out of several notable Omega rooms. The one Fry designed for Lalla Vandervelde is the best preserved. On the headboard of her bed he painted a coy female nude. Her wardrobe was splattered with giant flowers. No surface was left undecorated.

Lalla Vandervelde was the wife of the Belgian Minister of State, one of the 'smart motor-set ladies' whom Fry was reportedly so adept at charming. They and the Bloomsbury children formed the Omega clientele. The deliciously decadent mood of the whole enterprise is nicely captured in Vanessa Bell's advice for an Omega opening: 'We should all get drunk and dance and kiss.'

Loud, exotic, daring, Omega-ware was a way of avoiding the dullness of Custardland, of bringing some continental sunshine into the Bloomsbury home without travelling farther than Fitzroy Street where, under the sign of 'the emaciated Byzantine youth', you could buy a screen painted by Roger Fry with a view of mountains in Provence.

Most of the exhibits cluttered densely around the two shows – Omega's approach to design was always accumulative, never reductive – look as out-of-place in the English winter as a lemon-yellow frock. The Omega spirit, its favourite motifs, were imported wholesale from Post-Impressionist France – blue nudes, pink flowers, bowls of exotic fruit. Every object on view seems to have been painted in a loose English approximation of that dazzling French touch. William Morris would have shuddered in his grave. Ruskin would have choked on his sermon about the necessity for good design.

But the Omega Workshops was no descendant of the Arts and Craft Movement. Rather it was Fry's way of introducing his beloved French Post-Impressionism not only to the walls of Custardland but also to its tables, screens, even the legs of its chairs and the fabric of its umbrellas. The Omega artist treated pieces of furniture as if they were strangely shaped Post-Impressionist canvases.

Fry's insistence that all Omega objects should be enlivened by 'the nervous tremor of the creator' was never backed up by any coherent training policy aimed at turning his band of colour-drunk painters into craftsmen. Omega pottery, particularly Fry's own, has the wobbly uncertainty of the novice potter as its distinguishing feature. The only Omega objects whose beauty seems to come from deep within their structure are the delightfully simple wicker chairs gathered around one of Duncan Grant's lurid lily-pond tables at Anthony d'Offay's Gallery.

The d'Offay exhibition is the livelier in spirit of the two. Whereas everything at the Crafts Council is preserved behind glass this show is a jumble of Omega produce exposed to the fresh air, pottery and pictures, fire-screens and boxes, cabinets and chairs, dining room tables and portraits of Bloomsbury celebrities. Many of the colours have faded and some of the paint has peeled, but you still get a sense of the crude excitement which must have been generated by the opening of the work-shop in 1913.

On the Mantelpiece is an exquisite still-life in which for once the objects do indeed appear to have the light of Provence trapped inside them. Duncan Grant could paint it in them but not on them. The d'Offay show is rich in pictures and it is here, free from the strain of pretending to be designers, that the dominant Omega artists, Grant, Bell and Fry, are seen at their best.

One of the extraordinary features of the Omega's activities is that no hints of war were ever allowed to darken the bright colours. No wonder Wyndham Lewis and his friends walked straight out of Fry's enterprise and into Vorticism. The dazzle from all that aesthetic unreality must have become unbear-able.

In theory these two exhibitions and the shelf-load of literature which accompanies them are intended to celebrate the Omega Workshops' lasting achievements. In practice there weren't any. Even the bright colours, the thrill of a new decade, seem now to have dried out and withered. The Omega's ideals were paper-thin and easily torn to shreds by the Bauhaus.

There was never any serious attempt to affect the union between beautiful colour and beautiful form, which Fry wrote about so eloquently in his essays on Cézanne. All that remains now is a handful of genuinely beautiful objects, a marquetry cabinet inlaid with giraffes, a coiled green cat designed by Gaudier-Brzeska. And of course there are always the Blooms-bury anecdotes.

There's the one about how Arnold Bennett ordered an Omega table for his mistress which was sent by mistake to his wife. Or when S. S. Koteliansky ran amok at a party and attacked Mark Gertler with a tray – supplied by Omega of course.

18 January, 1984   **Waldemar Januszczak**

Power failure at Potsdam

'You should get a majority of about 80,' suggested Stalin reassuringly to Churchill. They were sitting together at dinner during the Potsdam conference on the outskirts of bomb-destroyed Berlin in the middle of July 1945, waiting for the votes to be counted in the British general election.

Churchill replied that he wasn't sure how the soldiers had voted, but Stalin told him that as armies always prefer strong governments, they would certainly vote Conservative.

'Churchill's popularity probably assures him of a majority of about 50,' Attlee told Molotov a few days later, just before returning from Potsdam to London to hear the election result – of the first general election for ten years.

In spite of his doubt about the soldiers' vote, Churchill himself was optimistic. 'I am led to believe that the present Government will obtain a majority,' he wrote to Lord Halifax, the British ambassador in Washington, the day after the poll (held on July 5), 'but . . . electioneering is full of surprises.'

Even if there were to be an adverse vote, Churchill – it appears from the record – had no intention of resigning, 'unless it amounted to a very extreme expression of national displeasure.' Churchill wrote that he would 'await the result of a confidence vote in the House of Commons on the King's Speech, and take my dismissal from the House.' This would not occur until the middle of August. As a result Churchill would have been able to return to Potsdam to complete the work of the Three Power meeting – the first great summit conference of the post-war era.

In the event, the KGB and everyone else were proved wrong. National displeasure was overwhelming. 'What an astonishing turnover,' wrote Gladwyn Jebb, an FO high flier, to a colleague in London from Berlin. 'We are all agog to know who is going to come out . . . to represent His Majesty's Government.' When the result was declared, on July 26, the Labour Party had secured an overall majority of 146 seats. Mr Attlee returned to Potsdam accompanied by Ernest Bevin, replacing Eden as Foreign Secretary.

'The silent voters' had been forgotten, Attlee told Molotov in explanation of the upset. 'The middle classes and technical classes had voted Labour.'

These insights into the often erroneous calculations of politicians are revealed in the first of a major new series of foreign policy document volumes, published today at the Government's command.

The decision to publish was taken originally by Sir Alec Douglas-Home, then the Foreign Secretary, in 1973. He told the House of Commons that the Government had decided 'to extend into the post-war period the practice adopted for 1919–1939 of publishing documents on British foreign policy.' The new series would be called *Documents on British Policy Overseas*.

The preface to Volume 1, which deals solely with July 1945, is full of wonderful phrases about 'the established criteria for the selection of documents', and how everything to do with the editing has been 'in accordance with previous practice'. But how did this great tradition begin? And what is the purpose of the operation, apart from allowing the Foreign Office to blow its own trumpet? For official publications derived from the archives often have, according to that cynical old diplomatic historian A. J. P. Taylor, 'a propaganda purpose. No government pays for the production of many volumes merely from a disinterested love of scholarship. Sometimes it seeks to justify its predecessors; sometimes . . . to discredit them, even, more remotely, to revive national pride by displaying the glories of the past.'

Previous collections of such documents were published in order to explain and justify policy in the run-up to the last two world wars. The original series, edited by Gooch and Temperley, dealt with the world before 1914 and was actually called *British Documents on the Origins of the War*. The next series, *Documents on British Foreign Policy 1919–1939*, edited by Woodward and Butler, was designed (in the words of Anthony Eden in 1944) 'to make available as soon as possible documents dealing with events most relevant to the outbreak of the present war.'

Another more high-minded and improbable purpose was 'to enable the people of Great Britain to read for themselves a documentary record of the conduct of foreign policy, under the direction and control of Parliament, in the years between the two Great Wars.'

Such a purpose would raise a hollow laugh in the reader of the current Potsdam volume* (price £85), where the conduct of foreign policy seems often to be almost wholly in the hands of civil servants – bearing out the thesis of G. M. Young that diplomatic history is simply 'what one clerk said to another clerk'.

Presumably the current series, starting nearly 40 years ago with the Potsdam conference of July 1945, should – in line with its predecessors – be called *Documents on the Origins of the Third World War*. But in practice it is obvious that the real purpose behind the decision to publish – taken just after Britain had

Documents on British Policy Overseas, Series 1, Vol. 1: The Conference at Potsdam, July–August 1945. HMSO.

joined the European Common Market – was to look back over thirty years of Anglo-European relations, allowing the Foreign Office to show how percipient it had always been.

'I should like to thank successive Permanent Under-Secretaries of State,' writes the editor Rohan Butler, 'for their support in planning and launching the present publication.' Not surprisingly, for those who flit through the pages of this 1,278 page volume nearly all made good in after life – Harold Caccia, Gladwyn Jebb, William Hayter, Patrick Dean, Norman Brook, Pierson Dixon, Oliver Franks, Frank Roberts – and many of them passed through the House of Lords on their way to the grave. It must be gratifying for them to have their early signs of promise retrospectively, if expensively, acknowledged.

Europe, and Britain's plans (or rather their absence) for the post-war world, is certainly a major theme of this volume. A more intriguing and elusive one is the failure of Britain – or its mandarins – to come to terms with its own relative decline and the emergence as a far more important Great Power of the Soviet Union. When told that there was an assumption in the United States 'that Great Britain was now definitely a second rate Power', one diplomat minuted angrily, 'What does he mean by this?'

Advice about the Soviet Union, particularly from the ambassador in Moscow, Sir Clark Kerr, and his deputy Frank Roberts, was shrewd, but it often seems to have fallen on deaf ears at home. 'Despite the trials of the war,' wrote Kerr from Moscow on July 10, preparing his political masters for Stalin's arrival in Potsdam, 'the Soviet Union is teeming with vitality and bent upon making her influence felt, even far from her own frontiers . . . Russia of today is rejoicing in all the emotions and impulsions of her early manhood that spring from a new sense of boundless strength and from the giddiness of success.

'It is immense fun to her to tell herself that she has become great and that there is little or nothing to stop her making her greatness felt. Why resist therefore the temptation to put a finger in every pie?'

Back at the Foreign Office, it was still felt that Britain could play in the big league, even though, in the words of Sir Orme Sargent, one of the wiser diplomats of the older generation, 'we shall have to take risks, and even live beyond our political means at times.'

The tentative Foreign Office-supported moves towards forming a West European bloc in the post-war world were partly the result of this perceived sense of weakness. The Foreign Office favoured such a development, said Oliver Harvey, at a meeting held on July 25 to discuss the question, 'in order that we and our Western European allies should carry more weight in the counsels of the Big Three.' Yet no one seemed to be pushing for this politically.

A similar air of unreality hung over the discussion of military bases and Britain's future global role. Attlee, at least, seemed to have clear ideas. 'The attitude towards the defence of Gibraltar and the Suez Canal,' he minuted to Eden on July 18, 'seems to me to be unrealistic in view of air warfare and to be based on an obsolete conception of imperial defence derived from the naval era. . . . I am afraid of us undertaking responsibilities which we shall be little fitted to undertake in the economic conditions of the post-war period.' Attlee hoped somehow that these 'responsibilities' could be shouldered by the embryonic United Nations Organisation.

Eden replies sharply: 'It does not seem to me that, on the showing of this war which has proved them vital to our national existence, it is unrealistic to hold that we should continue to maintain our special position in these two areas. I should be sorry to think that we could not undertake to maintain the necessary minimum forces for this purpose.' A decade later, this unresolved argument was to blow up in Eden's face and cause his own downfall.

Over the entire volume is cast the long shadow of the atomic bomb, at first a secret known only to Churchill and Truman, and subsequently, after the successful test at Alamogordo on July 16, shared with Stalin. Mr Attlee only got to hear about it after the election result. There is little new here except detail – one of the disadvantages of a publication printed 40 years after the event when the archives are already open.

But it is rather striking to find the new Prime Minister's interest in the subject almost solely restricted to the wording of the press release to be issued after the bomb had been dropped.

'The problems of the release of energy by atomic fission have been solved,' wrote Mr Attlee on July 31 (a week *before* Hiroshima), 'and an atomic bomb has been dropped on Japan by the United States Air Force.'

The decision to drop the bomb, or the non-decision not to not drop it, had already been taken. Diplomats and commanders in the field were now wholly preoccupied with 'our total lack of preparedness should the Japanese decide to call it a day', as Mountbatten's political adviser in Southeast Asia put it.

The problem 'frankly appals me,' he went on. For on July 19, the Combined Chiefs of Staff had agreed that 'the planning date for the end of organised resistance by Japan be the 15th November 1946' – more than a year ahead. Now Mountbatten, the Supreme Commander in Southeast Asia, had suddenly in late July directed his staff 'to examine urgently the possibility of a walk-in were the Japanese to surrender at short notice.'

The possibility had arisen as a result of the appeal to the Japanese from the Big Three at Potsdam on July 26 to proclaim an unconditional surrender. 'The alternative for Japan,' the appeal went on, 'is prompt and utter destruction.' Ten days later, the alternative was dropped on Hiroshima.

One other country deserves a mention from the archives. In early July 1945, Sir William Strang travelled around it with Goronwy Rees. 'A smiling countryside,' he wrote, 'beautifully farmed with bountiful crops growing to the roadside and hedgerows; villages and small towns off the main road quite intact. . . . The population more healthy looking, better dressed, and showing less sign of strain than one would have expected. . . . It is strange to see people going serenely and even cheerfully about their business. . . .'

Where could be this still point at the heart of the turning world? It is none other than the serene picture of the rural areas of the British zone of Germany.

It would be unfair to conclude on such a surprising note. Philip Nichols, for example, the ambassador in Prague, had sadder things to point out: 'To one who has some former knowledge of Central European conditions, one of the most striking difference between today and yesterday is the almost complete absence of Jews. I remember well the very large number of Jews to be seen in Vienna after the last war. I have scarcely seen a Jew in Prague today. Comment is unnecessary.'

And Pierson Dixon, dealing with the problem of the return of Soviet citizens to the Soviet Union against their will, minutes that 'privately, we very much dislike sending some of these people back, particularly as we know that some of them are executed on arrival, but the decision to do so was most carefully considered. . . .' Comment here, too, seems superfluous.

And not all Germany was spared like the countryside that Strang had observed. Geoffrey Harrison, a young diplomat in Berlin in September 1939, returned there in mid-July 1945, and produced a more familiar picture: 'The overwhelming impression we got flying in on Saturday,' he wrote to an old friend at the FO, 'was of the total devastation and stillness of all the built-up areas. In the whole flight over Germany I did not see a single train moving . . . There is literally hardly an untouched building in Berlin . . . We walked round the corner into the Wilhemstrasse and poked about in the ruins of the British Embassy (incidentally I found the remains of my old Vauxhall car in the garage).' Not even Graham Greene could have invented a line like that.

28 February, 1984   **Richard Gott**

A Country Diary: Keswick

October so far has been rather a let-down. The rain and wind, no digging done in the garden, and the wood pigeons took the fine elderberries – earmarked for use – from outside this window between one day and the next. There is never any lack of pests. The cold wind soughed over the fell breast one day lately, so I retreated to a welcoming cottage kitchen to hear how mink had come up the little beck beside the garden to get among the hens and even kill a cock for good measure. Mink can be seen on any lake, river or beck here, and so far they seem to have attracted no natural predator. However, there was one small bonus: they have wiped out almost all the rats on the two farms down the valley. Indeed, in that easy warmth with the storm shut out, nothing seemed wholly bad. There was even a grudging good word for carrion crows. They mate for life and build their nests together with, first, a layer of fresh sticks, then a plaster of 'muck', usually cow manure, and more sticks well tamped down before the lining. It sets to rock-like hardness so that a shot, fired from below, cannot get through.

Foxes are a constant topic here, too, and like other 'pests' have ways of surviving. A new man, a new broom, came to an army unit in the North and, seeing a derelict tank bogged down in the forest, ordered its removal. Heavy equipment came and at the first grinding heave, a fine dog fox shot out of the gun turret. The one that got away?

I came home, warm, with a big bag of tomatoes and one apple in it. The apple was not for eating but to ripen the tomatoes easily and quickly.

24 October, 1983   **Enid J. Wilson**

'I dare say I am a bit of a thug'

'I plan,' said Denis Healey, 'to be the Gromyko of the Labour Party, for the next 30 years.'

Ha! How old was Gromyko? 'I'm 66. I guess he's 76, and he's had a harder life than me. He's been foreign minister the whole time, and I've been luxuriating in Opposition. He's a bloody good foreign minister, and he's still there. He's outlived Brezhnev, Khrushchev, Kosygin.'

And did Mr Healey intend to outlive his leaders? 'I don't *intend* to, but I think probably my genes condemn me to it.'

Mr Healey's genes may indeed condemn him. The above passage came about two thirds the way through a long conversation with him, a conversation into which he introduced Victor Hugo, John F. Kennedy, Pitt the Younger, Churchill, and Pericles, a conversation which began with his telling me that his father died at the age of 92, and that his mother was still thriving at 95, having recently read the whole of Turgenev.

We met at Mr Healey's London house in a Georgian square near the Elephant and Castle. If this one meeting was a fair example, he has developed the preliminaries of conversation to an art form, taking a spectacularly long time to pour drinks and place them on British Airways Concorde table mats, and keeping up a running commentary all the time on where is the whisky, where is the soda, where is the gin, and throwing in the information that these houses were originally built for the doctors who worked at Bedlam (the madhouse, now the Imperial War Museum, nearby) and that George Brown went to school on the corner, though that, he said, was something he didn't cherish.

He also said he had recently done a television programme on photography, had liked Don McCullin but thought Patrick Lichfield a bit of a pseud. His (Mr Healey's) paternal grandfather had been a working tailor and a Fenian, and Auntie Maggie had been a mill-hand all her life. Perhaps his first memory was of his father opening a tin of sardines.

Mr Healey's youth is well documented. He won a scholarship to Bradford Grammar School, where Delius went before him, and Hockney after. He got a first at Balliol. During the war he was a beachmaster at Anzio.

He fought the 1945 election, his poster showing a young Major Healey, in uniform, and with the inscription 'BA (Oxon.)' after his name.

He said that of course he hadn't put the degree there, and that as to the use of his army rank – and he never used it again afterwards – well, it was a safe Tory seat and his Conservative opponent was a brigadier, an RAMC pox-doctor, and the Liberal was another brigadier, a heavyweight boxer and the nearest thing to Neanderthal man.

When I remarked that he must be one of the few remaining politicians to have had a humane, classical education, he said there were a few around: he'd met one the other day, much to his surprise.

That was why he was sometimes called Renaissance Man? 'Oh no, that's because I'm so brilliant at everything outside politics. Nothing to do with my education. I like philosophy, paint a little bit, very keen on music. . . . Winston, you know, was like that. He was a Renaissance man. He painted very well indeed, and he wrote well, and he liked building walls.'

63

Wasn't his own second name Winston? 'My father believed in lost causes, and I was born when Winston was in the doghouse over Gallipoli.'

So he was named after a lost cause? 'That's right. But it (Churchill) turned out to be a winning cause. You never know, you know, you never know.'

After 1945, Mr Healey became International Secretary of the Labour Party, publishing pamphlets like *Cards on the Table*, and *Feet on the Ground*, and *The Curtain Falls* (in Eastern Europe that is). He said then, and still believes now, that the curtain will eventually rise.

He had gone into politics because he was a chap who only thought and worked well under pressure, and would go to seed otherwise. That was why he did not return to Oxford, as he was invited to do, even though he wanted to write 'the world's great book on aesthetics'.

It came out here that, just before the war at Oxford, he had organised an exhibition of Picassos, at a time when you could buy a good etching, of the Minotaur period, for £5.

Had he? 'No, I didn't have £5. Don't be silly.'

What would his advice be now to someone in such a situation, Borrow? 'Yes. Borrow, save, steal, anything.'

But to borrow was unsocialist advice? 'Yes, and I personally, like most people from my background, you know, I've never borrowed myself except for a house. I actually paid off my first mortgage early, which was financially insane . . . It took a long time for me to accept the economic and intellectual validity of Harold Lever's attitude to life.'

In the mid-50s Mr Healey wrote a pamphlet on Neutralism, a concept he carefully distinguishes from neutrality. Neutrality is the policy of such a state as Switzerland or Sweden. Neutralism, as I understand the idea, is the attitude of an individual who, disliking the facts of the world as they are, opts out. I asked Mr Healey how far his concept of neutralism described the state of mind of CND members.

'Well, I think the weakness of the CND approach is basically trying to isolate one element in the total international situation, namely nuclear weapons, from the rest. It's sort of single issue politics; in that sense it's rather like giving up the whole of your life to saving the whale, or stopping seal culling.'

Mr Healey said he was at the moment obsessed with the nuclear winter, in which the world might starve in a continuous Arctic night. 'But,' he said, 'you can't opt out of the thing by being neutral, or even getting rid of your own nuclear weapons, because the other buggers can start the war. So somehow or other you've got to concern yourself about this appalling problem. . . . You can't contract out of that, because you're on the same planet, and you can't step off.'

We touched on Austria, whose domestic policies Mr Healey admires. Now Austria, he said, had started off as the head of one of the greatest empires the world had ever seen, and in some ways one of the most benign. The Austro-Hungarian empire was still yearned for by people living in Yugoslavia.

As the British Empire was still yearned for? 'Oh, yes it is.'

To jump from the Austrian to the British empires was permissible. To jump from social democrat Austria to the SDP was not: when I did so, Mr Healey asked me for heaven's sake to keep the conversation clean. In that spirit, therefore, I went instead to a speech of his made some months after the defeat of 1979, in which he mentioned the brotherhood of the Labour Party.

'I know,' he said. 'We don't make a good shift of it.'

Knives out? 'Yes I know, but, you know, we have a turbulent love life actually. . . . We bash one another about, but there's a great deal of underlying respect.'

Quite simply, the public manners of the Conservative Party were better, then? 'That's right. I'm glad to say, though, that democracy is invading them and they're becoming much the same.'

I took a second point from the brotherhood speech. How, he had asked himself, could Labour ensure it did not lose the next election, and had answered that it was not by lurching to the opposite extreme of policy from the Conservatives and jumping into the trenches of the class war.

'As you jolly well know,' he replied, 'I had three miserable years trying to oppose this tendency.'

I said I was not convinced he *had* fought against it, at which he looked at me and laughed.

Very well, I said, let's take what must surely have been one of the most entertaining documents of the last many years in politics, the 1983 Labour manifesto. 'Yes, the one which I did *not* describe as the longest suicide note in history.'

But that was a pretty apt description, and what had he done about that manifesto? 'Fought it every inch of the way.'

'On unilateralism?' I asked, and here things got complicated, I saying there was a fudge and Mr Healey that there had been a straight contradiction in terms. For me to condense what was said will inevitably oversimplify it, but there's no help.

So, he said, there was agreement on no cruise and no Trident, but then it came to Polaris. 'Now just listen . . . This is where there was not a fudge but a straight contradiction. Because if you were absolutely committed to getting rid of Polaris . . . obviously you can't negotiate with the Russians if you say you're going to get rid of it anyway, and there was always an implicit contradiction, which of course came out.' He said Mr Foot had agreed in advance that if the question arose, what would they do if the Russians would not negotiate, then the line should be that a new situation would have arisen, which would be considered when it presented itself.

Yes, but Healey hadn't stuck to that line, had he? 'With great respect, I did.' When Mr Healey says the words 'great respect,' watch out.

We reverted to the manifesto. 'It wasn't out-and-out unilateralism. But it's equally true, and this is the problem you face, that the Labour Party had committed itself to out-and-out unilateralism at its conference. Now you say I didn't fight. I fought. So did Peter (Shore). But Peter didn't refuse to contest the election for the party. We were in a minority. There was no chance of changing that.'

But then, in the middle of the election, Mr Healey had made a local radio broadcast saying that if the Russians wouldn't negotiate, then we'd keep Polaris? He replied that it had been a slip; that he had said he thought that would be the case; and that it had been a mistake. So what? What was I trying to prove? And had I read an article he had written in *Encounter* in 1956?

No.

'I've always thought the question whether we have our own

nuclear weapons is a question in the end of cost benefit. What does it cost? What do we get?'

So it was not a moral issue? 'Oh no. Of course it isn't. Because if I thought it was a moral issue I'd think the Germans had to have one too.'

What about the Falklands; what about his having said Mrs Thatcher gloried in slaughter?

'A bad mistake.'

'Senseless,' I suggested.

'It was a very bad mistake.'

Here Mrs Healey, who had been sitting at the other end of the room throughout the interview, interjected with some heat: 'If you were followed around . . .'

Mr Healey: 'Oh well, never mind. The plain fact is that the television recorded every word, and they didn't find a word they could use against me until that. But still, I don't claim to be perfect, and this was a bad mistake. Although funnily enough my own supporters said my mistake was withdrawing the word. But I thought it unfair (to Mrs Thatcher).'

But my question remained. How, with the Falklands a crucial issue, and very much to the Conservatives' advantage, could Mr Healey, with 30 years' experience in politics, make such a mistake? He said that Mr Wilson, with even more experience, had made the mistake of saying the pound in your pocket would not be devalued. And Mr Kinnock, for whom he had the greatest regard, had had to apologise twice during the campaign, over the Falklands. 'I only had to apologise once. It was a very bad mistake, and I was not so much ashamed of it as very worried about all the damage it would do the party.'

And Mrs Thatcher, next morning, had called him a political thug? 'With great respect, the real trouble is that the only politician who doesn't make that sort of mistake is the sort who tries never to say anything, and my great weakness as a politician is I always say too much . . . I dare say I am a bit of a thug . . . On the other hand, you know, every party needs some people who will rough it up from time to time, don't you think?'

When had the realisation come to him that he would never be leader of the Labour Party? 'Never's a big word. We don't know that even now.'

I just looked at him. He then said he supposed his chance came and went in the leadership election of 1980, when Mr Foot narrowly beat him. But that was life. That was show business. It was a disappointment.

Just a disappointment? 'You will exaggerate it . . . I certainly would have been glad to be Prime Minister and leader of the party if that had come my way, but it's never been in a sense the focus of my ambition. What I like is doing a job well, and I think I was a bloody good Secretary of State for Defence, and a bloody good Chancellor too. The first is generally recognised, the second not.'

He then repeated that he was not saying he had had it as Prime Minister, and it was at this point that he said he planned to be the Labour Party's Gromyko for the next 30 years.

Well, after the general election, when the party needed a new leader, he had supported Hattersley, but it had turned out Kinnock. 'I like him a lot. Edna and I both like each of them (Mr and Mrs Kinnock).' People, he said, had needed a break with the past and a new face, and, besides, Mr Kinnock had shine.

Shine? 'Yes, something glamorous and exciting.'

Now glamorous Mr Kinnock simply is not. And as for exciting, what was exciting? 'That's why they chose him . . . What they've got is something more than that. I think Neil is very influenced by the Kennedy example.'

Kennedy? Kennedy had been a Yankee aristocrat, surely? 'His role in American politics was to excite a generation of young people with politics, after Eisenhower and Truman. He excited young people not only in America but all over the world.'

He was comparing Kinnock with Kennedy? 'In that sense yes.'

But a successful leader of the Labour Party over the next five years would have to be a most talented trimmer? 'Oh no, that is not the right way to put it . . . Moving forward in politics, it's like being carried down a river; you can't suddenly start swinging across to the bank. You have to wait until the river divides and then decide which way you go.'

That, I said – thinking that a moment before he had been describing Mr Kinnock as exciting – was just anodyne. 'It may be anodyne, but it has the unfortunate demerit of being true, and so it's terribly dull, *terribly* dull. But it's awfully true, and it's been true right through history, from Pericles on.

'Kinnock, not Pericles, is going to be a very good leader.'

I mentioned lack of experience. 'You know, William Pitt was very inexperienced when he was Prime Minister, very much younger than Neil.'

Well, Pitt had been 24, but he had, I said, been the son of his father. 'I don't think Neil's illegitimate, you know.'

At this point, what with J. F. Kennedy and Pitt the Younger, it seemed to me we were drifting down rivers of political fantasy. 'You sound baffled,' said Mr Healey. 'But have another go; or have another drink.'

I said I'd have another go, and asked about the idea, which I'd heard put about, that Mr Healey, now he was no longer deputy leader, felt born again. '*They* say I'm born again. The Return of the Heli, they call it.'

I mentioned a book of Mr Healey's own photographs, called *Healey's Eye*, which was published in 1980, saying that in it he had described as a rictus of hypocrisy the false smile that some people put on when they pose for the camera. (Here my memory was inaccurate: what he wrote was rictus of stupefying dishonesty, but the sense is much the same.) 'Yes, yes,' he said, 'rictus is a word I adore,' and did I know these lines of Victor Hugo, one man addressing another:

– Pourquoi ris-tu?

– Je ne ris pas.

– Alors tu es terrible.

Ah, yes, but he had just told me, earlier, that he didn't think Labour had a chance in the June election? 'Nobody did.'

But there he had been sitting on the platform smiling, for God's sake?

'Yes.'

Was that a rictus of hypocrisy? 'There's an element of rictus in it, certainly, but, equally, I think your only chance of winning was to convey confidence and aggressiveness against the Government.

'Let me tell you about rictuses. Edna and I were sitting in my room, which is like a cell block in a lunatic asylum, where the Shadow chaps live (this was during the 1980 party leadership

69

election), and someone came up with the results of the poll. And I was told I'd lost by eight votes, whatever it was.

'Now, so I felt, well, I'll put a brave face on – that's not a rictus, a brave face – and I walked smiling down the corridor into the room where they announced the results a couple of minutes later, and everybody thought I'd won. Michael shambled in, looking desperately unhappy; everybody thought he'd lost. . . . That's a comparison which I wish I hadn't made, but there you are.'

30 January, 1984   **Terry Coleman**

Through the nonsense barrier

On Northwest Orient's flight from Prestwick to Boston the steward invited us to 'deplane' at Shannon, but to remain seated while the 'food module' was in the aisle. It was a foretaste of the language I was to learn. I was actually on my way to JSC (the Johnson Space Centre, Houston) for an LDS (Long Duration Simulation), covering the 'timeline' for the first four days of the nine-day Spacelab Mission now scheduled for the end of November.

All the PIs (Principal Investigators, originators of the 70-odd experiments on board), and their teams, were expected to be there. We were there to learn how to man the consoles and speak proper space language. The space crew, and all the ground teams, were divided into two 12-hour shifts – known as the Red Shift and the Blue Shift. The Red crew are OC1, MS1, and PS1, and the Blue are OC2, MS2, and PS2 (Orbiter Crew, Mission Specialists and Payload Specialists).

The real names of the Reds are John Young (commander), Bob Parker and Ulf Merbold; and those of the Blues, Brewster Shaw, Owen Garriott and Byron Lichtenberg. It is their first names that really matter, since that is what they are called over the 'voice loops'. PIs do not normally speak directly to them, but pass on messages through the APS (Alternate Payload Specialist). The APSs, or back-ups, have trained to perform all the experiments along with the Spacelab crew, and play a crucial intermediary role on the ground. They are Wubbo Ockels (Red) and Mike Lampton (Blue).

Most of the Spacelab management personnel are located in the POCC (Payload Operations Control Center) in Building 30. Most of the PIs are packed into crowded user rooms there, where they clamber over apparatus and bags, searching for a spare headset and space at a console. The Germans would like to see lists drawn up stating who is entitled to be at a given console at a given time; the Americans believe it can all be settled by a little give and take. There are too few British to have a concerted opinion.

Luckily, 025 (my experiment number) was not in the POCC but in the SMA (Science Monitoring Area) along with most of the other Life Science experiments. The SMA is in Building 36, some five minutes' walk away or seven minutes' drive (2 minutes' drive, and five minutes' walking round car parks). Most Americans prefer to drive. The SMA has enough room and a fairly relaxed atmosphere: there is coffee always on the brew, and space to chat. We were given a special SMA Life Sciences training and SDS (Short Duration Simulation) before the start of the LDS. We were taught how to operate the voice loops, and what to say. We were told to speak briefly and clearly, and use the approved language of 'Affirmative, Negative, Roger, Wilco, 025 copies.'

Americans were also told to avoid the use of cute expressions like 'Between a rock and a hard place' (when they really mean Hobson's Choice), and Europeans were asked to avoid saying 'Can do' and 'Can't do' since these sound the same to Americans. I complained that this wasn't just a European problem, since we couldn't hear the difference when Americans used these words. 'That just confirms that it *is* a European problem,' said 102 (an American).

The 025 team had increased by 100 per cent for this visit to JSC. 025 is normally a one-woman team, but I did not see how I could manage to operate as both Red and Blue for several days without sleep. The Medical Research Council (who fund the experiment, which is about adaptation to weightlessness, and the difference between weight and mass) were very understanding, and agreed to pay the expenses of my research assistant,

Eric Brodie. I was to be Red and Eric Blue. That was until I discovered that Red was to be the night shift during the actual mission. I decided to be generous and let Eric take the Red shift: he would be flying over only for the days of the mission, so he could stay on GMT and avoid jet lag. I would be staying longer in the States, and could not avoid a circadian shift. The only snag was that during the LDS the relation between MET (Mission Elapsed Time) and CST (Central Standard Time, as in Houston) was different: Blue ran from 10 pm to 10 am. Having signed on as Blue, there was no way out. So Eric did the day shift, where he was kept busy with various simulated disasters, including a spot of SAS (Space Adaptation Syndrome – it sounds pleasanter and more beneficial than 'space sickness').

My shift ran smoothly enough, but I spent most of the night trying to chase up the tapes. The crew were supposed to read out the results of X (experiment) 025, and somewhere this should have been recorded on a voice tape. I received lots of fascinating tapes, but none contained any reference to X025. The wrong time, perhaps? (GMT instead of MET?) The wrong voice loop? Should it be A/G 1 or A/G 2 (Air-to-ground 1 and 2), or perhaps ICOM B (Intercom B)? Or was it 'sim-peculiar' (the communications system not functioning as it would in the mission)? No one seemed to know.

During the next performance of X025 it became clear that the crew were recording their answers on their personal tape recorders instead of A/G, and I would not get the data till after the mission. I explained that I would like it during the mission. 'Why do you want it realtime?' asked Mike (the Blue APS). In the small hours of the morning diplomacy deserted me, and I could only think of the most compelling reason. 'Well, if you all crash, at least I'll get my data.' There was a horrified silence.

'I don't think Owen would like to hear that,' said Mike. (Owen was about to perform X025.) Various negative things were said by management personnel. 'How does this impact your science?' asked one of them.

'What?'

'Repeat, how does this impact your science?' (impatiently).

'I don't understand the question.'

72

'What difference would it make if you got the data during the mission or afterwards?'

'Ah, now I understand.'

But I was unable to produce instant and compelling reasons for wanting the data now, and the opportunity to record the answers from Owen was past. I felt depressed, and wondered whether I was in danger of being 'descoped' for using improper language. (To be descoped is to have the scope of one's experiment reduced. The phrase is often used euphemistically for total removal from the mission.)

I had a cup of coffee, and a new idea, and was soon back on Mike's loop. 'Mike, this is 025. Listen, I've had an idea. I can see that 20 minutes is too long to occupy the A/G loop while the crew member is doing the experiment. But if he waits till he's finished and then reads out the answers quickly, he can do it under two minutes. Do you think that might be allowed?'

'Oh, Helen, what a *super* idea. You've got Byron coming up next, from 6.30 to 7.0, but that's mostly LOS. But at 7.06 we go AOS with KU, and there are four minutes before his next operation on the timeline. He could do it then.' (LOS is Loss of Signal, or no voice communication. AOS is Affordance of Signal. KU is one of the signal bands.)

Management reluctantly agreed to give it a try on this occasion. There was a long silence, but at 7.06 Byron could be heard reading out the data, 'Charlie, X-Ray, Foxtrot, Delta . . .', and I was able to check it all off on the corresponding record card.

'Byron, we hear you loud and clear,' said Mike.

'That was 1 minute 36 seconds. Real neat,' came a management voice, with a touch of pleasure in it.

'Mike, will you pass on 025's thanks to Byron?'

'Sure will.'

The night had passed, and it was morning. I felt very confident that things would work out during the mission. The crew want to achieve as much science as possible. A large part of the achievement will be due to the behind-the-scenes work of those interpreters and negotiators, the back-up Payload Specialists.

20 October, 1983   **Helen Ross**

73

Florence of Arabia, the Desert Rat herself

In spite of the usual assault upon him of visual aids, video tapes and verbal interactions, it appears that Lee is still of the opinion that Louis Armstrong was the first man to set foot upon the moon. One small step for man, one huge leap for Satchmo, and one almighty poke in the eye for the schoolteacher.

Little wonder, then, that the teaching profession is in a demoralised state. So much so, that when these weary men and women meet, at what are called conferences, courses, or seminars, much time is now spent not simply on listening to lectures of the 'Adolescent role-play in a mixed-ability group situation' kind, but also on sharing tales of woeful ignorance. Such meetings, in other words, often become a form of therapy whereby all teachers, in turn, talk freely about their experiences of Louis Armstrongs, Christopher Cullodens, or of the Desert Rat herself, Florence of Arabia.

The teacher is supposed to take comfort from such discussion. But as the stories are divulged, it soon becomes evident, not to say disturbing, that many of these hitherto unknown figures from world history are mentioned not by one child alone but by children from all over the country. An unpleasant thought then begins to haunt the minds of all present: Is it they, and not their charges, who have failed to do their homework properly?

Take, for instance, the apparent nationwide popularity among the young of a distinguished historical character by the name of King George. If we collate the reams of exercise book evidence on him, we must conclude that King George was so monumental a figure that he was able to protect Britain from dragons, the Turks, and a man named 'Hitlar' all at the same time. 'Hitlar,' again, is another celebrity on whom the young are able to write with an authority rarely seen outside amusement arcades. This man 'Hitlar,' it is widely held, was involved in dairy production, until someone suddenly realised that all his dairies were forgeries – though there is one school of thought, in some northern part I believe, which suggests that on the whole the dairies are genuine and that it is 'Hitlar' who was the forgery.

In one recent examination, a teacher asked his students to name four of the most important people in history and to say why they thought each of them was important. Overall, God and Jesus won hands down, though the Queen came a comfortable third. Other royals probably took fourth and fifth place, too – Annette's famous four, for instance, were the Queen Mother ('because without her we would not have a queen'), the Queen ('because she is the Queen'), Prince Charles and Diana ('because they will be King and Queen' – Annette only counted them as one person, incidentally), and Jimmy Savile. In the final reckoning, however, I understand that Savile and 'Hitlar' were just pipped by 'Maggie Thatcher' into sixth place.

Certainly Margaret Thatcher is more familiar to us all than her hitherto unheard of medieval counterpart, 'Magner Carter,' a woman who seems, according to a girl in the West Country, to have been a crucial figure in 'stopping bad King John and bringing the country to its senses.' Although perhaps not quite of the top four calibre, Magner might well require R. J. Unstead to consider rewriting a few hundred of his school text books, quite apart from her causing mayhem among medievalists in the senior common rooms. There is sure to be trouble too over Jason's discovery that 'King Henry' in fact had eight wives, not six, all of whom had their heads chopped off.

One cannot help wondering how the great 'Carter' might have fared against other fearsome figures from history such as 'Attila the One,' 'Mussli,' 'Frankenstein,' or even against the King of Lusitania. Who, you doubtless ask, is the King of Lusitania? Plainly you have not read Darren's long and lurid account of the outrageous adventures of 'The Sin King of Lusitania,' written after a history lesson of uninterrupted slumber somewhere in the Thames Valley. Darren argues cogently, and with eye-watering attention to detail that the Sin King not only broke every rule in the book, but also 'had the cheek to start the first world war' – a war which, incidentally, many young students of the subject now believe to have begun in the Falklands, not in the Balkans as had previously been suggested.

There are some teachers, nevertheless, who will stubbornly continue to believe that 'Magner Carter' is an old document and was never a person, just as there will be others who cling to the idea of Wellington once being a man, and not merely a boot. But how much longer, we might ask, will the young politely continue to ignore such nonsense? Move over AJP, here comes Darren.

18 October, 1983   **Stephen Petty**

Gentlemen of the Press

Mrs Margaret Thatcher is a refined woman. She wears smart frocks and discreet jewels, has very tidy hair, and speaks in a modulated voice with a ladylike accent, so it is sometimes hard to see exactly how she has managed to coarsen the fabric of our society quite as thoroughly as she has. We have, after all, been through worse times, suffered more adversity, endured loss of jobs with far fewer compensations. Perhaps it is not entirely her fault, perhaps there is something inadvertent in the timbre of her voice that has penetrated the caves where the beasts live, waiting, as dogs wait, for their day.

However that may be, their day is now. They are slouching out, beetle-browed, knuckles dusting the ground, grunting glottal figures who are not yet familiar even with fire. They are invading the country, pushing in everywhere and nowhere more successfully than into journalism.

There appears to be a gentlemen's agreement among workers and professionals of all sorts that birds of a feather, however vulturous some may be, must stick together. Myself, I am no gentleman. Nor do I feel at all inhibited in criticising the Press because I work for it. My own newspaper no more resembles most of that degrading use of trees than a lion resembles an infestation of fleas so let us not flounder about pretending false modesty. The fact is that of all the callosities produced in Thatcher's Britain, a majority of our Press has become the most callous. Americans – I mean *Americans* – think it the pits and, given their Press, that is saying something. Yet we continue to accept it as if it were the weather, bad but inevitable. And many decent journalists who could take action against it fink out and, instead, praise it with faint condemnation.

The protective professional buzz word with which they do that at the moment is 'predictable'. 'Mr Michael Foot' (or whoever), goes a typical news item, 'predictably claimed today that the debasement of journalism was worse than at any time in his predictable recollection and he predictably attacked . . . predictably deplored . . . predictably denounced . . . blah blah blah.' The idea seems to be that by calling any criticism of the Press 'predictable' you have uttered the last word on the subject, finally summarised it, brought all discussion to an end, don't call us we'll call you. Curious reasoning, that. Rather like reporting that a child predictably screamed when beaten by a parent or that Jews predictably objected to concentration camps, the implication being that the child and the Jews are at fault and extremely boring for carrying on so.

I have two main reactions to the present state of the Press. One is work centred. I deeply resent what should be an honourable job being so debased, particularly on behalf of a few very fine and courageous journalists who have, in every corner of the world, drawn our attention, often at the risk of their lives, to terrible injustices. That they should have to call themselves by the same name as the Neanderthalers of their profession is a nonsense. At another level, I find I am not as disturbed by the wholesale distortion of truth or the outright lies or even the obsession with tits and bums as I am about the truly astonishingly low level on which this takes place. For instance, throughout the seventies the Press howled with fury about the women's movement, made vitriolic jokes and drew vitriolic cartoons. At the time (predictably) I reacted with equal fury. But now, looking back from the new low of the eighties, I feel positive nostalgia. Those attacks, however infuriating, had gusto, real emotion. Brains were cudgelled, wits were sharpened, battle was joined with all flags flying.

That is no longer so. Now we are colonised by journalistic muggers with cabbage ears and blocked noses who beat at their typewriters with leaden coshes. Under those indiscriminate blows the keys weld into mere slugs of metal within which there is no decipherable meaning other than hostility. The muggers do not forge words but blunt instruments with which to render those who read insensible, if not permanently brain-damaged. When you actually handle the newspapers for which they commit their acts of aggression, holding them away from you as you might an old sock, you realise that, indeed, time has a warp. Fresh from the presses each issue may be, but it already smells of its near future, the contents of dustbins and the wrapping of fish.

These muggers have their gang leaders, of course, the Private Eyers, the Spectatorites, superior folk who specialise in callousing their readers' skin with humour. They are the doormen of Thatcher's Britain; they ushered it in. Some can make you laugh like a drain, meaning that when your laughter dies you feel exactly like a drain – a conduit for their rubbish. Used. Others, resting on the laurels earned in more civilised times, feel free now to resort to common abuse, purging themselves in the process of the detritus of their private lives and most particularly, one cannot help noticing, their unimaginable sex lives.

But the really extraordinary thing about these people who consider themselves in the business of communication is their startling lack of the essential talents for that business. To communicate requires empathy, imagination, an intuitive understanding of what other people feel. You do not need to agree with them but any literate debate or argument must stem from this understanding. If it is not there, mere thuggery results. As a trifling example, the editor of the journalists' own paper, the union organ, could not seem to take in at all why union women objected to the use of the Varoomshka unclad-lady cartoon in that paper. This failure of imagination is reprehensible because it makes almost impossible the really important intellectual debate (one, I may add, that we on this paper conducted when the lady resided with us). You cannot argue with any passion against someone who does not grasp the ground rules, any more than you can hope for light to dawn upon the Labour Party bigwigs if they – like the Press – cannot understand why women attempting to speak at the rostrum object to being sexually kibbitzed by loutish colleagues.

The worrying thing about journalists on papers like the *Sun*, the *Mail*, the *Star* is not that they attack – that is their privilege – but that they cannot understand their victims' case and so let all the potentially interesting issues go by default. Thick as planks they are, I fear, their heads jammed with sawdust, only able to wave their flippers and bark like seals. One would like to leave them alone with their personal afflictions but unfortunately, given muscle room as they are by Mrs Thatcher (*her* case they do understand, which speaks volumes for her case), their influence is widespread. Newspapers create a climate, they emit an odour that encompasses us all, like effluent from a factory chimney that we cannot help but breathe in.

Are we to live in it forever? Must we accept it as the English way of life? Is it *this* they mean when they talk so proudly of the freedom of the Press? Some freedom. Some Press.

11 October, 1983   **Jill Tweedie**

All Our Working Lives

In the century when Britain built 80 per cent of the world's new ships, the great steel hulls would tower above the shipyard towns like beached whales in Lilliput. Time and forgetfulness have turned the great days of the industry into part of the British sea myth. Shipbuilding was Brunel on the deck of the *Great Eastern*, it was royalty smashing bottles of champagne on the snouts of liners, and the world queueing at the British ship-yards' doors to place their orders.

The Japanese ordered their warships from Vickers on one side of the Tyne, and the Russians ordered theirs from Hawth-orn Leslie on the opposite bank, and those two fleets sailed half way round the world and fought each other in their war of 1905. The armourers thrived all right. (Later when the Swedes did that kind of thing, the British upper lip would curl in disgust. And wasn't there some similar Argie-bargy not so long ago?)

The first part of Peter Pagnamenta's series *All Our Working Lives* (BBC-2) looked at the shipbuilders, from that heyday to now, when we build just two per cent of the world's new shipping. If it had an invisible sub-title it was How a nation's pride became a nation's downfall, and Angela Holdsworth produced a rich and sharply detailed mosaic out of archive film, old documentaries and present day interviews.

Ships contained everything that symbolised the industrial revolution, put together by all the skills available in such plentiful, and dangerous supply. Dangerous because where there were fewer skilled men, competitors like the Germans had to invent machines and better methods; and because the sheer abundance of them in British yards meant they were treated as squads of sweated casual labour, to be hired when needed, and paid off at an hour's notice when they were not.

The squad system was invented by employers in the spirit of Adam Smith's division of labour, and divided it fell. The squads guarded their corners with a jealous passion that turned into the rivalries of the 20 odd trade unions in the industry's maturity, and the suicidal demarcation disputes of its decline.

And like some crude cartoon of Capital, management took its profits, unwilling to invest while the orders poured in, unable to do it when they stopped; while the Admiralty turned Nelson's eye on innovation, and the Marine band played on the poop. In this synoptic reading, after the traumas of the thirties and the boom of the war years, it was too late: the industry had destroyed itself because its fear of slump was greater than its faith in prosperity. The rest of the world sailed by, admiring our craftsmanship. Hearts of oak. And between the ears, solid mahogany.

14 April, 1984   **Hugh Hebert**

Hobson's blind spot

Oxford and Cambridge men are said to suffer 'the needle' once they are in sight of Putney Bridge on Boat Race day. The Cambridge cox, Peter Hobson, got an overdose on Saturday, when he attacked a 500-ton lighter with a £6,500 plastic racing shell powered by his university's finest.

He was warming his eight up with a practice start when he hit McCann's barge and sent the bows of the yellow craft into a parody of a fascist salute, delaying the race by 25 hours. Cambridge lost by 3¾ lengths to Oxford, who set a record time yesterday of 16 mins 45 secs.

The Cambridge lads stuck gamely by the 21-year-old Yorkshire mite after the accident, saying that he was too little to be expected to see through the 105 stone of beefsteak and muscle towering in front of him, and that they would all go to their rooms and miss the Boat Race ball at the Savoy. 'The barge was in my blind spot,' said the 7½st maths student at Christ's, thus establishing a record in blind spots.

Hobson listed 're-shaping barges' among his interests in the race programme. This was not only prophetic but based on experience. Last summer he piled a brand-new college eight into a barge on the Cam, wrecking another fine example of the boat builders' craft. This precipitated him out of the Christ's rowing congregation into the eager arms of the university boat club, who recognise a truly aggressive cox when they see one. Ian 'Gonzo' Bernstein, Cambridge's cox for the past two years, was displaced by Hobson in the ill-fated Blue boat.

Hobson survived Saturday night with his crew, who watched the film *Raiders of the Lost Ark* in their Putney headquarters. That was also prophetic. The ark was lost for the ninth successive time from Putney to Mortlake. Cambridge nevertheless broke the old record to become the fastest crew in Light Blue history. Hobson received two warnings for bad steering from the umpire.

Members of the coxswains' secret society – blindness, deafness, and loquaciousness are the essential qualifications – would recognise Hobson's close shave with Oxford and the warnings as good coxing.

Hobson's choices have not been made for him, but he has surely steered his way into history.

19 March, 1984   **Christopher Dodd**

The place where you can't sit on the fence

I went to a party last week in that Sloane Rangerland I once knew well. A Hooray came up to where I stood, nose stuck in a glass of bubbly, and invited me to another round of champers the next day.

'Do come, darling, we'll have a few giggles,' he said.

'I can't,' I said, 'I'll be at Greenham Common.'

The room erupted into silence, jaws sagged, bottles splintered, mirrors cracked across.

'Greenham? You're joking, darling.'

'No.'

'But you can't believe in . . . all that? I mean. I mean . . .' the Hooray wailed, 'the women. They're so *ugly.*'

'You've been reading the *Sun* again, naughty,' I said. 'If you don't give up that filthy habit you'll get hair on your lovely white hands.'

In cool Belgravia we said a cool goodnight.

Greenham Common is a theatre of war, as choc-a-bloc with significance as a bad play; the symbols come at you like hailstones, bouncing off your brain and making it ache. Within the high curved fences, behind the rolls of razor wire, on that weird wide stage where the missiles are, everything is as neat as death. It looks like a new crematorium in a rich part of the shires, with manicured lawns and broad access paths for the mourners. The brush of leafless trees at its borders glow oddly pink and brown, lit from behind. Here and there, on the man-made pyramids of grass at the gates and along the meshed perimeter, young soldiers stand in their dappled costumes, unreal as Action Men, their faces under the perky berets smooth and expressionless, their eyes professionally blank.

Outside the fences, where the missiles aren't, there is turmoil. Fly-sheets flap in the wind, trestle tables groan with pamphlets, cards and badges, the plastic domes of bender huts spew forth mounds of sleeping bags, cars nose their way into clearings and men in vans dispense paper plates of beans and curry or take on children to mind. And of course there are women everywhere, long entangled skeins of coloured wool wound around the empty inner ground. Young women dancing and piping on recorders or sitting in circles round open fires or playing with children or gathering firewood. Middle-aged women in anoraks and ski-ing gear and Agricultural Show tweeds, hanging onto each other's arms. Elderly women with grey curls who squat under banners proclaiming 'Grannies Against the Bomb' and wave cheerfully at the passing throng. One of them puts a loose piece of fencing to her face and says, 'Please don't feed the Grannies.'

All day the women trudge through churned-up mud beside the fence, talking, laughing, eating, stepping carefully across the boggy ground and always, at their sides at the miles of fencing, there are lines of women standing still, their fingers hooked in the wire, their faces pressed against it, staring solemnly across the plain inside, thinking their thoughts. A woman with two little girls threads silver string in and out of the mesh in an intricate ever-growing glittering web. Two women dig with a small trowel and plant a little tree. Another ties a Christmas tree up and stands as if in her own sitting room, decorating it. Other women pin up photographs of themselves, their men, their children, reminding me of the bright snapshots you see on Russian graves. Slowly, the fence fills – banners from every part of England, Scotland and Wales, chips of mirror that wink in the sun, swathes of embroidery full of quilted doves and collage flowers and cross-stitched letters that say things like 'Cruise Will Cost the Earth.' Further over, where the soldiers gaze impassively ahead, a cut-out family in full-size cardboard, hands linked like doily dolls, is painstakingly pinned up by its still-living counterparts.

Later, when the sun is setting, the women join hands and sway and sing, rank on rank. 'You can't kill the spirit, she is old and strong, she is like a mountain, she goes on and on.' The voices rise into a high ululation, the ancient sound of grieving women, and the soldiers gaze over the heads of their sisters and their mothers towards the blood-shot horizon. Then the women

12 December, 1983

at the fences hang in and start to move, back and forward, back and forward, pulling and pulling. Away along the line the ten-foot mesh begins to undulate, in and out, in and out, carrying with it in and out the burden of banners and snapshots and silver threads and cardboard families. Overhead, the spirals of barbed wire plunge up and down and in front of us the soldiers stir uneasily, their eyes flickering from side to side.

The women breathe heavily, it is heavy work but once begun, no-one gives up. As one woman falls away, panting, another woman takes her place, hooks in and heaves. In, out, in, out. From the end of the line dark figures move up, the police, plucking the women away. Wherever they go, an outbreak of ululation marks where they are. The women fall back and fall against the fence again and go on. In, out, in, out. The police go up and down, plucking again and again at the women, not hard, not ungently, almost resigned, almost smiling. No-one is angry. It is simply that everyone has a job to do.

The eyes of the soldier opposite us suddenly click into focus. As I watch, his face flushes and a spasm goes through him. He

leaps for the wire and hits out at our fingers, short hard jabs from the chest. I feel pain as his knuckles hit mine and look at him. He is about the same age as my sons, there are flecks of hazel in his eyes, he is a handsome lad and his breath smells sweet, milky. I cannot understand why he is angry. Young men like him do not, in my experience, usually identify so readily with their employers' interests. Can he feel protective about the death they have stored at his back? Have they taught him so well? To myself I intone 'he is only doing his job' but the flushed face, the furious jabs, belie that. There is more here than meets the eye.

As I am thinking, hanging on, heaving, another soldier lunges forward, pushing his face at the face of the woman beside me. The two of them are, I suppose, the same age, they could be twins. The mesh rears between them, wicked little spikes of wire rise to their chins. 'Gi'us a blow job,' he hisses and, amazed, she laughs.

With a creak and a grind, the wire peels off its concrete posts and folds to the ground. Startled, a woman whispers, 'Oh, they can get at us now,' and instantly the soldier reaches out, closes

85

his fists round her shoulders and tugs her across the barbs of the wire. She cries out, five women close around her, he opens his fists and lets her go. Nobody moves. In the silence the soldier, eyes fixed on the ground, stretches his hand out and gives her back her camera which has fallen at his feet. 'Thank you,' she says. There are beads of blood at her throat.

In seconds the soldiers, with the police, have got the mesh up and fastened it again. We stand and stare as we did before and they stand and stare through us. It is well known that the relationship between male and female animals behind bars in zoos often becomes seriously disturbed.

20 December, 1983   **Jill Tweedie**

The folk who bring you cruise

It is no accident that United Technologies arrived on the British sponsorship market at about the same time as the Cruise missile reached Greenham Common. They help to build the things. And assorted other missile defence systems, and helicopter gunships and jet fighter engines. And Otis lifts, points out the latest United Technologies brochure, to restore the balance.

We first heard of United Technologies as a sponsor at the Arts Council sculpture show last summer. They paid for all the posters, the ones with 'sponsored by United Technologies' on them. The Arts Council said it was grateful for the free publicity. Free publicity? For whom? Later this year United Technologies will be sponsoring the George Stubbs exhibition at the Tate Gallery, which is like hitching a tank to a dappled grey.

But at the moment they are truly in their element as sponsors of an exhibition of home-made knick-knacks and jingoistic slavering called American Folk Art – Expressions of a New Spirit. The cover of the catalogue nearly says it all. It shows a wooden gate carved in the shape of the stars and stripes. Made in 1876 for the centennial celebrations of American Independence, the gate has lost its original red, white and blue paintwork and gone very grubby indeed. The white in particular has started to peel and turned an ugly yellow.

The thing could do with a lick of fresh colour. But it turns out that back home in America it is exactly this appearance of old age, the patina, which makes such objects so valuable. Their value in the market place drops dramatically if you attempt to restore them.

Expressions of a New Spirit feels like an exhibition with a mission – to boldly go where no exhibition has gone before. United Technologies are touring it around the world or 'outside our own borders' as Harry J. Gray, the chief executive officer of the corporation puts it.

What the world's visitors will see includes a giant eagle, bald of course, with its wings outstretched, holding a carved model of the globe in its talons. They will see an Uncle Sam whirligig: every time the wind blew Uncle Sam would rattle up and down on his bicycle waving a stars and stripes behind him. Hurray, hurrah.

Visitors can also see a game called Auctioneer and Slaves. This is a small box with ten numbered doors, on top of which stands the white figure of the auctioneer. The idea was to put money in the slot and then bet on which nigger would come out of which door first. The catalogue twists its tongue into a knot trying to disguise the true spirit of the game.

'A growing concern for slaves and abhorrence of the institution of slavery ran high in New England as the 19th century progressed. Each individual representation of a slave on this game of chance is a compelling portrait in itself.' If by 'compelling' they mean ugly, generalised, de-humanising, then I agree. Quite how this nasty little bar-room game was supposed to champion the anti-slavery cause I cannot imagine.

But it is some time since I mentioned the name of our sponsors, United Technologies Corporation. Since someone ran after me specially to remind me to do so, I must oblige.

The arguments for sponsorship are obvious. To put on exhibitions you need money. If the government won't give it to you then private enterprise will. The arguments against are much more complex and would require more than a passing reference in a review to do them justice. They have to do with morality and the long-term consequences of a short-term solution.

The symbol for the sponsor's new power is the gallery official who runs after you and asks you not to forget to mention the names of his benefactors. This is not a gallery official's job. Few of them do it with dignity or confidence.

Sponsors don't usually know much about art but they know what they like. This show would have us believe that there is some intrinsic artistic value in building a gate and painting it with the stars and stripes. We are told that folk art is 'direct', 'healthy', 'enthusiastic' and all those other adjectives which people use when they want to avoid the word 'crude.'

Folk art is presented as some sort of honest expression of the human spirit, an art of the people, which in some way becomes more profound than the stuff produced by the highbrow artist whom nobody understands. As Jean Lipman – 'one of America's most adventurous pioneer scholars in the field' – tells us, 'A number of gifted folk artists arrived at a power and originality and beauty that were not surpassed by the greatest of the academic painters.'

Now it would be churlish of me not to admit that there are some fascinating and charming objects on display. With its whirligigs, home-made toys and nodding heads it is a fun show in the same way that a visit to the fair is fun. But power and true originality? Where?

In the giant weather vane, shaped like a Red Indian, with which the exhibition greets you and which the catalogue boasts was used for target practice and is riddled with real bullet-holes? In the cigar-store Indians who keep the black slaves company, behind the numbered doors? It appears that real American folk art is the stuff which the Wild West hero whittled out with his bowie knife in between gun fights.

For true power and originality I advise Jean Lipman and the entire United Technologies Corporation to go and look at the portrait of Margaret Gage by John Singleton Copley which is currently on display at Agnew's. This is a magnificent example of what American art can achieve when the artist searches for the sublime rather than the sublunary.

Copley (1738–1815) was the first great American painter. Mrs Gage was the American-born wife of a British general. That she was also so much more than that I know from having stared into her plain face and dreaming eyes for three-quarters of an hour

88

trying to decide whether she was about to cry or about to smile. How long could you sit in front of a painted gate?

The point is that folk artists carve the best they can, they paint the best they can, they work to the ends of their ability. Their art expresses this honest human endeavour. But achieving the sublime is not one of their ambitions. They deal with the outside, not the inside, of the human spirit.

I don't expect the United Technologies Corporation to understand that. They help make missiles. But if they really want to prove to us that they are a benign, art-loving corporation then they should stop building helicopter gunships and electronic defence systems, and strive for enlightenment. They can even use one of their own lifts.

15 February, 1984   **Waldemar Januszczak**

It sounds offal

The Day After (ITV), a disaster movie about how everybody went bald in Lawrence, Kansas, provoked a massive retaliatory response from five Heseltines – plus one malfunction on TV-am – to show that there was no need for anybody to lose their hair.

Mr Heseltine, I know not how it is, shows a unique ability to get up the nostrils of even the most experienced interviewers. It may be something about the way he sits there looking as if 'Very authoritarian, secretive, declamatory, amazingly tough, unbending, unyielding' was a character reference. Even Brian Walden, the politician's pal, was driven to an uncharacteristic yell, 'What the devil does it matter whose terms they are as long as the talks get going?'

Some 15 million saw *The Day After* here and 16 million were asked their views on it, including Admiral Elmo Zumwalt Jnr. (who presupposes, one realises, amazed, an Elmo Zumwalt Snr.); Mrs Bowers, who has a bunker at the bottom of her garden; Sir Leslie Mavor, the Civil Defence Coordinator who thought 'Civil Defence was at a very low ebb in Kansas', unlike the song which reckoned that in Kansas City they'd gone about as fur as they kin go; Sir John Hackett ('Despair is not on the agendah!'); and a chap called Fred from European Nuclear Disarmament who carried a *Guardian* in a marked manner.

Not one of them said it was as cliché-ridden a film as ever insulted its subject. In the words of Queen Elizabeth I (according to Mark Twain at least): 'Verily in mine eight and sixty years I have not heard ye fellow to this fart.' No-one who saw *The War Game* – well, eventually, the BBC not being keen to show it at the time – could make deferential noises about this sort of thing.

The best was the worst: evidently genuine film of two big soft toadstools taking their time to form Minuteman missiles, making pale rainbows, skeletons on X-ray exhibition, a firestorm and afterwards a silent fall of something like soft snow. It was positively interesting to see – you knew, but to see – that because of the EMP factor anything electrical dies after a nuclear explosion, and that the key to launch strategic missiles is marked 'Gently'.

Otherwise *The Day After* was about a bunch of characters fatally confusable from the start and completely unidentifiable when their hair fell out. Jason Robards, what with the pale make-up and the thinning wig, changed ineluctably into Alastair Sim.

Meanwhile back in the cellar, Dahlberg, a farmer, is cursed with two hysterical women – 'Now listen, Denise, getta hold of yourself!' – and the most revolting child in the history of the American film, Jolene.

Mom is irritable because her cooking is not appreciated – 'Eat that up or it will go bad'; Denise is sobbing into her wedding dress; Dad in his simple fashion is trying to explain the situation to Jolene: 'Honey, we're going to have to get used to things being a lot different.' 'It sounds offal,' replies Jolene, a shrewd judge.

At the first commercial break we had, with doubtful tact, a Russian being twitted on his inability to pronounce Cockburn. At the second, after Jolene's, 'Oh Daddy, there isn't going to be a war, is there?', it was straight into the Cod Crumble and Chunky Codpie. After the last shot of Kansas City reduced to two old winos on a patch of rubble, the commercial for hair driers may have been a mistake.

It had at times a faint spectral look of *Gone with the Wind*, all those groaning extras, but as Alan King's father said of his late brother-in-law, Nat, 'Dead don't make you better.'

12 December, 1983   **Nancy Banks-Smith**

Mr Reagan scatters his allies

'The struggle for peace is indivisible. We cannot pick and choose where we will support freedom.' Thus Ronald Reagan on Monday afternoon in Washington, adding a new gloss to America's beleaguered role in Lebanon. Now, within hours, we have a further example of 'the indivisible struggle', as 2,000 or so marines (with a few tatty trappings of multilateral bunting) drop in on Grenada. More soldiers die; so do more civilians. And America's underlying perception of the world order is encapsulated again in that single quotation. It is Them or Us. The dark forces of the Kremlin against the White Knights of Washington. To blazes with Grenadan independence; to blazes with consultation with allies; to blazes with peace-keeping when there is a Commie to be given a bloody nose. Even Mrs Thatcher and Sir Geoffrey are left spluttering at the end of the day, expressing 'considerable doubts' and havering reservations. They weren't even told until it was too late, and the fllimsiness of the cover story rips like tissue paper.

Let us take Grenadan circumstances first. A speck on the Caribbean map which, four years ago, saw a peaceful coup and the expulsion of a notably unpleasant regime. Mr Maurice Bishop, a proponent of Caribbean socialism, took over. He was, of course, blown hither and yon by events. He did not run a free society. He leaned, perforce, on Cuban advice. He built a suspiciously large airport. He never got round to holding elections. But there was little doubt, amongst the Grenadan people, that he was working for them. Had he ever managed to hold an election, he would have won it. After Eric Gairy he was a breath of fresh air. But Grenada is a tiny state, where personality struggles become magnified. Bishop fell out with some bizarre colleagues to his left. He was deposed and then most brutally murdered. The Cubans, far from rubbing their hands, were visibly discomfited. The lesson was not that a neutral little island had fallen under Kremlin domination, but that the Caribbean socialist route was just as loopily factional and wantonly bloody as any rightwing revolutionary path across the sea. Mr Bishop's murder was a jolting setback to leftwing idealism, the quenching of a torch. But now, uncomprehendingly, that

'*President Reagan doesn't like your choice of eight gramophone records.*'

27 October, 1983

message is thrown away. The message that will live on when the pall of smoke covering Grenada has cleared is that this United States administration will impose the regime of its choice by force anywhere its writ may be taken to run. Talk of restoring 'law and order' seems laughable in the circumstances. They were 'leftish thugs' said the President yesterday, as though that settled everything. Are 'rightish thugs' – like the El Salvador government gun squads who sent even Dr Kissinger home shocked last week – then the only symbol of 'freedom' we can hang on to? It is a question to scatter America's allies in confusion.

The temptation, of course, must have been irresistible to those in the White House who see the superpower world just black and white. There is an election in the gearing up. (Remember the glory of the Falklands and how that helped win a victory at the polls?) There was, on Sunday, a crushing military reverse in the Lebanon: an enemy who could not be identified and thus lashed back at. But here was a tinpot island far from outside assistance, a target of minimal risk which could be swatted with vigour. A handful of nasty lefties; a smattering of Cubans and Soviets in situ; a cluster of other little states around who could be counted on to ask Mother America to move, to lend a further surface smear of the 'indivisible struggle'.

It is always a mistake to stand in the wider world and seek reasons from that world by which to interpret Mr Reagan's policies. To the contrary, one must begin in the suffocating atmosphere of his office and work outward, through America's insular preoccupations and paranoias. Viewed from afar, Grenada may prove a devastating blow to America's eventual influence. A Commie with a bleeding nose may, or may not, stir the crowds in Pennsylvania Avenue. But at a stroke it throws any moral arguments about Afghanistan into the trash can of history. It fatally infects perceptions of the Lebanon situation. It kicks European susceptibilities about missile deployment and good intentions into the gutter. From the inside, working out, it may have seemed a sweet, applause-worthy move. From the outside, working in, it is a disaster.

The precise nature of the wider repercussions will have to wait for the moment. Too much, on the ground, remains unclear. But one can already catch scent of things to come from yesterday's extraordinary exchanges in the House of Commons. Here was Mr Reagan's greatest admirer in the Western world – unhappy already about the flailing plunge ever deeper into the Lebanon and now visibly distressed about Grenada. Our views – when offered – had been of no account. Our expertise in the

Caribbean utterly disregarded. We hadn't been told until there was nothing left to do but bleat. And the greater wisdom of the Caribcom countries, too, had been cast aside. Like everyone else, Mrs Thatcher and Sir Geoffrey found themselves on the outer periphery of White House concern. They were, and are, humiliated. They cannot condemn; they cannot approve. They are irrelevancies when Mr Reagan sees something he wants. America's friends over many decades – like this newspaper – can only watch in anguish at the heedless division wrought in pursuit of indivisibility.

26 October, 1983   **Leader**

Christmas cards

This is the season of goodwill and bad debts. It is the time for New Yorkers to add up exactly how much money they can pay out that does not belong to them. It is frankly amazing how much of it is within the graft of the average irresponsible spendthrift. Thanks be to the charge card and instant credit: without them it would be a very different Christmas.

American Express, of course, appears to not set a limit upon it. Perhaps one binge of unpaid bills would alter that happy state of affairs and, of course, all accounts are payable in full on receipt. It is regarded as highly sensible, therefore, to hold Visa and Mastercard plates through as many banks as possible. Just an ordinary couple who have moved about America opening bank accounts hither and yon – Michigan at school, Ohio the postgraduate, California in the winter, Aspen in the summer, bits of New York the rest of the time – could theoretically have between them not less than 30 such charge cards with an upper limit each of US $1,000–$3,000.

Department stores press cards upon likely customers. Gimbels has just finished a highly successful telephone campaign in which representatives of a marketing firm in Philadelphia called thousands of shoppers in Manhattan urging them to accept that store's charge card. A random check of the first person encountered in our elevator produced a list of charge accounts at the

94

following: Bloomingdales, Gimbels, Altmans, Bergdorf Good-
man, Sears, Bonwit Teller, Alexanders, Macy's, Saks Fifth
Avenue, and, tucked away, Gumps in San Francisco.

Banks, sensibly, do not recognise the word overdraft, such a
thing does not exist in New York. There is, instead, a service
known as 'privileged credit', an established arrangement for
writing cheques on an empty account with no questions asked
awarded to special customers who have a good enough record of
going into debt and back again. Some banks have recently
extended privileged credit to its logical conclusion, which is
ambassador service. A special cheque book is issued with loan
cheques in amounts up to $10,000 or, in some cases, $25,000.

These merely have to be written out in order to activate the
arrangement, and the amount borrowed then has the status of a
normal bank loan. Since, of course, it is illegal in America to
send an unsolicited anything to anyone that grants a credit line,
it is necessary to fill in the odd form or two to qualify for all these
wonderful plastic goodies. At last count, for instance, I worked
out in an idle moment, that this household could spend just
under $200,000 using only the credit line and cards now avail-
able to us. Ingenuity could possibly push this up another
$100,000 or so. At that exciting thought I fell asleep, counting
credit having much the same relation to New York nights as
counting sheep might elsewhere.

Courage alone stands between the middle classes and a life
decorated in its entirety by man's bounties. The faint heart
merely makes do. What weak and pallid creatures they seem to
those who can seize the challenge of going gloriously into debt.

The worst aspect of choosing to spend only what one has
saved up is that at Christmas such timidity has the appearance of
horrid parsimony. The thought does not count over here.
Manhattan is a small island where the big gesture is all. There is
somehow a feeling that nothing worth giving may cost less than
the largest note of the currency. At present, alas, that amount
stands at $100 and it is exactly what the average building
superintendent expects to find in the envelope pressed into his
hand by each grateful tenant who might like to enjoy some heat
for Christmas.

The idea of Christmas is of a huge six foot tree garlanded with priceless baubles beneath which lies a heap of store-wrapped gifts, each one looking more lavish than the last. Package decorating is no sport for the amateur. This is a land where, on the index of children's gifts, the norm was always taken to be the bicycle. Anything that costs less than a 10-speed bicycle short-changed a child.

Last winter, disconsolate sons roamed the empty streets lamenting that they had been given only table-sized models of the best-selling video games. This year, every child is meant to have a home computer. Such is the pre-Christmas pressure on these that Macy's ran out of favoured models days ago. Anxious parents rush from store to store, place phone calls to distant New Jersey, searching for the vital microchip without which no eight-year-old will be able to survive maths in years to come.

It is a general guide line that it is in bad taste to give anyone a present that costs under $25. That is the accepted minimum amount, or was this year at least, for a baby gift or wedding present to be offered to someone one knew so slightly as not to expect an invitation to view the infant or the marriage. Present giving is the good manners of today, subject to a strict etiquette. As a result, one no longer gives truly for joy and happiness. 'I like her enough that maybe I shouldn't send her anything' was a lovely remark overheard in a gift shop on Columbus Avenue this week. How well the world stands on its head sometimes. Meanwhile the relentless rush goes on to get ready for Christmas and further in debt. It is a time when in spite of the qualms of conscience, New York is an exciting place to explore. Restraint is not in this city's character. Windows sparkle with irresistible decorations – many of which are given over to the bear. For no particular or discernible reason, teddy bears are the superstars of this year's gift array. Every store for children and adults has its display of them – in beds, houses, gold, silver, all sizes, as stick-ons, adorning Christmas cards, in books, and hanging from necklaces.

Cabbage Patch dolls, the Farrah Fawcett-Majors of the teeny set, are in the last throes of their popularity, is the feeling on Columbus Avenue. What a person really needs at a time like this with the thought of next month's finance charges, is a vast, furry, cuddly, understanding person called Teddy who never answers back and never sends in the bill for his services.

And just in case there is any credit left at the end to the month, one store on Long Island is already advertising a sale to be held on December 26 and 27: its plastic Norwegian pine Christmas trees and all tree decorations at half price for two days only. Goodness. It is almost Christmas 1984 already.

14 December, 1983   **Linda Blandford**

A long road that had no turning

Bright lights were seen in the night sky around Epping Forest on Christmas Day. Local inhabitants emerged from their homes and stared at the yellow glow which bathed the countryside. It was the promised sign they all had dreaded: the motorway lights of the M25, switched on a month too soon. The illuminations stayed on over the festive period. Cold turkey would never be the same again.

On January 25 Nicholas Ridley, the Transport Secretary, will open the eight-mile link in London's orbital motorway, which passes through the northernmost part of Epping Forest. It is one of the few great 'relict' forests of England, with perhaps the largest surviving stand of hornbeam in Europe, granted by Queen Victoria to the people of London for all time.

Before the official junket, and in the week that Environment Minister Patrick Jenkin pledged that the Green Belt is now inviolate, it is timely to say a few words over the buried hopes of a tiny community which took one of the most extraordinary campaigns in motorway history into the House of Lords. It is a saga of betrayal.

There are more horses than people in the Essex village of Upshire (pop. 350) on the fringe of Epping Forest. It was a farming community until comparatively recently, its inhabitants traditionally exercising their rights to lop firewood and graze their animals in the forest. They were galvanised by the threat of the motorway, which was to sever the village from the forest.

When the M16 public inquiry, as it was then called, opened

97

explosively in Epping on December 3, 1974, the Upshire Village Preservation Society had raised most of the £21,000 bill for counsel and expert witnesses. Much of it came from poor people in inner London who enjoyed the forest at weekends. The Society's chairman, Mrs Joyce Woods, was also elected to lead the Alliance of objecting groups. She was and is still a magistrate at Waltham Forest, whose incisiveness and decency impress all who meet her.

Uproar ensued on that first day among the 300 spectators when the anti-motorway millitant John Tyme rose to challenge the inquiry's legitimacy. DoE officials were chased from the room. But when the inquiry reconvened next morning, the Alliance's counsel announced that his clients repudiated John Tyme's views and wished the inquiry to continue.

Mrs Woods now concedes that she might have been mistaken. 'John Tyme is a fanatic and very often such people get things done. They get publicity, but usually that's all they do. Then they fade away. We set our face against that sort of thing. We thought we could do it by proper argument and by appeals to reason. We played it by the book, straight down the middle.'

Another trauma was in store. The Upshire Society's then president, Sir Williiam Addison, is also the Verderer of Epping Forest, one of the Conservators charged by Parliament with the task of preserving the character of the forest and sternly resisting any new roads.

'It was a terrible shock to discover that even when he became president in 1971 he knew all about this road,' said Mrs Woods. 'He had been one of the principal negotiators with the department as to where the road would go. We went on having our suspicions, but trusting him, for years. We couldn't believe that anyone could behave like that.'

After the inquiry was lost, it was Sir William and his Conservators who paved the way for the M25 link by promoting a Private Bill to enable forest land to be sequestered for the road.

Why had he done it? 'The powers the Conservators enjoy were conferred by Parliament,' Sir William, 79, said this week. 'Unfortunately what Parliament gives, Parliament can take away. It was inevitable that something had to go. We felt obliged to accept the least harmful route, provided they tunnelled under the forest.'

What of the Upshire Society of which he had been president? 'At that stage all these village societies were anxious to push the road through someone else's cabbage patch. We would have had to make value judgements. I am not certain about who felt I had let them down. I have enjoyed very great respect.'

But why had the Conservators, pledged to protect the forest, promoted the Bill instead of allowing the Ministry of Transport to do so? 'We would have lost our negotiating power,' he said. He admitted that he had known about the proposal since 1967, but claimed Upshire was informed.

Still playing it by the book, and armed with sweet reason, Upshire petitioned a Select Committee of the House of Commons in 1979. Ranged against them was a phalanx of experts, including Sir William Addison. On the second day Mrs Woods's husband died, and her crucial evidence was read out in her absence.

Richard Padfield, a retired diplomat born in Upshire, witnessed the hearing. 'We were treated in a very hostile manner. The Establishment, as represented by the ministries of Environment and Transport quite clearly regarded us as a confounded nuisance that had to be got out of the way as soon as possible.'

They were caught in a classic pincer movement. Separate sections of the motorway had advanced on both sides of Epping Forest, each disgorging traffic. By this time, largely due to the efforts of the British Road Federation, the Epping Forest link was seen as part of an orbital scheme, never originally envisaged. It was planning by stealth.

In an unprecedented move, Upshire then petitioned a House of Lords select committee whose chairman Lord Derwent, they were surprised to discover, was a former chairman of the British Road Federation. Mr Padfield found this tactless, to say the least.

'The larger part of our evidence was ruled out of order by the chairman,' said Mr Padfield. 'Time and time again, important and relevant facts were refused a hearing. The evidence given by the department witnesses, though it was no more substantiated than any other, was always preferred to that given by objecting expert witnesses.'

This week, the motorway glares emptily. At Epping Forest it enters a tunnel, which according to engineers is packed with electronic equipment to detect breakdowns. On top of its concrete roof rests an eight inch layer of peat and topsoil. This will barely support the cricket stumps of the pitch that is to be reinstated, let alone the roots of hornbeam, oak, beech and birch.

The M25 experience has turned a community which believed in it, against the Establishment. It is astonishing to hear Mrs Woods express admiration for the Greenham women. In another time, in another place, one feels she would be fining them. 'I no longer believe in anything I am told,' she said. 'There are powerful and selfish forces ranged against you. A lot of what we predicted has materialized. One could say "I told you so." But that gives me no satisfaction at all.'

14 January, 1984   **Stuart Wavell**

On the spot

Mrs Finchley was at a Festival Hall carol concert when the Harrods bomb went off. Selected broadcast media representatives were invited to the Hall to hear her reaction. My Man on the Spot, who doubles as a *Tribune* legman, carelessly switched on his tape recorder earlier than was strictly necessary and, on playing it back, was surprised to hear the following: 'Now then, gentlemen, how would you like me to play this? Would you like me to set it against the background of the carol concert I have just been attending? Would you like me to tie it in with Christmas?' And she did.

The Harvey Nichols, Knightsbridge, windows near Harrods featured – at least on Saturday – a display of alarm clocks wired up to sticks of mock gelignite. Doubtless this has since been removed. Prize for the press coverage goes to the FT headline: 'Bomb Blast Damages Retailers' Record Hopes.' Shock! Horror!

20 December, 1983   **Alan Rusbridger**

Battery de cuisine

It popped through the letterbox last week – this stern reminder from a local vicar that Christmas Day had a greater and deeper purpose than cooking ovenfuls of food and stuffing it down the Family Throat. And so say I, vicar, dear. In fact, I'd go much further and say that every day has a greater and deeper purpose than stuffing food down the Family Throat.

For years I didn't think so, though. For years I was a sort of food Moonie, a gastronomic groupie worshipping at the altar of the omnivorous oven. I have approximately 150 cookbook bibles to prove it, their pages stuck together with grease, blotched with blood and sweat and tears. Silent witnesses to a quarter of a century of obsessive cooking, thousands of hours crouched over a hot stove producing rather a lot more than 20,000 meals to be eaten in rather less than 20,000 minutes.

We have to eat, naturally. A mother has to feed her family, naturally. But there was nothing natural in the fervour with which I approached this everyday task. I blame Elizabeth David, it was she who began it all, she who initiated the whole foodie thing and its accompanying paraphernalia, she who fired all those who read her with the ruinous desire to turn their poky kitchens into four-star Michelin eating shrines and their three mundane meals a day into epicurean feasts. Cooking as Art. Cooking as Self-Expression, as Status, as Snobbery. Cooking as a symbol of the Good Life, of everything rich and positive and caring and Earth Mothery. Brainwashed, I believed that if you didn't cook in the most committed way possible, you were dead.

What I didn't realise was that if you did cook in the most committed way possible, you were also dead. From exhaustion, mainly. The mind sagging with the weight of foodie thoughts, the body loaded with foodie activities. Check the recipe, check the cupboards, go out, buy the stuff, chop and peel and boil the stuff, stuff the stuff into other stuff and stuff it down the waiting throats.

No short cuts allowed, either, to us followers of David. Grind your own curry powder, knit your own pastas, clarify your own butter, make your own shrimps, lay your own eggs. Tins were anathema, stock cubes a mortal sin and white bought bread a capital crime – I even had my own yeast culture, nipped off a piece being carried by an acolyte like the bones of a saint around the world. Food was a sacred object, it hung from my beams, it lay in ornamental plates and it required special reliquaries for each of its manifestations: curved omelette pans, clay briquettes, antique moulds, copper bowls, daubieres, cocottes, salamanders, mandolines, tripières and marmites large and medium and small.

I had things to stone olives with and crush garlic with and lard pork with and drain cheese with. The whole boring batterie de cuisine dangling round my ears, cluttering up my drawers, bursting from my cupboards and getting on my nerves. Enough gadgets to overcrowd the kitchens of the Connaught all crammed into a six-foot length of damp kitchenette five floors up in Paddington Green.

And, of course, a real food groupie could not be confined to English fare. The world was one huge voracious oyster and every day demanded another weirder ethnic dish. Italian, Chinese, Indian, French, Spanish, Hungarian, Turkish, Jewish, Thai, Caribbean, North African. Even South African. Whenever I travelled I filled my suitcase with rare khaki dusts from Arab bazaars and genuine paprika and the most virginal of olive oils. I lugged back samphire from markets, sheep cheese from the Pyrenees, blue leg mushrooms from Gloucester and a shrimp paste from Indonesia that smelled so bad it made the cat faint. Still unsatisfied that these real things were real enough, I began to smuggle in seeds and cuttings, plum tomatoes from Italy, basil roots from Greece, mange-touts from Brussels, to be planted in my backyard and die of soot-rot. One corner of an English plot that was forever foreign.

Then, one day, I went to stay in a friend's house to work, alone. A unique and shameless friend who never cooked. A food heathen. Too tired to cook for myself, I rummaged through her cupboards and for the first time in 20 years opened a tin of made-up food. Spaghetti in bolognese sauce. Furtively, behind drawn curtains, I spooned it down and fell back, stunned. It was delicious. Next day I bought three frozen dishes, went home, stuck them in the oven, ate them and they were wonderful. No preparation, no cooking, hardly any washing up and a taste treat.

It was my Road to Damascus. A huge revulsion against everything connected with food rose from my guts. I peered back through all those years of cookety-cook and heaved at the sheer enormity of the needless labour. As in a dream I saw my children's faces clearly, gathered round the table, saw not anticipation in their eyes but alarm. Oh God, what's the old bag going to stuff us with today? Why can't we ever have lovely fish fingers, heavenly baked beans, marvellous mushy peas and Heinz spaghetti like other children? Not even on our *birthdays*. Not even at *Christmas*.

I went home. I stormed into the kitchen. I cleared the counters, emptied the drawers, threw out the hundred spices and herbs and dumped the cookbooks in the attic. I piled up useless gadgets and pretentious pots and pans and sent them off to jumble sales. I said to the assembled family, 'I shall cook no more' and, tears of relief brimming in their eyes, they gave me a round of applause. It was a magic moment and I have stuck to my word, pretty well. I roast something occasionally, I boil potatoes and grill things now and again and I use every cooking aid I can lay my hands on, tinned, frozen, pre-cooked, pre-mashed, pre-mixed, powdered, ground, condensed, stoned, minced and bottled. And now, instead of chaos, calm reigns. Smiles greet me round the table as the family blooms, freed of the constant pressure of having to say goodness me how wonderful how do you do it what *is* it? In the garden, flowers dance where once there lurked the baleful bean and plain English parsley grows where once coriander wilted.

Cry your eyes out, E.D.

13 December, 1983

Jill Tweedie

103

A hell of a hotel

The hotel looked seedy, but respectable, from the outside. The plate glass doors bore stickers welcoming Diners Club, Mastercharge and American Express. Just inside the door was a rack filled with brochures for the National Theatre, the Royal Opera House, and West End shows. But this hotel's residents were unlikely to be paying by credit card for a night at the opera. The only 'Dining' available to the Diners Club card holder was a regulatory roll and cold coffee in a dank basement room at breakfast.

This is one of the notorious bed-and-breakfast hotels where the homeless are crowded together in squalid misery, dumped by local authorities with nowhere else to put them. The occasional bemused tourist does stay here too, usually by accident, not design. The brochures and credit card signs keep up the shabby pretence that this, and 50 similar others in London's crowded Bayswater, are still hotels. In fact they are tenement slums, many of them plagued by rats, mice, lice, bed-bugs and constant outbreaks of gastro-enteritis in the children. Other cities have their own such hotels to house their growing numbers of homeless – now officially put at 73,600 households (not individuals).

The hotels have grandiose names. This one housed 500 homeless people, most of them families with children. The old stain-sodden carpet gave off a sour smell. The banisters were broken in places, leaving lethal gaping drops for small children. The partitioning of rooms made the place a warren of corridors and cramped winding staircases – a death trap from which few residents could hope to escape in a fire. The bathrooms were squalid and shared by five or more families. There were no cooking facilities at all – though most families had an illegal electric ring in their room, another perpetual danger to their children.

Each room had just space for the beds and a sink – a double

bed and two bunks in the first one I entered, but not enough room for the whole family to stand up at once. They had nowhere to keep food, but a small cupboard which also held the few clothes and possessions they had room for. Some of the hotels have a cooker in the basement six floors down for the use of scores of families – no fridges or laundries. Washing has to be dried on the radiator in the room.

I was asked not to mention the names of the hotels I visited. The residents feel too vulnerable, both to their local authorities who placed them there, and the shark-like hotel proprietors, to dare risk being accused of having brought in a visitor, let alone a journalist. Who owns these hotels, none of the residents had been able to ascertain, but several were part of a highly profitable group. Since each family was being charged more than £120 a week for their tiny, sordid box rooms, the landlords' profits must be colossal. (One woman returning to the hotel from hospital with her three-day-old baby was charged an extra £35 for having the child in her room.)

Down the winding passages, each narrow hotel room gives onto a scene of human misery and despair. A woman, her husband, and three children under the age of six were crammed into one room with a rough constructed sleeping platform taking up the top of the high ceilinged space. They had been living in a caravan before, and had now been in the hotel only a couple of months. But they had a five month stretch in the place before, when they were driven to such despair that they left to camp out again – a serious error. Now they had to begin the waiting all over again, and that five months had all been for nothing.

One woman had just come out of hospital with a new tiny baby. There was not enough room for her to put up the cot stacked in one corner and the baby slept curled up on the bed. The curtains were shut, and she scarcely went out, having no pram. She was told she had to go to register the child, collect his National Health card, register with a doctor, take the baby to the clinic, go down to the DHSS and apply for a grant for a pram. She didn't know this part of London, seemed vague, depressed, alone, uprooted, and utterly unable to cope.

These people have no social workers to help them through the complex bureaucracy of poverty. They belong to the distant authorities who have dumped them here, and not to Westminster where the hotels are. Westminster do not regard them as their responsibility, so they appoint no social worker to help them.

How did they come to be so utterly homeless that one tiny room was the only alternative to the streets? Sheila is a nurse and her husband a plasterer. They have two small boys, of two and three. They have been living in the hotel now for 19 long months, waiting and hoping for the chance of a flat. When they first married they lived with friends, but then they had a baby and Sheila became accidentally pregnant again soon afterwards. 'We couldn't stay. They told us to go. We had a row in the end when the council tried to get them to take us back. So the council sent us here – for a few weeks they said. Now it's been 19 months.'

She is a woman of great energy and resource, determined that her children should not suffer. She has seen plenty of women fall into lethargy and deep depression in their hotel rooms. So she takes her children out all day every day, to the library, swimming, round the shops and to a play group. 'I keep them awake all day so they'll sleep as soon as we get back to the room. Sundays are worst, with my husband home, and everything shut, nowhere to go, all of us in the room. We try to sleep as much as we can.'

Sandra also keeps out all day with her two children. Her husband works and they have been in the hotel for 16 months. They were evicted from their one-bedroom private flat, though they fought it through the courts. Her oldest boy was in his first year at school, and she didn't want to move him away. 'The council said we'd be here a few weeks, and the school left his place open. That was 16 months ago. It's impossible to get him into a school here. There are no places.' She describes what it was like arriving at the hotel. 'I couldn't believe it, such a small space for all of us, nowhere to cook. I wouldn't use a ring, as it's too dangerous with small children. I felt dead, dead inside. I couldn't believe this was happening to us.'

In the hotels too, there are those given temporary housing for being 'vulnerable', usually those released from mental hospital.

Sheila and Sandra described drug addicts and deranged people wandering around the corridors, frightening them and their children. 'One battered on the door the other day, shouting and yelling to be let in. I screamed at him to go away, but no-one came.'

These, believe it or not, are among the lucky homeless. They have, at least, been taken on by their local authorities. They are on the waiting lists for a flat, their authority has shouldered responsibility for them. These are among the 73,600 that appear in the official figures. Most experts estimate the actual number to be three times that figure – a fact not disputed by a Government spokesman in the House of Lords recently. The Homeless Persons Act allows authorities to turn away those deemed to have made themselves 'intentionally homeless', and some authorities use this loophole ruthlessly. All the families I spoke to had been grilled about this and some of them were indignant: 'Would you put yourself here if you had anywhere else to go?' one said fiercely.

The bed-and-breakfast hotel is the modern equivalent of the old workhouse. It serves the same purpose and is punitive in intent. It tests the genuine desperation of families awaiting rehousing. While they hang on, squeezed in with their parents, or friends, or cramped in tiny bedsits, they have no chance of getting a flat, with waiting lists growing and available housing shrinking. Making life hell for these homeless people is supposed to act as a deterrent against others throwing themselves on the mercy of the local authorities. Like the workhouses of old, these hotels keep the poor from freezing to death in the streets, but they keep them so miserably that only the utterly destitute would avail themselves of this form of state aid.

It is an immensely expensive way to house people atrociously and the cost is rocketing as the number of people in bed and breakfasts grows. In London alone the boroughs spent £4.3 million on bed and breakfast in 1982. This rose last year to £6 million – money pointlessly thrown away, enriching the hotel proprietors grotesquely, as it debilitates the housing budgets of the boroughs. It is accounting madness, since that money would pay for housing those people in flats permanently. A private person paying that much rent a week would do the wise thing, borrow money for a mortgage, and pay for a capital asset that will last for several generations. The Government's obsession with preventing borrowing means throwing away money in a way that no-one would advise for any individual family.

Meanwhile, 136,000 houses stand empty in London alone, boroughs deprived of the money to renovate them, falling into worse repair year by year. The housing crisis deepens. The Government has cut housing expenditure by two-thirds, while half a million new homes are needed. Housing has gone cold as a political issue, since the early heady days of Shelter and *Cathy Come Home*, yet the numbers of homeless multiply year after year. 'Do they know, do you think, do they really know what it's like living here?' said one distraught mother. 'I have to think they don't, otherwise what sort of people are they?'

5 March, 1984   **Polly Toynbee**

Henry in the breach

Anyone who has seen two-ton Tessie O'Shea singing 'I've a little bit here and a little bit there and it all belongs to me!' might be led to think that great possessions presuppose a sunny and outgoing nature.

It is not so. The word that comes to mind while watching 'Down and Out at Calke Abbey', *First Tuesday's* account of the last stand of the Harpur-Crewes, is crustacean. In their tendency to pull their house over their ears and give intruders a nasty nip, the Harpur-Crewes suggest something you might find on the seabed in a shell. Perhaps the horseshoe crab, which comes of so old a family its blood is actually blue. You must have seen one last week pointedly ignoring David Attenborough.

Or, of course, the hermit crab. Sir Vauncey, the last Harpur-Crewe but one, known politely as the noted naturalist, seems to have filled Calke Abbey with stuffed ducks, startled stags and seashells. He hung on to horses and hip baths when the popular fancy was for motor cars and modern plumbing. Charles, Henry's brother, reluctantly admitted electricity in 1960.

He died leaving Henry a house untouched by the twentieth century and a tax bill for £8 million.

Now this is where a remarkable mutation was apparent in the Harpur-Crewes. Darwin would have been interested. In defence of the most important thing in his life, his house, Henry seems to have reversed the habits of 300 years.

He offered the Abbey, its contents and grounds, to the nation. The Treasury, with a sharp exclamation of distaste, held out for hard cash. Henry began to cultivate publicity as assiduously as all his ancestors had avoided it. He welcomed the press and television. Yorkshire filmed him cooking (courgettes and a nice bit of beef) and eating (an otter with its face full of fish – more of Sir Vauncey – peered over his shoulder).

They filmed him in action (the hare first, the hounds second and Sir Henry in a woolly weskit, a sturdy third) and in repose (climbing into bed with what grace he could muster). The picture that glimmers in his bedroom all night is that of his own moon-bleached grounds. It is a burglar alarm.

He considered bigger and better ways of making an exhibition of himself: 'I thought I might tie myself to the railings at Westminster.'

In the churchyard the Harpur-Crewes turned over. 'I'd like,' said Henry, 'to end my days at Calke Abbey or somewhere on the estate. It will be cheaper when the end comes. The church is near.' He did think of getting married once, but 'We saw too much of each other and she got sick of me.'

So, for that matter did the Treasury. He conducted a solitary sit-in for three years. Large lumps fell off the Abbey. Large lumps of interest were added to the tax bill. On budget day Nigel Lawson accepted Henry's argument and his Abbey. The last Harpur-Crewe is a man, as Wodehouse put it, at whose name even the blood-sucking leeches of the Inland Revenue are accustomed to raise their filthy hats.

It is probably a mistake to imprison a poet or to let him go. In *Arena* (BBC-2), Breyten Breytenbach's seven years of political imprisonment in South Africa were released in an astonishing torrent. This is his description of life or rather death in Pretoria's maximum security prison.

'The first thing one notices is the clinical atmosphere of death and the people chanting their own death. They help one another by singing continuously. You hear the absolute raw beauty and despair of life in the voices of those people. Sometimes you can hear by the quality of the voice – because you never saw anyone except, in the slit between the steel partition and the wall, the naked feet of the person who brought you your food – but you can hear as they go up to the gallows that sometimes there is a young man among them. Maybe 17 or 18 years old and how his voice is breaking with the fear. And then how the older ones carry him with their voices, how they insert him in their rhythm, how they support him up the steps.'

As it says on Dylan Thomas's stone, 'I sang in my chains like the sea.'

4 April, 1984   **Nancy Banks-Smith**

A good day out

John Foreman is a postman and, on the face of it, not much to write home about. He is light, slight, with neat blond hair and a downy moustache. He seems meek – and each Saturday afternoon, on the streets of some football town, he inherits the earth.

That's the time when he fights. It's the point where he proves that, at least in the estimation of his friends, he is hard and swift and extremely clever.

He is hard enough to inflict the maximum damage in the shortest time on any rival team supporter who stands in his way. He is smart enough never to have been caught. And on Saturday afternoons the only team that truly matters to him is the pack of friends with whom he runs.

They are veterans of hundreds of street fights, with a fixture list as clearly recalled as any playing record kept by Chelsea Football Club, the team to which Foreman and his friends also claim allegiance. Portsmouth is where, after a pre-season 'friendly', the home fans wanted trouble and he helped to oblige; Burnley is where he was hit over the head with a housebrick. Preston is where a mate died when, during a running battle, he jumped a wall concealing a drop on to a railway track.

This London suburban postman delivers flying fists and an elegant boot. If a soccer match street fighter wants to stay smart, and remain out of trouble with the law, then he must *look* smart. Appearances count for everything in this violent and menacing underworld which has become almost an institution attaching itself to the legitimate sport of football. And the first rule today is that the really serious trouble-makers take considerable care to look anything but football hooligans. They disdain club colours; treat with contempt the skinheads in heavy boots who will, at best, have their laces removed when they arrive at the ground and who, if trouble erupts, will become the obvious and visible targets for police retribution.

John Foreman (not his real name) is aged 22 and lives with his parents in a small semi-detached house – and an atmosphere of constrained respectability – in North London. His mother and father are still unaware of his Saturday activities and the exact nature of the conviction which, finally, came his way after the Brighton rumpus. Foreman is quietly amused that he was arrested for running on to the pitch while drunk, having evaded more serious charges for years.

In his terrace tribe there is ritual and a sort of code. Each 'good day out' follows a similar pattern; invariably the violence is fuelled by a mixture of lager and cider. Fist fights are acceptable, knife fights are not. 'They are out of order,' he said. 'For away games I usually catch an early train or go by coach and stop off at a place out of the town and have a few drinks with my mates. Towards 2.30 you start making your move to the ground,' he said.

'We used to go in other people's ends but that's not so much of a thing now. Terrace violence is out with the people who have their heads screwed on properly. You are in a closed space and you are going to get caught. It is on the street at the moment. We come out of the ground and break away, a group of 50 or 100 of us. There is always someone who wants trouble. We go to find our way back to the station not by police methods but by ours. We walk the streets.

'There has been 100 of us and we have fought twice as many. I have never really got hurt. I don't know about other people. You don't stand around and find out. There are so many people about and so many bodies. You are just fighting.

'I don't hate the teams. I just hate them on the day. Their mob are out for the same as what you are. I have never hit a person who is not looking for it. I wouldn't say I was a great fighter but you just do what your body tells you.

'Trouble is expected everywhere that Chelsea goes now. They have such a reputation that people want to be better than they are, harder than them. It's a challenge to everyone, more or less.

'You get more satisfaction knowing you have got away. I have had loads of fights. A lot of it boils down to impressing your mates. I know it sounds stupid. Drink is one of the main routes to all evil. It causes 90 per cent of the trouble.

'In some cases you are just defending yourself or your friends. The generation who live today have to be prepared for it. No matter where you go there is always someone who wants to have a go at you.

'It's a good day out. You have a drink, go to the game and we usually stay in the town for a drink until late. A fight? It's all part of the day. You disappear before you get nicked.

'I don't think there is a motive. It happens everywhere, up and down the country. It's happening right now as I'm talking to you. If there was no football violence there'd be more street violence.'

But what about the impact on football and the reputation of Chelsea, the team whose name is tattooed on his right upper arm? Does he really care that much for the game or for that club?

'Sometimes I'd rather stay in the pub. Sometimes I'm more interested in having a good drink than watching the football,' he said.

Then, at 5 o'clock on Monday morning, he rises and quietly returns to his postman's walk in London. And, meanwhile, Chelsea have been promoted to the First Division.

11 May, 1984   **Andrew Moncur**

A Country Diary: Howgill Fells

As youngsters we thought the Wasdale flank of Kirk Fell the steepest grass slope in Lakeland although more than half a century of widespread exploration has since yielded steeper places. But I don't think there are any grassy fellsides in the national park as steep as several in the soaring Howgill Fells, just across the Lune and the motorway. Of course, there are Lakeland fellsides of rock and scree at punishing angles – the east face of Helvellyn or the top of the Blencathra gills among dozens of examples – but grass slopes where hands as well as feet are needed for upward progress are rare. Whereas, in the smoothly domed Howgills, bare of crags except at their Black Force and Cautley corners and even unmarked by dry stone walls, the ascent of many of the towering grass slopes that sweep above a score of becks would demand rock-climbing postures. No point, though, in clawing up grass clumps when the ridges leading to the rounded tops are all straightforward walking. But the adventurous Rough Fell sheep, seeking sweeter herbs, cross these precipitous places on nine-inch trods with the aplomb of alpine chamois. An afternoon across The Calf and other heights, enlivened by a bitter east wind and brief showers of horizontal snow, had me traversing some of them and calculating, for example, the length of a fall from a slippery snow-hold, to Calf Beck, looking almost vertically below my boots. There's nothing like this in the Lake District – or even in those steep bits in the Brecon Beacons – and, under the right lighting, these hanging velvet draperies of mountainsides, sleek as sealskins in the evening sunshine, give to these lonely fells a rare beauty not seen even in more famous places.

16 April, 1984   **A. Harry Griffin**

Slightly unreal estate

A wealthy Egyptian added to his eccentric British estate yesterday by buying a mountain in South Wales. Mr Oncy Nathan already owns a disused lead mine near Aberystwyth and several half-submerged Scottish reefs. He paid substantially more than the £250,000 reserve for the Black Mountain, which lies between Ystradgynlais and Llandovery in Dyfed. Severe planning restrictions cover the 35 square miles of heather and whinberry which are wholly within the Brecon Beacons national park.

Mr Nathan, who is 28 and lives in London, bought the mountain by private treaty while an auction in which it was one of the lots was under way. The transaction infuriated a group of Welsh farmers who had come to London to bid for part of the land. Ten of them claimed compensation for a wasted journey which the embarrassed auctioneer, Mr John Barnett, offered to pay. He apologised to a roomful of bidders who had been attracted by national publicity for the mountain sale. 'I don't like this sort of thing happening at all,' he said, forlornly clutching a pebble from the Black Mountain which he had planned to show the room as a joke. 'Unfortunately there is nothing to stop a vendor selling privately right up to the time his lot is taken.'

The president of the Council for the Protection of Rural Wales, Baroness White, was among those who protested, although her group had decided not to bid because of legal uncertainty about the land's title. The vendor, a Mr Randall, has not completed his purchase from the previous owner, the Earl of Cawdor, whose own claim to possession has been challenged by a local farmer.

Mr Barnett said that contracts had been exchanged between the earl's estate and Mr Randall, who therefore had legal title. The Cawdor family had owned the land for 100 years and their rights had been upheld by the Commons Commissioners, he said.

Mr Nathan, whose purchase is officially part of the medieval Commot of Iscennan in the Lordship of Kidwelly, is a property speculator and import-export dealer. 'My father is a church minister who has renounced earthly things,' he said. 'It seems that I have gone back to them.'

He has yet to visit either the Brecon Beacons or the Hebridean Isle of Lewis, where he bought two more sea rocks yesterday as well as the 40,000 acre Valtos estate. He said that he had no plans to do anything controversial to his mountain, and he looked forward to meeting the local graziers. One of them, Mr Reg Haydon of Myddfai, Dyfed, who had hoped to bid with his fellow farmers, said he looked forward to introducing Mr Nathan to his 450 sheep.

The purchase may not be entirely whimsical. Another frustrated would-be bidder, Mr Peter Jones, asked the auctioneer if the price had been £1 million. When told it was less, he replied: 'Then the vendor has lost himself some money.'

4 April, 1984   **Martin Wainwright**

Leaking is what other people do

One of the nice things about being a member of that fashionably unpopular body, the Parliamentary Lobby Journalists, is that one is virtually entitled to wear one of those 'by appointment' signs when it comes to receiving leaks of information. We are, in a sense, the licensed and officially authorised drip tray beneath a notoriously leaky contraption, the machinery of Government.

Put like that, it perhaps does not sound quite proper. Not the kind of thing that respectable parents would wish to see their treasured offspring take up as an occupation. But the really attractive thing about it is that we are, as a group, uniquely protected as we go about our business by that notoriously ill-defined concept, Parliamentary privilege.

Unlike other forms of journalistic life with an equal interest in leaks – general reporters, say, or crime correspondents, or perhaps even City Editors – we lobby correspondents are allowed into the Palace of Westminster to pursue our trade on the strict understanding that we will *not* reveal our sources. Part of our secret initiation rites, more arcane even than those of the Freemasons, is the presentation of a small leather-bound booklet in which this duty is enshrined as holy writ.

The beauty of this is that, should a piece of information which we have seen fit to share with our readers get up the nose of some officious minister, we have the perfect let out. All we have to say when the inquisition starts is 'I heard it in the lobby of the House of Commons.'

In theory, at least, that should be sufficient to end all further enquiry about the source of our information. For it is only on the understanding that we will protect our informants in all circumstances that we enjoy the unique privilege of access to the troughs and watering holes frequented by our elected legislators. In other words, we are fireproof.

Yet the source of our information is not invariably a member of Parliament. All too often, if we were to crack under the pressure of official thumbscrews and electrodes, the words we might reluctantly let slip would be: 'I heard it from Mr Bernard Ingham, the Prime Minister's Press Secretary.'

Mr Ingham, of course, has let it be known (a phrase, by the way, which is normally a euphemism for 'he said it, but doesn't want to be quoted by name') that when he or another Government spokesman is the source of our information that is not a leak. Leaking is what other people do. What Mr Ingham does is to offer 'guidance'.

Now I have the utmost admiration and affection for Mr Ingham. Indeed, I once shared a room with him in this newspaper's former offices in Gray's Inn Road, when Bernard was the *Guardian's* deputy Labour Correspondent. I can reveal that (like me) he was not much of a typist, and used to scribble out his stories in shorthand and dictate them over an internal telephone to the *Guardian* copytakers.

But the simple truth is that, just as unofficial leaks are sometimes wrong, official guidance occasionally misdirects its recipients. This need not involve telling outright whoppers – an activity which is a great deal less common than the adherents of the conspiracy theory or history like to think.

For as Stephen Leacock once remarked, half truths are often

better than lies – like half bricks, they carry further. And official spokesmen are not under an absolute requirement to tell the whole truth, even if they are wise to avoid lying. In a long journalistic career, both in Britain and abroad, it has never occurred to me that an official spokesman for any kind of institution was likely to tell me the plain unvarnished truth in its entirety, except in the unusual circumstance that it suited his employers.

Nevertheless, official spokesmen can be roughly divided into two categories – a separation which often has more to do with their character and intelligence than with their status. There are those whose whole approach, either due to timidity or because of bloody mindedness, is to ensure that journalists (and there-fore the voters) know as little as possible about what the Government is up to. There are others who will tell you as much as they think they can, within the constrictions imposed from above.

Mr Ingham, who was brought into Whitehall by Mrs Barbara Castle during the 1966/70 Labour Government and who served several senior Labour ministers before being appointed to 10 Downing Street by Mrs Thatcher, belongs by instinct to the latter category. He has retained the respect and affection of reporters, in spite of a notoriously short fuse on a spectacular Yorkshire temper.

Indeed, the Ingham temper has frequently served as a source of information in its own right. Like all effective Downing Street press secretaries, he is known to have not only the confidence of the Prime Minister but also (no less important) unhindered access to her presence. When Bernard turns pink and starts to shout, we can be confident that we are on to something close to Mrs Thatcher's heart.

But the Ingham blood pressure has been on a rising curve of late, and the cause is not difficult to establish. The Prime Minister is more than usually angry these days, and the cause of her bad temper is partly the drip, drip, drip of innuendo about her son and the Omani university contract, and partly the increasing frequency of unauthorised and damaging disclosures from Whitehall departments about the direction of Government policy.

It is possible even for a journalist to feel some modest degree of sympathy for Mrs Thatcher. All politicians resent their vulnerability in relation to their families, and virtually all ministers firmly believe that they have a right to discuss policy matters in private without risking discovery and disclosures in the public prints. But sympathy is one thing; endorsement of her red-necked over-reaction to recent leaks is quite another. The business of gathering such information, and ultimately of publishing it, has been part of the newspaper trade since the seventeenth century. It is one of the essential features of an informed democracy, and the attempt to suppress it will inflict long term damage far more serious than the temporary embarrassment suffered by ministers at the time. So Mrs Thatcher needs to ask herself why her Government has been the victim of leaks on a scale far more extensive than anything experienced even by notoriously leaky Labour Governments like the 1964 and 1966 Wilson administrations. For there is a relatively simple explanation, and it has everything to do with the personality, the political persuasion and the historic thrust of the Prime Minister herself.

To appreciate the point I am making, it is necessary to reflect first on the nature of virtually every post-war Government, whether Labour or Conservative, and also to contemplate the nature of the British Civil Service. Those Governments have operated within a band of opinion which once used to be described as Butskellism. It was a viewpoint which covered a considerable consensus, even though the boundaries on the left and the right could alter significantly as intellectual fashions shifted. The British Civil Service gained its reputation for impartiality within that consensus tradition. The mandarins and their assistants were able to carry out policies with which they did not wholly agree because even the policies they disagreed with were within hailing distance of the ones they would have preferred. It was a comfortable, workable system which left only a few radical socialists complaining that the Whitehall machine was there to block fundamental changes.

That, at any rate, was the state of play until Mrs Thatcher overthrew Mr Heath and hijacked the Conservative Party for a new kind of radical Toryism. Hers was an ideology which bore a much closer resemblance to nineteenth century liberalism than anything understood by civil servants brought up on post-war Butskellism. With mounting horror, they began to realise that Butskellism was not just out of fashion; it was the main target of the new management.

It would be an exaggeration to say that this overt and aggressive abandonment of the post war consensus has caused the entire Civil Service to adopt the view that all previous bets are off, and that they will now repudiate the concept of an impartial administrative class. The great majority of senior civil servants continue to do their job as best they can in the new atmosphere, acutely aware that the Yes Minister image of their role is the one which Mrs Thatcher genuinely believes. But a small number clearly see the new atmosphere as a repudiation of what they regard as the implicit contract between successive Governments and their supposedly impartial servants.

Some of these people regard the policies pursued by the present Government, many of which are designed to dismantle the Butskellite edifice of social services, as intolerable. And that is why some of them, rightly or wrongly, are now resorting to the judicious and damaging leak as the only weapon they possess.

I am not saying they are right. But Mrs Thatcher has her share of responsibility for the destruction of a system which was once the pride of Britain's constitutionalists.

16 March, 1984   **Ian Aitken**

Six months in the climate of 'these times'

Sarah Tisdall was sent to prison for six months yesterday. That is a savage sentence, and what was said and done at the Old Bailey merely increased its savagery. For the first time, the world—and we—knew more about Miss Tisdall. She was not, she said, a Greenham woman. She was 'not at all' against nuclear weapons. She had merely, in her photocopying work at the Foreign Office, read two letters from Mr Heseltine to Mrs Thatcher concerning the orchestration of arrangements for cruise arrival last November and found them 'indecent' and 'immoral'. In an 'isolated and misjudged action' (the words, if you please, of the prosecuting counsel) she had taken a couple of extra copies and delivered them to this newspaper. There was no financial gain to her. She was 'not a spy'. She simply felt the public had a right to know. When the office she worked in came under suspicion she told her parents what she had done, and then confessed. The superintendent from Scotland Yard who persuaded her to confess thought she had been 'a silly girl'. And yet she must now serve six months in prison.

That is savage: and savage even by the standards of modern times. For example, the defendant in the ABC trial only five years ago—and dealing in an area where true national security was clearly at issue—was sentenced to a six-month suspended sentence. Yet any comparison of what the State itself claims about the 'seriousness' of the two cases indicates a dramatic reversal of priorities. 'In these times,' said Mr Justice Cantley delivering his verdict yesterday: by 'these times' he means times when we have a Government obsessed by loyalty and leaks and self-evidently determined to make an example of whoever comes to hand. It is Miss Tisdall's profound misfortune that she arrives on the scene in 'these times'.

That misfortune is underlined by the change in the Ministry of Defence's tune in the four months between the High Court case against the *Guardian* for the return of the document and the hearing of the Crown Court case against Miss Tisdall. Then we were all—fatally—in the dark. But the Ministry's mind was made up. Here was a 'matter of great significance' and of 'the gravest importance to the continued maintenance of national security'. The future of Nato, we were floridly informed, seemed to hang by a thread. Only the 'innermost circles' of Government had enjoyed access to Mr Heseltine's thoughts about how to catch Labour on the back foot at Westminster. Mr Justice Scott, it is fair to say, was sceptical of these prot-estations; and he was utterly right. For 'national security' barely featured in yesterday's proceedings. What we heard instead was that the Government had been caused 'embarrassment' by this leakage of 'politically sensitive' material. And yet, though the charge is utterly diminished, the sentence is at a level beyond even ministerial prognostication. The atmosphere of 'these times' is black and unfeeling. And consider, for a moment, the implication. Miss Tisdall was not the 'innermost circle' of Government. She was not one of the seven dignitaries to whom the letter in the case was addressed, not one of their closest mandarins. She was one of 300,000 clerks in Whitehall who had been formally read the Official Secrets Act. But she was only 23 and young enough to be shocked by an account of how Mr Heseltine proposed to outmanoeuvre Mr Kinnock. If the two documents in the case had been genuine matters of national security, then this Government would have been seen to have shot itself in the foot, spraying such secrets across dozens of junior clerks throughout Whitehall within 24 hours. But they weren't of such significance: they were only said to be of that import.

And there is, to repeat, a savage hypocrisy about the spread of charges and assertions of lofty international confidences. If Miss Tisdall, to take that charade of a Western security argument for a second, had been in a court of our greatest ally, the United States, yesterday, then on the evidence produced—the evidence of a young conscience momentarily outraged—she would have had a perfect defence under the 'Whistleblowers Act'. But the whole thrust and approach of British law is different. It wasn't for her to blow any whistles on her own, said the judge. She should, by implication, have asked Mr Heseltine or Sir Geoffrey Howe first. And neither her obvious innocence of the world or political calculation, nor her age and inexperience—so much younger, for instance, then either of the Prime Minister's children—was of any account. She was sentenced explicitly to discourage the others. She was sentenced to make clear that the public interest lies, 'in these times', only with the Government of the day.

There is one further area we would wish to explore. 'She stands,' said her counsel yesterday, 'in the box alone.' The newspaper that published the stories she anonymously supplied was not in the box with her. We publish today on page 4 a full and often painful account of the circumstances that led up to the surrender of the document in the case last December. But Mr John Mathew's point remains a solid and emotive one. Miss Tisdall fell prey to Section Two of the Official Secrets Act—

that 'mess' of an Act, as Lord Franks called it, a mess so open and admitted in legal circles that the Government declined in the end to use it to prosecute the *Guardian*. We were arraigned under Copyright and Interference with Property, and then in the end with the full, escalating financial penalties of contempt of court. But we could have been charged under the same Act as Miss Tisdall—except that it was at no stage argued that we had acted against 'the public interest' or that what we had published was not in 'the public interest.' At once one sees the hypocrisy and desuetude of a ramshackle legal area, where bits of widely different acts can be pointed against different defendants—bound together at the end only by judicial thundering about 'betrayals of trust'. Mr Mathew was dead right. The *Guardian*—as the receiver of stolen goods—should have been in the dock too. The fact that it was not—because to have put it there would have utterly undermined the case against Miss Tisdall—exposes a miasma of statute in an area where the climate of freedom—in 'these times'—has suddenly and dramatically deteriorated under Governmental attack.

This grey area of uncertainty and creeping repression cannot, we now feel, be cleared piecemeal. It was one awkward feature in this case that a specific statute—a new statute for which we had argued ourselves—provided a defence that was left in manifest disarray at the first test. We intend to exercise our right of appeal to the House of Lords in this matter, and we believe that Miss Tisdall herself wants the wider issues to be kept alive and tested to the full. That will be done. A law which seemingly demands respect and offers protection is a smouldering pistol whilst it remains in such confusion.

But there is a still wider issue. Since December, the climate of repression has grown chillier week by week. Reporters' saddlebags are searched in the street. Scotland Yard is in sweeping operation against every Whitehall tremor—or supposed budget leak. There is an atmosphere, in some ministerial circles, almost of paranoia—and savagery grows easily in such a greenhouse. The British press is divided and bitterly competitive. Such competition means, alas, calls in some papers for the 'hunting down' of all leakers: and in the difficult aftermath of our own case, other papers wrote that we would have done better to hand over the document without a struggle. That is a patchwork foundation on which to build. But the message of yesterday is clear enough. The Government is in hot pursuit, and the press and television—and those who deal with them —will be pursued. Meanwhile, the law offers no coherent protection. One does not, as an ordinary citizen, have to approve of every leaker—case by case—to realize that, in Lord Scarman's theme, there is a public and democratic interest in the bringing forward of material that authority does not wish to see published. There is a general theme and a general interest. It does not hang on specific instances and specific judgements. Sarah Tisdall is the victim of a case which constantly changed perspective. But in the end, alone in the dock yesterday, she was a victim. As she is a powerful symbol of what is profoundly wrong in our society, and what needs to be put right.

24 March, 1984   **Leader**

Subversion and the State

In May 1982 the Prime Minister gave Parliament her view on the role which the Security Service should play in countering the threat of subversion by domestic political groups. In a White Paper on a security commission report, she said:

'The internal threat has altered considerably. It has become more varied and viewed as a whole has grown more serious. The threat offered by the Communist Party of Great Britain has probably diminished as a result of the fall in the number of its members and the disillusionment of many of them with Soviet policy since 1968 in invading Czechoslovakia and, more recently, Afghanistan.

'The fall in CPGB membership, however, has been accompanied by the proliferation of new subversive groups of the extreme left and the extreme right (mainly the former) whose aim is to overthrow democratic parliamentary government in this country by violent or other unconstitutional means, not shrinking in the case of the most extreme groups from terrorism to achieve their aims.

'Membership of individual groups is small but, for the most part, active and conspiratorial.'

Mrs Thatcher's statement is a public clue to an unseen development which had for some years been taking place in the monitoring of political activity in Britain. To counter this perceived new, proliferating internal threat, a small force of civil servants and police officers have established a nationwide operation which has led them to defy the law and to evade their own rules in order to record the personal and political lives of broad swathes of the population.

At the heart of the operation is the Security Service, MI5, which celebrates its 75th anniversary this year: an extremely secretive organisation whose 2,000 staff work within the conventional Civil Service structure but without any of the normal scrutiny of their activities. They organise the tapping of phones and the opening of mail, the infiltration of political groups and the procurement of informers. They have a section whose main purpose is to break and enter private homes and offices, and they have gained access to confidential personal information held in supposedly private government files. The arms and legs of the operation are provided by the Special Branch which now has some 1,800 officers spread through every police force in the country. Working apart from ordinary officers, their main role is to investigate 'subversion', helping MI5 with local sources of information and their extra police powers of arrest and search. The Security Service and the Special Branch are linked at the top through the Home Office and in the provinces by a network of nine regions in which MI5 representatives direct the Special Branches towards new priorities and handle particularly sensitive case work.

Although the foundations of this operation have existed since before the First World War, its character and size have changed: new soft targets such as peace activists have been added to the old ones like spies and terrorists; new techniques of surveillance have invaded privacy and infringed civil rights. The concern of Downing Street and the Cabinet Office about its work has grown.

The morale of some of those involved has started to fall: although the leadership appears to be solidly committed to its work, there are now some people who are warning that in the long term it will suffer from its secrecy, its lack of accountability and its disrespect for the law.

Those concerned with the present state of the Security Service take differing views of these changes. According to one the service is 'cynically manipulating the letter and the spirit of its charter. The clear-cut definitions have been eroded and so a grey area has spread. There is now a dangerous and maybe irreversible slide; the momentum in that direction has perceptibly increased since 1979.'

Another recognised the change, but defended it. 'The change that has been required, which has been very, very significant for both the overt and the covert security forces, has meant that they are more and more intrusive. Some civil liberties do go by the board. When people are under suspicion then their privacy is intruded upon. I regret that this has happened, but I don't apologise for it because it's the only way that we can possibly begin to meet the threat.

'I regret that it is now necessary to spy on people to the extent that we do. I regret it is now necessary to vet so many people whereas before you could take their loyalty for granted. I regret that within the organs of Government you now have to be looking at almost everybody whereas before you looked at one per cent. But although I regret it, it is necessary.'

The headquarters of the Security Service is Curzon Street House, a squat, six-floor concrete building in Mayfair. At the head of them all sits the Director General, a remote figure who finds other people rather difficult to deal with and prefers to delegate to his chain-smoking deputy, an incisive man in his late 50s. He is well thought of in the Home Office and will probably take over soon. Between them, these two men determine the direction of the Security Service, and lay down its priorities. They link upwards to the Home Secretary and the Prime Minister and, through their secretariat and staff officers, to the other intelligence services and to their own officers abroad. Beneath them are the six branch directors.

There is 'A' Branch, in charge of field work and therefore, many of the Service's dirty tricks. A1 (technical operations) section includes the MI5 officers who burgle properties to photograph documents or plant bugs. They have no legal immunity to do this, but, so far, they have not been caught. Other parts of A Branch transcribe the tapes of tapped phone calls, run mobile and static surveillance on targets (in a section known as The Watchers), keep safe houses and listening posts, specialise in extracting confidential information from contacts in Government departments like the DHSS and the DoE, and from banks and hotels, and liaise with GCHQ to reap the benefit of their electronic eavesdropping.

The man in charge of A Branch is described variously as 'a character' and 'an eccentric' and infectiously enthusiastic. He is a devoted amateur musician.

'B' Branch is effectively the Service's personnel department. It is responsible for the recruitment and, therefore, the vetting of new staff and for the welfare and personnel management of all employees. It also looks after finance and the personal and physical security of MI5 officers and buildings. Its director is a shrewd, quiet man, described by one source as 'gnome-like in every sense'. He has extended the reach of the Service's recruitment by cultivating contacts in the Careers Advisory Boards of red-brick and plate-glass universities.

'C' Branch deals with the safety of official buildings and secrets, so it advises the security officers of each Government department, inspects their security arrangements and leads leak inquiries. It also advises private companies who work on classified contracts and runs the vetting system for Whitehall, the armed forces and the police. It has a special role in counter-sabotage and counter-terrorism which means that it draws up contingency plans to handle possible incidents – such as the occupation of a nuclear power station – and then runs exercises with the SAS and special police units to learn how to deal with them.

The director of C Branch is a very conservative figure who is little known to his colleagues because he is, by nature, quiet and self-effacing and also because he has spent almost his whole career inside C Branch.

From the point of view of domestic political surveillance, 'F' Branch is the most important part of MI5. It is responsible for handling 'subversion' and is currently run by a young and ambitious officer who made his name for his handling of the 1972 miners' strike. He was then in charge of the sub-section which deals with trade unions and he kept Whitehall briefed with a running analysis of the political motivation of the miners' leaders, their strategy, immediate tactics, expectations and internal divisions. He went on to run the joint intelligence operation in Northern Ireland.

F Branch is clearly subdivided: F1 investigates the Communist Party; F2 investigates trade unions; F3 investigates terrorism; F5 investigates Irish terrorism; F7 looks at other left-wing groups as well as right-wing extremists, MPs, teachers, lawyers and journalists. Two of its sections are hived off to a separate sub-branch, known as FX, which is responsible for long-term infiltration: F4 puts agents into political parties and organisations; F6 runs them into trade unions at all levels. The current head of FX was a surprise appointment who does not command the respect of all his colleagues.

While FX runs its agents into 'subversive' targets, the rest of F Branch monitors the same targets with all the other means at its disposal including taps, bugs, mail opening, break-ins and local investigations by the Special Branch. F's young director is regarded as a strong contender to become Director General sooner or later.

His main competition comes from the head of K Branch, which looks after counter-espionage – basically, the Russians and their allies. He is also relatively young – in his late 40s – and highly spoken of by colleagues and by the army with whom he has worked in Northern Ireland.

K Branch uses all available techniques to monitor the activity of Russian intelligence officers at the Embassy, the trade delegation and other centres as well as the work of other Soviet bloc intelligence services. It will sometimes use local Special Branch officers to follow Soviet targets who travel outside London.

The sixth branch, S Branch, runs a variety of back-up services, the most important of which is known as JCB, the Joint Computer Bureau which is linked to MI6, the Secret Intelligence Service. It also runs MI5's own registry, where dossiers on 500,000 people are held, as well as training and miscellaneous support services such as travel, accommodation and printing.

Its director used to be the head of the Northern Ireland operation.

The Northern Ireland crisis has forced many changes in the Security Service, and much of the hardening of attitudes and disrespect for the rules and the law is traceable to this. It has also created the need for a special intelligence operation.

This is run as an adjunct to the main MI5 structure by the office of the Director and Coordinator of Intelligence, who works from Stormont Castle in Belfast to link the intelligence effort of the army, the Royal Ulster Constabulary, MI5 and MI6.

The Security Service has foreign links. It keeps its own officers, known as security liaison officers, in Washington, Ottawa, Melbourne, Berlin, Cyprus, Hong Kong and BAOR headquarters at Rheindahlen. It also has a role in the little-known British Services Security Organisation where there are British troops on foreign soil, and has direct telex links to European security services.

The staff of MI5 live a strange and rather lonely life, surveying and monitoring the world outside but isolated from it by the strict security demanded by their work. Like any other Government department, they are a mixed bag. Some middle-ranking officers resent their superiors. There are junior staff who feel hidebound by the custom and practice of years and complain that initiative is discouraged. But, unquestionably, there is talent. An academic who wrote an article about arms smuggling was approached by an MI5 officer, who used the name 'Steve', for information about his sources. 'Steve,' the academic recalls, 'was very intelligent, a shrewd observer. He never put pressure on me as such and never offered money. He figured out very quickly what I drink and what food I like. I remember him saying, for example: "Those are very nice continental cufflinks, 18 carat gold, aren't they?" He said things about my accent, my behaviour, and asked very astute questions. If he is a typical operative then I'd say they've got a good team.'

MI5 has immense power. In domestic political surveillance, it rests principally on the freedom to decide who is the internal enemy. They draw the lines and define the criteria and, thus, establish the basis of a wide range of activities: they influence job

128

selection in the whole public sector and in sensitive parts of the private sector; the progress of new political formations; the conduct of industrial disputes; the access of journalists and academics to official information.

MI5 makes these decisions, always, with the absolute minimum of interference from Parliament and Downing Street. Their independence is preserved by the demands of security which, they say, make it impossible for them to share details of their work. Prime Ministers, Home Secretaries, senior policemen, senior civil servants are all told only what they need to know and, very often, that is nothing.

The Director General is responsible to the Home Secretary. The two men meet about once a month for a 'general chat,' which very rarely involves the disclosure of any operational detail. There is also a separate infrastructure of intelligence committees around the Cabinet Office. This structure has got much stronger since the Blunt affair of 1979. The key figure now is the Cabinet Secretary, Sir Robert Armstrong, who sits on all the intelligence committees, and represents the needs and views of the Prime Minister. Sir Anthony Duff, who is the Cabinet's Intelligence Coordinator, prepares regular briefing papers for Mrs Thatcher. But this Cabinet Office structure has no more operational control over the Security Service than the Home Secretary does. Its main purpose is to process the intelligence gathered about foreign powers by MI6 and GCHQ. MI5 is a customer, in that it will receive useful information through its representatives on the committees.

The Director General's links with Downing Street remain ad hoc. He is likely to meet Sir Robert Armstrong several times a week at meetings of intelligence committees and he may ask for direct access to the Prime Minister if he wants it.

The Prime Minister and Sir Robert have two levers which may be used in extremes: they appoint and can dismiss the Director General and they can scrutinise his budget through the Official Committee on Security which Sir Robert chairs. The Prime Minister has recently brought pressure on the Director General to keep her informed about security lapses in MI5, but there is no sign that she has persuaded him to disclose more about the Service's operational activity.

When it comes to the selection of targets and the means of dealing with them, there is little friction between the Security Service and the current Prime Minister and her intelligence committees. The leading figures share a common point of view and often a common past, particularly through Northern Ireland.

Sir Robert Armstrong was previously Permanent Under-Secretary at the Home Office, responsible for signing phone-tap and mail interception warrants and liaising with the Deputy Director General, who is now the Director General. Before that, Sir Robert was the Home Office Deputy Secretary responsible for security liaison, terrorism and subversion.

The Permanent Under-Secretary at the Home Office now is Sir Brian Cubbon who has served in Northern Ireland, as did Sir Brookes Richards, the last Cabinet Intelligence Coordinator, Sir Howard Smith, the last Director General of MI5, as well as two recent Home Secretaries, Merlyn Rees and William Whitelaw, and the present Commissioner of Scotland Yard, Sir Kenneth Newman. It is a tight circle.

Much of the ground work for MI5 is done by the police Special Branch, which over the years has become virtually an extension of the Security Service. The relationship is not always an easy one, the Oxbridge background of MI5 against the more down to earth style of the Special Branch.

The Special Branch's biggest single area of operation – and the reason for its creation in 1883 – is Irish Republican terrorism on the mainland. In this one area, it has precedence over MI5 and works as a national force, running its own informers, taps and mail intercepts, making its own investigative initiatives and arrests. MI5 would rather be in charge, and has succeeded in getting control of the monitoring of Loyalist activity on the mainland.

Regular police Anti-terrorist Squad officers have little affection for their colleagues in the Special Branch and often complain that the Branch does not share the intelligence which it collects and also has no concept of gathering admissible evidence to run a prosecution in court.

In other areas – spies, terrorists apart from IRA and INLA, the left, the right, trade unions – the Special Branch is the willing servant of the Security Service, with which it has far closer connections than has generally been realised.

At the top, F4 division of the Police Department of the Home Office makes policy on counter-subversion in consultation with senior officers of MI5 and key policemen – the head of the London Special Branch, the Scotland Yard Commissioner, and the leaders of ACPO, the Association of Chief Police Officers. But this policy is limited. For practical and political reasons, the Home Office has never given the Special Branch a list of those political groups or trade unionists whom it considers are worthy targets. Instead, in 1977, it provided general guidelines and left it to the individual Special Branch officer to decide which threats he should counter. However, this policy vacuum is filled by MI5. In each of its nine regions, MI5 has an intelligence officer and a police liaison officer, usually a retired senior policeman who has been taken on to MI5's payroll. Their job is to influence the local Chief Constable and the local Special Branch officers to secure their help in ways useful to MI5.

One senior policeman told us: 'The liaison man will pop in to see the Chief Constable and have a cup of tea, talk about things. He'll say: "They're a bit worried up in London about so-and-so." And the Chief Constable will talk about what should be done about keeping a better eye on so-and-so and generally reassure him.'

MI5 deals directly with Special Branch officers, who often attend seminars or training sessions to bring them up to date on targets and techniques. New technical aids are introduced by the scientists of MI5 and MI6 working together and passed on to the branch. On specific investigations, MI5 will bring in Special Branch officers to make local inquiries or to carry out a time-consuming surveillance, to open a file for them or to help them to conduct a burglary.

Special Branch leaders are just as resistant to political control, and local police authority members who have tried to discover information about them have generally been rebuffed. Some Chief Constables even find they cannot discover what their branch officers are doing. 'They only tell me what I need to know,' said one, 'and that's not much.'

MI5's upper hand is reflected in the relationship between

officers of the two organisations. Special Branch officers try to nurture MI5 officers as valuable contacts and speak of them with some awe. MI5 and the rest of the intelligence community, however, make little effort to hide their lack of respect for Special Branch officers, particularly those in the provinces.

The folklore of Britain's internal security apparatus is replete with tales of Special Branch bungling and ineptitude – the overkeen officer who is not happy just to tail a target but has to break into his car as well; the cunning, covert approach to a suspect which immediately raises suspicions and gives the game away; the targeting of obviously harmless people.

This may reflect the recent growth of the branches and, as some suggest, recruiting of less able officers. In the late 1960s, there were some 300 in London and less than 50 others, concentrated in large airports and docks around the country. Now there are estimated to be more than 400 in London, a further 850 in the rest of the country, another 100 in Scotland, and some 400 in Northern Ireland. Special Branch's growth is also reflected in a series of now independent police off-shoots: the Illegal Immigrants Intelligence Unit, the Drugs Intelligence Unit, the Diplomatic Protection Group, the Anti-Terrorist Squad, and the D11 firearms squad have all been spawned by the Branch to concentrate on some of its functions and they continue to work closely and to swap staff.

In addition to its direct work with MI5 and with Irish Republican terrorism, Special Branch is heavily involved in VIP protection, watching ports and airports, registering aliens, vetting naturalisation applicants and enforcing the Official Secrets Act, the Prevention of Terrorism Act and election law. Two years ago it was given a special responsibility for investigating racial attacks.

The Metropolitan Police Special Branch remains the most professional and the most important. Its head, Colin Hewett, has the rank of Deputy Assistant Commissioner – more senior than the head of any other specialist squad. It has two commanders – one for administration and another, Peter Phelan, who used to be in the Anti-Terrorist Squad, for operations. Beneath them are eight Detective Chief Superintendents organising its various roles with the 24-hour watch on Heathrow Airport and the demands of VIP protection absorbing most man hours. London officers tend to stay with Special Branch for most of their careers, moving from desk to desk within it. All SB officers must be positively vetted.

Counter terrorism is a major priority. After the Irish threat the Middle East provides most work. A section of 12 officers keeps permanent watch on Iranians, Libyans, Palestinians and others and relies heavily on contacts with MI5 and the embassies of target countries and political exiles living in the UK. Subversion is nevertheless an important preoccupation. Half a dozen officers spend so much time following the National Front that their names and faces are well-known. On the left, they or their informers are involved in the same groups as MI5, working with the Security Service to build up the picture. Like MI5 they target trade unionists, particularly national officials in London, and peace activists and defend their behaviour by saying that even if these targets are not genuine subversives, they are likely to commit public order offences, which is another of the Branch's special responsibilities.

But secret bureaucracies have innate dangers. They can go off the rails, like the Special Branch in South Australia, which was formed along the lines of the British force with advice from the former MI5 Director General, Sir Percy Sillitoe. In 1977, Judge J. M. White conducted a thorough inquiry and found it had run completely out of control. The judge found that the Special Branch had deliberately lied to politicians to conceal the existence of thousands of dossiers containing information on members of the Australian Labour Party, any university academic who could be classified as left-wing, vicars, trade unionists, civil libertarians and judges and magistrates.

The dossiers had been compiled, the judge concluded, 'on the unreasoned assumption that any persons who thought or acted less conservatively than suited the security force were likely to be potential dangers to the security of the state.' Many of them, he added, were hopelessly inaccurate and laden down with irrelevant information. As a result, the South Australian Special Branch was disbanded.

17 April, 1984   **Nick Davies and Ian Black**

Arlott at 70

His wife, Pat, brings him a cup of tea at 7 a.m. and on comes Radio 4's *Today* programme. By 8.15, in his bottle-green corduroy bags and anorak over the great blanket of a Swedish sweater, he is having his first solemn, plodding constitutional 'over the top' on the hillocks. Such is the minuscule one-mile-by-three rocky blob of Alderney that at most places you can see the choppy Channel fuming and frothing on the rocks at every point of the compass.

Later in the morning he will turn in the other direction from his wide, bright white house and this time the parade takes him up and down the cobbled little doll's house main street. 'Mornin' George!' 'Mornin' Margot!' 'Mornin' David!' They all reply with a hoot and a wave and a smile.

First call is to the post office for the wad of letters and pile of parcels. 'Ahh,' comes the satisfied, familiar old growl, 'I do like my post.' It remains one of the most enduring, endearing, evocative voices known to Britain and beyond.

The telephone never stops. Indeed the volume of Alderney Telecom business that obviously increased the moment John Arlott retired to the Channel Islands gives absolute lie to the very idea of 'retirement'.

It was only day-in, day-out, cricket reporting for this newspaper and the BBC that ended with such wrenching finality in the early autumn of 1980. 'I can't sunbathe or sit in the garden or go on cruises. Not that I'm trying to build a career, I've come as far as I can. But I still love writing. Now I'm just coasting, not downhill, but just coasting along on a *loverly* level.'

There are strong hints that he is to embark, at last, on an autobiography. He has already decided on the first sentence – 'It was a fat baby of seven pounds that Nelly Arlott gave birth to in the Old Cemetery Lodge, Basingstoke, at 4 a.m. on the morning of February 25, 1914. . . .'

Exactly 70 years on and the birthday is celebrated today with a

Drawing by Peter Clarke

family party for his wife, his two surviving sons and their women – and his favourite friend and cricketer, Leo Harrison, the former Hampshire wicket-keeper. And tomorrow at noon it seems that half the island will be popping in to raise the hairs from the dog with a further bracer or two. 'Mornin' George!' 'Mornin' Margot!'

This week, the old spaniel's soft-boiled eyes still shining bright, the birthday boy showed me round his green-grey granitey island. We sat in a picture window watching spectacular waves snap and fret at the sea wall. It was like the royal fireworks. 'Ooh, look at that one!' 'Golly, there's a beauty for you. Wow!'

It was calmer up the cobbled street. I had, of course, to be introduced to the bearded young man who kept the DIY shop and who last season scored 216 off 51 balls on the island's little cricket pitch. 'Even Frindall says Jessop never matched that!'

After a pre-lunch bracer in the Albert – Fino sherry in tomato juice – back home for cold meats and the accompanying myriad of honest bottles – reds, whites, rosés, all the way from France and Germany and California, from Spain, Lebanon, New Zealand and even England. We tasted, in slugs large and small and long. On the whole I think wine correspondent might be a better job than cricket correspondent.

The newspapers have arrived from the mainland. He goes straight to *The Times* obituaries. Then to the *Guardian* sports pages. 'Good God! Lillee's put Miandad in hospital. In a benefit match too. The bastard!'

Then an afternoon's work. He taps at his typewriter, sometimes dictates to Pat. 'I'd go mad if I didn't work.' He first discovered Alderney some 30 years ago. 'It is the most beautiful place I know. So quiet. You can only realistically arrive by air. We enjoyed many family holidays here when my late son and wife were alive.' His eldest son was killed in a motor accident. The sorrow of his loss still pains him intensely.

The isle is full of silence and the house full of treasures. In the hall is a grand and ancient old wireless set – it belonged to Haley when he was the BBC's Director-General. There are watercolours of Winchester and needlework of Worcester.

In the kitchen is Toynbee's lively and glorious oil of 'The

Nets', drawings of Hardy and Dylan Thomas and a striking portrait of Elizabeth David. In the Long Room there are the first editions – Hardy, Hazlitt, Betjeman and all – and on the walls Lowry and Rowlandson, Lancaster and Beerbohm.

John Arlott's beloved father, Jack, ended up keeping the graveyard neat at Basingstoke. He wanted the boy simply to get a job with a pension. He began in local government and then in the police force. When the young man started making his name with the BBC father and son embraced, 'and cried together at the wonder of it all.'

His third cricket book, on the Australians of 1948, was dedicated 'To my father who knows nothing about cricket and cares less but who wos werry good to me.'

The last sentence in that book reads: 'Is there, I wonder, anywhere in the world such a human, generous, unenvious, shop-talking, enthusiastic, mellow, craft-versed sporting community as English cricket professionals?'

He still loves his cricket, though since that famous day at Lord's when the ground and players stood to him in farewell he has only seen one day's play – at Taunton when Somerset made him a life member. Hampshire have not done him similar justice.

And of course he still loves cricketers. 'Of all of them over the years I think I have only known four bad ones. Yes, only four.'

Supper, beautifully cooked by Pat, is served with another swill and clink of honest bottles. You start with sherry to brace up the soup. And the stories and opinions keep coming. You ask about Yorkshire cricket. 'The only thing that can sort them out is five tons of napalm!'

You wonder if you will be steady up the stairs. You leave, early to bed, with John solemnly munching and dictating to Pat his Cheese Column to be typed on the morrow. You stagger upstairs and below, the old voice is gravelly dictating – 'A deep, intense nose . . . pungent taste . . . but deep, creamy and satisfying. . . .'

And in the morning he will be up far earlier than you to greet the day. 'Mornin' George! Mornin' Margot!' Happy Birthday, John.

25 February, 1984   **Frank Keating**

A kind of dog's breakfast time

And we're going straight over to Parliament Square and our reporter, Rodney Smooth, who has been following the siege of the so-called British People's Cabinet all afternoon. Can you tell us what's going on, Rodney?

– I certainly can, Selina. The Opposition has had the occupiers of the self-styled Cabinet surrounded now for over two hours. Obviously they want to know how an unarmed policewoman came to be shot in the back by a member of the Diplomatic Corps, and who arranged to escort the murderer out of the country.

I gather they've called on everyone inside the Cabinet to come out and co-operate with an independent investigation Rodney.

– That's right Selina. But they're only willing to hold what they call an internal inquiry, and you can imagine what that would mean among those kind of people. So it's beginning to look as if the chaps responsible are going to get away with it.

Do you have their names yet, Rodney?

– Well, unofficially we think that the man who did it is called Humiliation for Brittan, Humiliation must be his first name. He's issued a statement here and so has his colleague, an officially credited diplomat called Howe – interestingly enough, Selina, because he won't tell us How. When the Opposition tried to get further details over the landline they're not being very helpful. Keep referring questioners to each other.

Have they expressed any regret for their conduct, Rodney?

– 'Fraid not, Selina. Of course most of them are devoted supporters of their leader, Colonel Finchley, and they seem to think that whatever they do is entirely justified. Rather pleased with themselves, I'd say.

Some reports suggest that they're singing Land of Hope and Glory in there, Rodney. Would you describe the people inside as zealous fanatics chanting jingoistic slogans?

– To be honest, I think that exaggerates the mood here today.

Some of their supporters have been staging a demonstration outside the Cabinet, praising what they call a brilliant exercise in damage limitation. And they've been shouting 'Hindsight merchants' and 'Headline hunters' at the men in charge of the siege.

How did Gerald Kaufman, David Owen and Denis Healey take that, Rodney?

– Pretty calmly, Selina. They're all very experienced officers. Mr Healey has been particularly interesting. He was obviously trying to establish a relationship of trust with the men inside because he spoke for even longer than the self-styled Foreign Secretary. Almost rambling, you could say.

Did the strategy work, Rodney?

– Actually, no, Selina. They were laughing so much at the end that you couldn't hear the old chap's final appeal to give themselves up. Even Mr Kaufman was looking at his watch.

What you're saying, Rodney, is that this People's Cabinet deny being negligent before the shooting and having any alternative after it. And now they're banging the stable door after the horse has been escorted out of the country, as dishy Dr Owen put it.

– That's right, Selina, they've been nasty to so-called Libyan students and genuine midshipmen. It's rather more difficult to enforce the Vienna Convention or stop them taking arms out of the country.

You mean the diplomatic bag, Rodney?

– And the British defence contracts to Libya. Existing ones are being reviewed, but meanwhile they're continuing. Stopping them might cost jobs and we're short of them. That's why so many Britons are working in Libya.

Which means that we can't afford to get tough, doesn't it? If we do they'll start taking hostages and costing us jobs?

– You mean the Libyans or the Cabinet, Selina?

I'm sorry, Rodney, that's all we've got time for. With me now in the studio is Mrs Julia Miles . . .

2 May, 1984   **Michael White**

April is the hanging season

'The people are in power in Libya. How should I know what they are doing in every place. I don't know what happened at the university. Go and see for yourself.'

That he is not a conventional head of state, that he has no executive or administrative authority, is an alibi in which Colonel Gadafy frequently takes refuge when confronted with questions he does not care to answer.

And it was with this dismissive reply to an inquiry about the recent executions of two students at Tripoli University that he concluded an aggressive press conference devoted to the events at the London People's Bureau. Had it not been for those, the macabre university hangings on April 16 would never have had the publicity which they did.

It proved all but impossible to follow Colonel Gadafy's advice. After a considerable delay and a telephone call to higher authority, the People's Militia at the university gates let me pass, only to confront me with the far greater difficulty of finding just one of the more than 20,000 students who would talk at all.

'I know nothing about it,' said one. 'I was on holiday in Turkey at the time,' said another, slightly more forthcoming. 'Yes,' conceded a third, 'I did see one of the executions. Yes, it took place on that tennis court over there, just behind the agricultural faculty. Yes, we were obliged to attend. Yes, it was the revolutionary committees who made us. But please,' he begged, 'don't ask me about this problem.'

There seemed to be little choice but to go straight to one of the 'revolutionary committees'. These are what Gadafy calls the 'red nerve' of his revolution. They came into being in 1977, after the founding of the Jamahiriyah, the capital state of the masses, which set itself the task of ending all 'conventional' forms of government – 'authoritarian, family, tribal, factional, class, parliamentary, partisan or party coalition' – and replacing them, for the first time in human history, with 'people's power' in the fullest sense.

Gadafy has identified three things – political authority, resources, and arms – which the people have to conquer before their power is irrevocably assured. Even in the Jamahiriyah this has not yet been completed. Segments of the old, traditional structures – and, most problematically, the army and the police – remain in being. They co-exist with and are increasingly challenged by the new, revolutionary institutions, and in particular the 'revolutionary committees'.

According to their own statutes, these are composed of people who 'have been convinced, through the Green Book, of the fraudulence of contemporary democracy'. Their task, among other things, is to 'incite the masses to exercise their power', to practise 'revolutionary vigilance' and to organise people's congresses. They are, in other words, the eyes and ears of Gadafy's unique regime – the dedicated few who will follow wherever he leads, trying to take the whole of society with them.

The university, like everything else, is bedecked with the slogans of the Third Universal Theory – Authority, Resources and Arms in the hands of the people, committees everywhere, representation is a fraud, and so on – but the 'revolutionary committees' do not advertise their presence. They exert their all-powerful influence from the back-rooms.

It was in one of these, at the College of Education, that a third-year geography student, Jamila Durman, was thrust forward by her male colleagues to answer questions. 'They were not "executed",' she corrected me in response to the first, 'they were "liquidated".' She seemed to be disguising her gender in a kind of spaceship tunic, all zips and pockets, and was as aggressively unfeminine in her language as she was in her appearance.

It was a slight relief to learn later that this fierce, fanatical, but far from unfriendly young woman – for she seemed to regard every inquirer as a potential convert – was held in some awe, on account of her dedication, in revolutionary circles well beyond the university.

There was no secret about it. True, the news of the hangings had not been published in the newspapers. But why should it have been? This was an affair that concerned the university alone. For in the new era of 'people's power' and 'direct democracy' the students, like every other corporate body, were in the process of conquering their share of the 'authority'.

In April 1983, they had won an officially-recognised autonomy under the guidance of their revolutionary committee. These committees were not only egalitarian within themselves, Jamila explained. As the true expression of the popular will, they were strictly 'horizontal' as opposed to 'pyramidical' in their nationwide structure.

There was, it was true, a Revolutionary Committees Liaison Bureau, and this happened to be physically located – and even with a sign to say so – in the Azizia barracks, where Gadafy lived and worked. But its function was what its title suggested: liaison, and liaison only.

The two students – Jamila would not divulge their names – had been convicted as 'enemies of the revolution'. They wanted to 'take power for themselves', and, as was well known, in the Jamahiriyah no-one, not even Gadafy, held power except the people.

It had been fellow students who had unmasked the traitors. One of them, in the pharmacy college, had begun to behave very strangely. He had formerly associated with girls like everyone. Only reactionary Islam, she observed, discriminated between the sexes. But then he began to spurn them, refusing even to shake their hands. So his colleagues kept a watch on him, and discovered that he was meeting with Saudi diplomats in mosques. He eventually confessed – he was a member of the Islamic Liberation Organisation, an extreme fundamentalist sect which crops up from time to time in the demonology of many an Arab regime.

So the pharmacy students set up a revolutionary court, composed of members of their 'revolutionary committee', as well as some of those whose vigilance had first caught up with the traitor. The regular courts still functioned in Libya, Jamila explained, but they dealt with common crimes. This was a political crime, and a monstrous one, an attempt to overthrow a system so enlightened, she said, that its mission would only be complete when all the peoples of the world had adopted it.

The agricultural students had likewise tried, condemned and 'liquidated' their 'traitor'. His case seemed very similar – he had been conspiring on behalf of an organisation called the Islamic Vanguards.

Why had the investigations and trials taken so long? The two men had been apprehended in 1982 or 1983, Jamila did not seem to be quite sure, but she struck a note of compassion – one takes time when human life is at stake.

Any misgivings? No, and the manner of execution proved it. 'Only tyrants, only those who are afraid of the people, execute behind prison doors.' And she recited one of the rhyming slogans which had been shouted in the shadow of the gallows: 'We are the generation of anger, the generation of the cause. We have no mercy on the traitors, we hang them in the open square.'

There have been student executions before. April – traditionally associated with student revolutionary 'gains' – is the hanging season. But these latest ones seem to have been particularly well rehearsed in their exemplary intent. As such, they were symptomatic of the hardening battle-lines between the regime and its opponents. And so, of course, was the reaction from the opposition.

The hangings contributed to the demonstration outside the People's Bureau in London. And this had an unprecedented resonance inside Libya. 'Everyone listens to the BBC now,' said one of the rare taxi drivers to venture a political comment. The authorities are now trying to jam BBC broadcasts.

There are various accounts of what has happened in Libya itself. One certainty is the burning of the university auditorium. It was there, apparently, that students were obliged to watch a video film of the executions. The fire could – as Jamila said – have been caused by a short circuit, but that is not what other students believe.

Gadafy is reported to have been simultaneously burned in effigy and a dog let loose wearing a travesty of one of those richly-garnished uniforms to which, in recent years, he has taken such a fancy. There are also reports – denied by Jamila but widely believed elsewhere – that revolutionary committee members have been assassinated in reprisal.

One of the most colourful stories is that the woman, apparently another Jamila, who kicked away the platform beneath the gallows was found dead with a bullet through her forehead. Another committee member is said to be found hanged in the lavatories.

What makes the accident theory much less likely is that there have been other fires. If, in an arsonist's mind, the university auditorium represented a particularly apt symbol of a perverse and cruel political 'authority', the ammunition depot at Al-Abya, near Benghazi, could be seen to symbolise the 'arms' in Gadafy's trinity.

That blew up, with the loss of at least 200 lives, a few days before the university hangings. And 'resources' have had their turn too. Supermarkets, introduced a few years ago with great fanfare and immense expense, are one of the prides of the revolution, a practical expression of part two of the Colonel's Green Book, 'The Solution to the Economic Problem'. Unfortunately, they are also probably the world's best example of how not to run supermarkets. One of them, in the Tripoli suburb of Souk Al-Jum'a, went up in flames shortly after the university hangings.

It is not hard to understand why the Libyans are increasingly dissatisfied with their lot. And, judging by some of his own pronouncements, Gadafy sometimes understands it himself.

It seems that the visionary in him is too intellectually and emotionally exhausted, after years of exertion, to admit that his vision has failed. Make-believe is easier to sustain than reality to confront. Hence, it is not the theory that is unworkable, it is the executives and beneficiaries, the Libyan people, who have failed to make it work.

So, in spite of tactical retreats and compromises, and a continuing, very conventional sense of where real power lies, Gadafy ends up pressing for more of the same – more revolution, more disruption and chaos.

That, in turn, leads to more discontent, and to more repression, more of the executions which, in earlier, happier days – when he could reproach in others what he had not resorted to himself – he once roundly condemned as 'terrorism'.

7 May, 1984   **David Hirst**

Elections, yes. Democracy, no

There is a town in El Salvador called Happiness. One morning there, shortly after dawn, three people were found sitting on a park bench. None of them had heads.

In a country where 40,000 civilians have died in the past four years, three more killings are hardly worth a footnote. Yet there is something so chilling in that image of three headless bodies in a park that it may serve as a symbol of this small Central American country's agony.

So at least it seems to Cristobal Iglesias, the editor of *El Mundo*, one of El Salvador's four daily newspapers, who told me the story of the dawn discovery in (Alegria) Happiness. He is a man in his mid-fifties with greying swept back hair and an almost constant expression of despair.

I had gone to ask how a paper can function honestly in El Salvador, but he began with a ten minute monologue, a kind of Cassandra-like lamentation, against all that had gone wrong over the last four years. 'They say Africa is a continent where there are savages, yet it has not produced anything like the barbarity that we have seen here. I don't know how the war can go on and on like this, yet if the flow of arms into the country continues, then the war will continue. And whoever wins the war will find he has lost a country. There will be nobody left.'

El Salvador is a place of hunger, illiteracy, poverty and disease, he went on. It was the smallest country in Central America, half the land was unfit for cultivation. There was massive unemployment. The world price for its cotton and coffee exports was terribly low. 'We are practically just living on US aid.'

The election campaign was taking place under a State of Emergency. 'We have absolute restrictions on the freedom of the press. There is no pre-censorship, but the Armed Forces' Public Relations Office often telephones to complain of articles, so that an editor learns what can be said.' Anonymous telephone

145

7 June, 1984

threats are common, although – touch wood – there have not been any actual attacks on *El Mundo*.

Mr Iglesias's paper is the only one which publishes advertisements from Human Rights groups such as the Committee of Mothers of Political Prisoners and People Who Have Disappeared. It publishes the names of people 'captured' but does not write articles saying the security forces have been responsible for civilian deaths; it is the only newspaper which printed the recent peace proposals from the FDR-FMLN, the organisation of guerrilla groups.

San Salvador has some 50 radio stations but only the one operated by the Church, Radio YSAS, publishes communiqués and announcements from left-of-centre organisations. A bomb destroyed its premises in September 1980 and it was off the air for six months.

In spite of this lack of free expression, Mr Iglesias points out that El Salvador is having a presidential election this Sunday. Another man that finds it somewhat amazing is Father Ignacio Martin Barro, a political scientist at the University of Central

America, whose department has conducted public opinion polls for four provinces closest to San Salvador. Here there is no fighting, but the level of fear is such that close to 80 per cent of the people questioned either refused to say which party they supported or claimed they had not decided.

Father Barro says El Salvador has never had a free election and a fair result. People will go to the polls on Sunday in large numbers – out of custom, tradition, and the obligation to vote, and because of what he called an avalanche of propaganda in the media about the election. There is no tradition of open democracy, public demonstrations and debate.

'Look at the Spanish case,' he said 'The first election after Franco's death produced a result which favoured the Franquistas. It took another five years for the Franquistas to collapse and a genuine expression of democracy to emerge. But Salvadoreans are voting in an election in which half the political spectrum is not taking part and while the civil war is still underway.'

The only groups approaching Sunday's poll with excitement are the supporters of the ultra rightwing party, the Republican Nationalist Alliance (Arena). The blame for El Salvador's problems, they say, is due to the foreign press, the communists, President Reagan, Cubans, Nicaraguans – anyone except Salvadoreans themselves. Any Salvadorean who disagrees with them, such as the Christian Democrats' candidate, Jośe Napoleon Duarte, is branded a communist and therefore is not really a genuine Salvadorean at all.

Arena won 20 per cent last time but its supporters have worked themselves up to such an expectancy of triumph that it is terrifying to think what they will do if they lose on Sunday, or in the run-off which will follow later if no party wins 50 per cent this week. An Arena win will destroy any chance of negotiations with the guerrillas, for Arena is dressed to kill. Its party song, allegedly written by its leader Major Roberto d'Aubuisson contains the phrase: El Salvador will be the tomb where the Reds will end up. When they sing it Arena crowds do a gleeful thumbs down sign in unison. An Arena defeat could start a rampage of vengeance that will result in an upsurge of death squad killings.

The Christian Democrats won 40 per cent in 1982 and ought,

in theory, to have the best chance. Everything depends on how the lesser parties split, particularly the ironically-named Party of National Conciliation, which was the party of the one-sided military dictatorship of the 1970s. And if the Christian Democrats win, will things be any different from Duarte's two years in power in 1980 and 1981, which saw more death squad killings than any other recent period? On the guerrilla side elections have produced no significant upsurge in activity. Last weekend Commandante Joaquim Villalobos, head of one of the five guerrilla forces, announced a new offensive in response to the army's sweep of parts of the Eastern Provinces. It turned out to be a series of minor ambushes of government troops and an unsuccessful mortar attack on a barracks. The guerrillas may be planning something more dramatic.

The most important development was an apparent split in the guerrilla movement's political strategy. Members of Commandante Villalobos's forces, the People's Revolutionary Party, last week started to confiscate identity cards at road blocks and in house-to-house calls. They claimed they would return them after the election. Without identity cards people cannot vote and are treated by the army as subversive.

The tactics have been extended this week in several places in the East but are largely ineffective since people have been able to get duplicates at town halls these past few days. People interviewed by reporters made it clear that irritation at having to get a duplicate at a cost of the equivalent of a dollar for the card and a dollar for the photo has lost the guerrillas some support.

Guerrillas from the other main group, the Popular Liberation Forces, have condemned the taking of identity cards and are not doing so themselves. Neither group has been burning buses, an unpopular move two years ago.

So, when Salvadoreans vote on Sunday the war may not be visible nor will the death squads, and the other paraphernalia of nightly killings. But their presence will be felt as an inescapable backdrop to the polls.

By coincidence the voting takes place the day after commemorations for the fourth anniversary of the murder of Archbishop Romero at his altar. The murder is still unsolved and one of the candidates, Major d'Aubuisson, is a prime suspect as an organiser. As the front page headlines of the weekly paper of the archdiocese of San Salvador put it this week, 'Always elections, but when will there be democracy?'

23 March, 1984   **Jonathan Steele**

To the slaughter

On the eve of the issue of our first class stamps to celebrate British beef, I happened to see a film called *Meat*, made by Fred Wiseman in 1976, about meat rearing and marketing in the US.

Everything is vast. The herds, partitioned off by fences, all share a mile-long feeding trough, the grain is topped up by a tube attached to a lorry on the move. So much of this film resolved itself into images of the intestine, as if the technology which brings us the food we eat is one labyrinthine gut: the narrow channel the animals are channelled into to get them into the huge articulated lorries, the tubes, spouts and hoses of the slaughterhouse, the slippery trays filled with entrails webbed with blood, mucus and tendon, that disappear through dark tunnels then reappear in other rooms to be snipped, sliced, and sorted.

Much of the film deals with the storage and packing of the meat, the pricing and selling. Freezers in the home are on the whole a good thing, but if you have a bag of steaks in the freezer you are likely to eat more of them more often. When the sale of luxury objects declines, people spend more money on food. If there is a slump in limousines and second homes, there will be a rise in the sale of sirloin.

But the bulk of the film stayed in the slaughterhouse and concentrated on gory detail. I felt at one point that I was watching some classic tragedy. Potent images had a weird effect on my sensibility: the steers' heads, sliced from the bodies, hanging on hundreds of moving hooks. At first they retained their horned nobility but within seconds horns, ears, and hide had gone and they were bleeding flesh, eyes bulging, tiny muscles moving, looking in fact the very picture of life, but in death. They were spectres at our feast.

Nor can I forget the carcasses themselves, hooked to the

overhead line and ready for transportation, draped in great net shrouds, moving in a circle slowly, they too appeared like ominous ghosts, for each one shuddered slightly on its hook.

These images had an obscene poetry of their own, unlike most of the film which was just obscene. The humane killer more often stuns than kills. The slaughtermen are paid on how many animals they kill, hence to give the pig, for example, the legal requirement of the seven seconds of the stun gun would limit the number of animals slaughtered. The pig in the UK generally gets two to three seconds, is stunned, one hind trotter chained to a hook on the overhead line and a slaughterman waits with a stiletto knife to slit its throat. If the pig is lucky that will occur within those two seconds. But it is more likely that the pig regains consciousness, screams and then has its throat cut.

The recent dispute in Bradford about Halal meat in schools (should the council go to the expense of buying it for the Muslim community in schools?) is probably unnecessary, for, at a guess, most of the meat we buy has bled to death. But there is no way of proving it. How can you tell what level of consciousness the animal is at when it is hung upside down with blood pouring out of its gullet? The argument against a stronger electric current is that it could kill off the slaughtermen.

It was the speed of the whole process in the slaughterhouse that could not fail to impress. There was the beef steer in the fenced-in coffin, its head stunned, dead, perhaps; then the lid of the coffin closes, the fence rises, the carcass falls out. Two slaughtermen chain a hind hoof to the hook and the beast rises in the air, its head knocking against the wall, leaving a smear of blood momentarily looking like a cave drawing of a bison. There is, after all, something so ancient about the killing of a beast that something dark and uncomfortable stirs in the soul. The head is sliced from the body, impaled on its hook and starts its separate macabre journey.

Then rows of slaughtermen come into their own. Gowned, helmeted with hair sometimes tucked into a white snood, wearing wellington boots and often rubber gloves, they stand armed with a variety of knives and saws. As the carcasses pass, each worker has a distinct task. One might just nick at the neck, the rib cage, the knuckle, then tug at the hide. The hide was stripped from the flesh in stages; it resembled a gigantic, bloodied fruit being peeled. Another slaughterman might grow from his arm a vast mechanised lobster claw which in a deafening crunch would slice through the steer's thigh bone. Another would wield an electric saw and slice the carcass downwards. Another with one slash of the stiletto knife would disembowel the creature and the entrails would tumble out.

I had not heard before of the Judas sheep. In this film there was a Judas goat. It stood outside the slaughterhouse waiting for the sheep to arrive by lorry. The white goat looked elegant and distinguished. When the sheep arrived, the goat turned and treading with precise delicacy led the herd up an incline and into a concrete channel. Obediently, the sheep followed, crossing narrow bridges, down slopes, turning corners, and then reached the door. The goat stepped aside, waiting outside the door. Why did the sheep go through? But they did and were immediately stunned, chained and hooked to that grim overhead line. The white goat went back the way it had come to await the next herd.

The Bradford problem is that if they do not go to the expense of providing Halal meat in their schools, the Muslims will start their own schools for their own children, thus hampering racial integration.

I would suggest showing this film to the Bradford children: they might then all reject meat and the schools could enjoy good vegetarian cooking.

16 March, 1984   **Colin Spencer**

Secret papers

Here is an official secret: civil servants at the Department of Health and Social Security are to be denied soft lavatory paper. The decision has been taken on grounds of cost – an estimated £90,000 a year over the hard stuff. The officials responsible 'realised that this decision will be unpalatable to some,' and point out that they have considered 'the quality of life' argument. Further, they concede that, since so many other departments are changing to soft, 'it seems strange that the health department is amongst those who appear to be showing the most reluctance.'

This will be of mild interest to those who recall earlier Diary paragraphs on the subject and tough cheese on the 90,709 DHSS civil servants affected. As for the secrecy: well, after the last Diary mentions, whenever they were, the top DHSS toilet roll mandarin, Mr M. J. Boutal, would only discuss the matter verbally with the trade union side: 'Based on what happened to my previous letter on this subject,' he noted curtly, 'I am not particularly anxious to give a written response.' The unions protested they had not leaked to the *Guardian*. Mr Boutal was unmoved. He was not out 'to ascribe blame, but rather to avoid the possibility of any future embarrassment.'

Cruise missiles, toilet paper. . . . This country, 'in these times', has cause to be grateful to the example of Mr Boutal.
31 January, 1984   **Alan Rusbridger**

Hard times—with melodrama

Lord Northcliffe, a former owner of *The Times*, had an aquarium with a pike at one end and a goldfish at the other. Sometimes, when other entertainment palled, he would lift the hatch between the two. The result, like a battle between an owner and an editor, was never in doubt.

You might think that this grand old breed of press baron, so handy for frightening the children, had died out. Not at all. According to Harold Evans in *Bad Times at The Times* (Channel 4), it flourishes thanks to government connivance and a steady diet of editors. Choosing his time, Budget Day, Rupert Murdoch, the owner of *The Times*, called in his editor, Harold Evans, and said, 'Siddown. I want your resignation.' How fascinating—from a safe distance. Why 'siddown' when he evidently wasn't stopping?

Melvyn Bragg, thanking heaven no doubt that things like this are unheard of in television, described it as 'a tale of intrigue, treachery and power politics'. The cast was Evans, 'a mercurial ball of fire', former editor Rees-Mogg, 'amazingly well-informed round the wicket', the staff of the old *Times*, 'attached to their desks with cobwebs', and the sage of Auchtemuchty, who gazing into the entrails (he chanced to be dining with Mrs Evans at the time) prophesied, 'Murdoch will tempt your husband away from his power base at the *Sunday Times*. He'll ask him to edit *The Times*. He will be there one year.' It only remains for The Sage to buy a spotted bandana and set up in business as Gipsy Rose Junor.

What images rise to appal us in that year. The night the ageing Jim Callaghan was roused from his bed in the country at 4 a.m., made to write a thousand words on 'Anwar Sadat, My Friend', 'And,' added the features editor with characteristic glee, 'phone them over.'

Bad Times at The Times itself adopted the new broom style which caused such a dust-up when Evans tried it out at *The Times*. 'The Flight of the Bumblebee' with the editor doing everything. 'I'm just wild about Harry,' with Mr Evans laughing a lot and Mr Murdoch, who has Walter Matthau's hangdog face, looking cryptic. Martin Lambie-Nairn entertainingly animated *The Times's* lion and unicorn into a battle red in claw and horn. Mr Evans, who took a rather high moral tone about editorial independence, said sadly that every editor thought there was an idealist in Mr Murdoch trying to get out. There is, that's the last editor he ate.

It is only a couple of months since Channel 4 transmitted the National's fine production of *The Beggar's Opera*. Jonathan Miller's production for BBC-2 was, oddly, stagier. Props seemed to propagate before our eyes. No inch was unencrusted with authentic leather buckets and leg irons, gallipots and topknots, a game which seemed to fall somewhat heavily between snooker and croquet and women picking what I assumed to be genuine oakum. Some of the accents were rather less authentic.

It was, as Bob Hoskins promised, charmingly pathetic but personally I relished the performance of Peter Bayliss as Lockit, a jailer whose face suggested he was wearing a purple nylon stocking over his head, and whose singing made Lee Marvin sound like a boy soprano. Dr Miller has now left the theatre for a nobler calling, leaving the BBC quantities of firkins, bodkins, kilderkins, assorted querpoes (all authentic), a billiard table with hoops on it, several sacks of real oakum and no forwarding address.

2 July, 1984   **Nancy Banks-Smith**

GCHQ Diary

Electronic scientist? Applied Physicist? Computer Scientist? Plain old statistician? Humble old pure or applied mathematician? Never mind about Honours Degrees, HND or HNC might well do. Don't be put off if you're still at college. Yes! There's lots of jobs going at GCHQ, nestling on the edge of the Cotswolds in a busy and attractive regional centre. Just drop a line to the Civil Service Commission. But Hurry! Applications have to be in by February 24.

Thus goes the general drift of an advertisement in the current *New Scientist*. It is headed 'New Directions in Advanced Communications'. Mysteriously, the advert makes no mention of why this jobs bonanza should be cropping up just now.

8 February, 1984   **Alan Rusbridger**

A Bronx cheer for whitey

Unemployment was officially down to seven per cent when I went to the South Bronx. To judge from Washington's cheery announcement of the percentage, happy days are here again when anyone can get a job. Of course you can never be sure of unemployment statistics, especially in an election year, but even if the seven per cent is perfectly accurate, it is only a national average and the greater affluence of some of the suburbs has to be balanced against disaster areas like the South Bronx, where among young blacks and hispanics the unemployment rate is still closer to a crushing 50 per cent.

Presidents Carter and Reagan each made well-publicised promises to rescue the South Bronx, but the false fronts dressing up the windows of the abandoned buildings, making them look renovated and inhabited, are symbolic of how well the promises have been kept. Behind such window dressing, the grim reality remains the same.

But the media soon become tired of bad news, and all you hear about the South Bronx nowadays is that it is the home of breakdancing. There among the unemployment, abandoned buildings and graffiti was born this new acrobatic form of dance that has swept the country, and the implication is that this is surely proof enough that life in the South Bronx is much more upbeat than it seems.

Breakdancing may have begun as part of outsider-underground South Bronx black culture, but as always happens with American success stories, it has been taken over by main-stream Show Business. There have been two successful movies already, with several more on the way, innumerable TV features and official recognition by dance studios and white middle-class enthusiasts who have hired ghetto kids to teach classes in the suburbs.

Some black Show Business producers have presented them-selves as experts on this aspect of South Bronx culture, but this hasn't prevented them from giving their view a Hollywood gloss that prettied up the reality of the South Bronx almost a much as the political window-dressing. About the only genuine South Bronx breakdancing that remained after this massive takeover was from kids who journeyed downtown to put on sidewalk displays to raise money and often they prettied it up for their audiences, too.

Tracing breakdancing back to its source is almost impossible, though some black experts claim to have done it for the sake of TV or movies. Black ghetto teenagers are hard to reach, even if you have built bridges in the past. You may have gone to boxing matches with their fathers or visited their elder brothers in prison, but you still have to pass a test yourself to be trusted. The test may come in many forms depending on your colour, but basically, if you are white or a reporter or both like me, it will be a test of how close you come to their stereotype of you.

You may be challenged, as I have been, to follow them across subway lines, including the dangerous 'third rail', or be put in the company of alcoholics who keep telling you how much they hate whites or be taken to an Islam class in black history in which your own history is totally ignored. It is not that the teenagers themselves are such separatists, but they want to see how you respond when the advantage isn't on your side. If you pass, it is suddenly as if the barriers are down, and when you are introduced to their friends, you are presented as 'all right', the way a factory inspector stamps goods with his approval.

I was taken to an abandoned building where each room was occupied by black or hispanic teenagers, a similar building to the one depicted in *Beat Street*, the movie produced by Harry Belafonte about breakdancing, but with a much greater variety of people and interests. Several youths asked me what I thought of breakdancing, another test like being asked about Jesse Jackson or Ronald Reagan; if you are white, your answer is supposed to give you away.

I replied carefully that breakdancing had become too commercial for me and anyway, in the performances I had seen, its rhythm and movements were too nervous, too jerky, an uneasy mixture of dancing, acrobatics and martial arts, and reminded me of a macho man having a nervous breakdown.

They laughed, not feeling any need to be defensive. Breakdancing to them was already a lost art, no more to them now than a quick means of making money downtown from the square world. If it was ever a dynamic new means of expressing South Bronx culture or of challenging each other to duels instead of fighting the old way, it is no longer now that the square world has taken it over.

This attitude goes even for their personal slang. It is theirs only until the world that in their eyes has shut them out, that is less hip than they are, starts to use it and then they drop it and evolve something new.

'Everyone talks as if it all started with breakdancing,' said one youth contemptuously. 'My dad was doing something like breakdancing when he was a kid. But the media wasn't looking then. Go back to James Brown in the sixties and you'll find a lot of the same moves.'

I made the mistake of mentioning the Jackson Brothers'

multi-million dollar national tour due to reach New York early in August. Nobody was much interested. 'I've heard about as much of brother Michael as I want to for a long time,' was a typical comment. 'You'd think there were no other entertainers. Give me Lionel Ritchie any time.'

Was it because Michael Jackson had been taken over like breakdancing? 'Look,' said one youth, 'they charge $30 a seat and want people to buy no less than four—$120 for one lousy concert. Even with a job, you can't afford that. Those Jackson brothers don't live in the real world. I like someone who's more down to earth and knows the way we live here in the South Bronx.'

There was a great tolerance for any fellow blacks, at least in the face of whites, but underneath this tolerant attitude was a deep puritanism that came out obliquely in their satirising of con-men, pimps and addicts, their imitations, for example, of the frowning, irritable faces of drug addicts on the subways, brilliantly observed and disapproving.

They spoke respectfully of contemporaries who had found jobs whatever the jobs were—in the army, as security guards or labourers in the garment district—and some of them had held jobs themselves until they were laid off or quit when they weren't treated justly, another reflection of their puritanical code.

They had all been through drugs when younger, but you were considered less than a man if you remained addicted. Music, sports and martial arts were their passions, sex was carefully distinguished from love, many girls were criticised for only being interested in money, and friends were condemned for having kids too early, before they were ready to settle down.

When two youths went to a local store for some beer, they wouldn't take any money from me. I mustn't get the impression I could buy my way in. But when I talked to one shy youth about books, he offered to give me Dashiell Hammett's *The Glass Key*, which he'd just finished, and I gave him in exchange *The Great Gatsby* which I had in my pocket.

The next time we met he talked about the books. He liked *The Glass Key* because it was about friendship and loyalty, and *Gatsby* to him was a black man in a typical white society, finally

157

betrayed by the people he'd trusted. I said it wasn't racial, but was about the difference between an essentially decent person and his more selfish associates. He grinned. 'You look at it that way and I'll look at it my way.' 'Then we'll never communicate,' I said. 'Can't we live with our differences?' he replied.

He had been looking for a job for a long time because he had two very young children, their mother did nothing for them, and his mother only had welfare to live on. He had reached the stage of desperation. 'I'd take *anything*,' he said.

The next time I met him he was very excited. He had found a job at last. It wasn't much—he seemed embarrassed about it —but it paid well. He invited me to meet him and go to see him at work. We went downtown to a big colourful building —a sex emporium. His job was taking part in live sex shows four times a day. 'It's not what I wanted,' he told me defensively, 'but it pays the rent and my kids' food.'

I felt I had to say something. I asked him how he could manage it four times a day. 'You don't go through with it four times,' he said matter-of-factly. 'You fake it.' A ticket cost $6, but he found me a free seat upfront, but I suddenly decided I couldn't watch him go through with it. I left before he and his partner came on.

Next time I met him his attitude was different, far less friendly. It was useless to try to convince him I didn't like to see him having to earn a living that way. To him, I had acted white: I hadn't understood his desperation because I had never been in his situation. I had merely been superior and tried to make him feel ashamed. To him, I had failed my test.

1 August, 1984   **W. J. Weatherby**

Bean's means a dish of woe

American restaurateur Bob Payton, 39, was not happy. A perplexed frown creased his features as he gazed around his newly opened but empty eatery in Kensington early this week.

Payton is used to success: he introduced alien eating habits to Londoners at the Chicago Pizza Pie Factory in 1977 and the

Chicago Rib Shack last year. He is known for his biting wit: in Knightsbridge his customers wear bibs printed with the words Bone Appetit.

But now he wasn't laughing. He had run into something even more viscous than his revolutionary deep dish pizza—the British being beastly. His proposal to convert the Abingdon Arms into a new style eating/meeting/drinking place met vociferous opposition from the natives.

He thinks it might have been the name—Henry J. Bean's But His Friend's Call Him Hank Bar and Grill. Or the fact that it would be open from 11.30 a.m. to 11 p.m. At any event the local council recently turned down his application to alter the pub's exterior on the grounds that it was out of keeping with the locality and offended the local residents.

Payton forged ahead with the interior. Advertising signs, high oak tables and a Wurlitzer juke-box were imported from America. The old staircase and low pews were removed. American standards of hygiene were applied. On Sunday night he threw open his doors and cold air poured in.

In America, said Payton, people would flock to a new concept like this. 'Here they peek through the window. God forbid that they should come in and spend a pound. The British are afraid to try anything new. This says it all: Yanks go home. God forbid that we can do better than Scotch eggs. It doesn't mean we're here to pollute the area and poison the people.'

The old Abingdon Arms should have been blown up, he said. At that moment he was called away to speak to a policeman. A social call, he explained. 'One of the reasons I live in this country is I think your police are terrific.' The other reason is the Quality of Life. (He rides to hounds at his stable in Rutland.)

People ask him why he doesn't go home. He replies that if he didn't care so much he wouldn't waste his time. 'I just want to give everyone a good time,' he said.

Sadly that is not the British way.

17 December, 1983   **Stuart Wavell**

The razzmatazz they call democracy

Is there a man of sensibility who, having watched the Democratic Party convention deliberate for four days in San Francisco and elect its nominee for the Presidency of the most powerful state on earth, and having observed for four days the awesome processes of democracy in action—is there, I wonder, such a man who having witnessed this, would not be moved to mirthless laughter?

Now this was a convention which did, after all, choose not only the best, but by far the best, of the candidates before it, a good and decent man who at the end made a good and decent speech. But, oh, the tone of the convention—the piety, the razzmatazz and the bathos, and the sheer prolixity.

Before I explain this, I will say that nothing I write will be as scathing as H. L. Mencken's account of the 1932 Democratic convention that chose Franklin Delano Roosevelt. Niagaras of bilge, he said, implacable factions all hating each other, all sorts of grotesque female politicians with brassy voices, and a man chosen whose competence and good faith were far from clear.

But back to the convention of 1984. It was plainly a television event. The TV cameras had the only decent view, and all the best stuff was clearly rigged to fit in with prime time, but television cannot take the can for everything.

It was, I suppose, the Democrats themselves who got a preacher to open the last day's proceedings with an invocation that ended, as if the man were a candidate for the bishopric of Durham, with the words, 'Amen, Hallelujah, right on.' It was, I suppose, the Democrats who paid Jennifer Holiday, the star of a Broadway musical called *Dream Girls*, to shriek and maul the 'Star Spangled Banner', making it suffer as no national anthem should.

And it was certainly the Democrats who ran the aimless, sprawling proceedings in a way that made the Labour Party conference look a miracle of logic, order, and reason. In four days I did not hear more than a couple of hours of real debate. The rest was a series of harangues, mostly by obscure members of the House of Representatives from states you have never heard of and to whom nobody listened. And no man can just get up and speak. He has to be proposed, seconded, thirded, or in the Rev. Jesse Jackson's case seconded, thirded and otherwise introduced down to the sixth and seventh generation of seconders.

Certainly Mr Jackson displays every sign of believing he is a second Messiah, who says that God has not finished with him yet, but even given that, was it necessary for him to be introduced by an Arab, a Jewish woman who fled from the Holocaust, a Chinese girl, a Cherokee, a black bishop who ranted on about the land of Canaan, a disabled Hispanic woman who also announced that she was a single parent, and finally by a black man who spoke bitterly about the Middle Passage as if slavery were still a flourishing business? It was not as if these people each said a few words. Each made a speech.

Governors were incestuous in their fulsome introductions of each other too, and out of 50 Governors in the United States, 35 are Democrats. So you get the wonderful Governor of Kentucky saluting the wonderful Governor of Wyoming, who in turn calls on the talented Governor of Virginia. What they are doing is killing time so that the speakers anyone has heard of can appear in the prime time.

The Governor of Kentucky, incidentally, is a woman, born in Baghdad, Kentucky, and formerly a beauty queen. She was much seen because she took the chair for much of the convention. I will not go so far as Mencken, but these women were without exception shrill and aggressive. Is not persuasion one of the political arts?

One speaker who certainly was persuasive, as has been much reported, was Governor Mario Cuomo of New York who gave the keynote speech on Monday. He is a man of eloquence and sense, one of whose most telling metaphors was that of the wagon train. The Democratic wagon train (as opposed, he suggested, to the Republican one) did not leave the weaker members of the party behind on the trail.

This was an image much taken up by lesser speakers, who

readily latched on to the idea of huddled masses. One delegate said her mother came to the United States with 16 dollars, a featherbed, and an arranged marriage. This is telling. Another spoke about women being forced into 'stoop labour', which brought to mind a vision of Tess of the d'Urbervilles hacking weeds at Flintcombe Ash. That is not telling, because it overdoes it. Too often the assumption of the convention was that there are millions of exploited poor in the United States, which is simply not true. There are the poor, particularly in the eastern cities, and among general prosperity their poverty is all the more pitiful. But one truth which no one expressed these last four days is that America is an immensely prosperous country, and that people are better off now than they were ten years ago, or four years ago.

Every now and again there was some light relief, some bit of hokum. This is all in the game, and most welcome. Take Tip O'Neill, the friend of all Americans, the man we all love, the Speaker of the House of Representatives, announcing that the next regime, which would of course be Democrat, would not be remembered for its big limousines and chinchilla coats. Great applause. The next day Mr O'Neill, who drives round town in a common-or-garden car, was flagged down by a cop to let by Geraldine Ferraro in a vast limousine with police outriders. And it was Mr O'Neill who played a big part in her elevation.

To my mind the speech most typical of the convention was that made by Gary Hart on Wednesday. He was Mr Mondale's only credible opponent. He was given the spot just before the nominations, so that if he was to sway any delegates, as he had to, this was his last chance.

The course of the speech was as follows. Spotlights rotated in the hall, like Twentieth Century Fox searchlights. Senator Hart is from Colorado, so the music from an ancient film called *The Big Country* blared out. He praised Gerry Ferraro. Throughout the convention a sure way to achieve applause was to allude to Ms Ferraro. The Senator welcomed her selection and would, he said, have chosen her himself if Mr Mondale hadn't. Then he revealed that he had a daughter, Andrea, but he had always felt in his heart that, because she was a girl, she was 'frozen from attaining the highest office in the land'. Since Mondale's choice of Ms Ferraro this was, it seemed, no longer so.

Senator Hart continued. He was against 'toxic terrorism' (he meant the terrorism of trees or, as they are called here, the environment), against the nuclear demon, against human hunger, and against greed. He was for the torch of idealism. He had, in this last opportunity of his, nothing of substance to say at all. When he had finished, they played the theme from *Chariots of Fire*.

But I forgot. He did also say that we must look not to the past but to the future. Not look to the past? Why then, had everyone all week been quoting Tom Paine, Roosevelt, Kennedy, Truman, and even Jefferson? And Jefferson was a fastidious man, a man who feared the rise of an urban proletariat, a man who would not have been delighted to see delegates wandering about the floor during the pledge of allegiance to the flag with one hand held ritually over the heart and with the other holding paper cups of Coke.

In her acceptance speech Ms Ferraro, alone of all the women I heard at the convention, spoke softly. She made two rash and very American statements. There were, she said, no doors they could not open. (This is the old American hubris.) And America would stand by Israel, always. More safely, and like many before her, she made the obligatory Kennedy allusion, saying the issue was not what America could do for women but what women could do for America. The band then played for ten solid minutes, mostly not patriotic tunes—which can be assumed since 'My Country, 'Tis of Thee' is played to the tune of 'God Save the Queen' and 'Oh Maryland' to that of 'The Red Flag'—but just rowdy rock music.

When Mr Mondale came to make his acceptance speech he appeared greatly moved, though this will have been plainer on television than in the hall. He said the Republicans were a portrait of privilege, while the Democrats were a mirror of America. At home, it was time for America to have a season of excellence, so parents must turn off the television, and teachers must teach. Abroad, America should negotiate to 'control those god-awful weapons'. He wanted to talk to young children about their future, and whatever their religion, whatever their race, he wanted some of them to say what he was about to say, with joy and reverence. 'I want to be President of the United States.'

The band then played its awful rock music for ever, and I cannot imagine what it had to do with this sober man, a man from Minnesota, of Norwegian stock, who had told us only a few minutes before that his dad was a preacher and his mother a music teacher, and they never had a dime.

Whatever his sober virtues, Mr Mondale is stuck with a party which he calls diverse, which means that it is a wild and rickety coalition which spreads from the zealous Jackson on the far left to Mondale himself on the centre-right, and in the middle is a mish-mash of feminists, lovers of trees, and those who want to take the welfare of the Third World, and the sins of the whole world, on their shoulders.

Mr Mondale would do very well as a European social democrat. Minnesota is slightly eccentric in its politics, and he is normally a member of what is in that state known as the Democrat Farmer Labour Party. But this is not Europe, and he is not thought to be nearly aggressive enough. Why, it has been asked this week, has the Democratic Party produced no strong leader since Lyndon Johnson?

This takes me to the celebrated Democratic family of the Harrimans. This year's *Democratic Fact Book* has a foreword by Pamela Harriman, the wife of Averell Harriman. It was in her house in Washington, on the night of the 1976 presidential election, that two women, both life-long Democrats, told me after a few drinks that they had for the first time in their lives voted Republican that day, because they could not stand Jimmy Carter. This week, David Steel happening to be in San Francisco, I went to lunch and heard him explain that Roosevelt's New Deal had taken many of its ideas from Lloyd George's *Yellow Book* of 1929. My neighbour at the lunch table, a Democrat of many years' standing, told me after one glass of wine that she would, in spite of this, be voting for Mr Reagan in November.

18 July, 1984   **Terry Coleman**

Chris cross?

I dont know about you, Monica, but I feel strangely purged and purified. A finer, cleaner and, in some way, a *thinner* person. It is a phenomenon Aristotle commented on. When a playwright hits you with the old pity and terror, he said, you feel indistinguishable from a spun-dry sock.

Last night *Dallas* (BBC-1) converged as one man on one man—J.R. Ewing. Katherine Wentworth, grinding her teeth; Thingy the banker (the one who said foreclosing was thirsty work) grinding the poor; Sue-Ellen ('Snatching something from the drawer'); Peter her schoolboy lover ('I'll kill you, J.R.!'); Edgar Randolph the alcoholic child molester ('Edgar Randolph's been drinking again!') and Cliff Barnes, acting very strangely.

Around Dallas, bar keepers, eyeing their empty stools, said philosophically, 'They must all be out shooting J.R.,' Dallas Memorial turned down the bed reserved for Ewings and the *Dallas Bugle* dusted off the headline it keeps in permanent type, J.R. SHOT AGAIN.

And then, oh Monica, when that executive chair swung around it wasn't J.R. who fell out perforated but Bobby! It was like ordering chocolate and getting vanilla. You can say what you like—in a minute—but I think little Christopher did it. It has long been obvious to even the most uncritical child lover that little Christopher is not only seriously adenoidal but seems to be turning into something else, possibly a pig. It is typical of the action-packed life of *Dallas* that what with Mark exploding over the Bay of Mexico and Lady Mountford ('Apparently she snapped') not only setting fire to Clayton's first wife but stuffing his intended, Miss Ellie, into the boot of her car, that no-one has noticed that little Christopher would look his best with a lemon in his mouth.

Pam clearly triggered the whole thing by giving little Christopher a resume of the plot which he was, intellectually, ill equipped to digest: 'Oh God, I just wanted to do what was best for Mark and now look what's happened! I trusted Katherine and she betrayed me! Christopher, I don't even know where I belong any more. You don't understand any of this, do you?'

None of us understand any of this but Christopher listened with avid attention and open mouth. He evidently decided, in common with half the adult population of Dallas, that the world would be a purer place and Mommy would stop talking to herself and wearing her dress back to front if he shot J.R. That he got it a little bit wrong is understandable in view of his tender years and adenoids.

You purse your lips, Monica. It is, I know you won't mind my mentioning this, something you are far too apt to do. I need only add that little Christopher is really the son of Kristen who, two years ago, shot J.R. Ah, ha, you'd forgotten that hadn't you?

23 May, 1984   **Nancy Banks-Smith**

Medals galore

The US Army is apparently determined that its victory in the Grenada campaign, when it took a week and a large show of sea and air power to subdue a motley band of revolutionaries and Cubans, should be celebrated in grand style.

It has determined that 8,612 of its men were heroes of the invasion worthy of receiving medals, even though there were never more than 7,000 enlisted men and officers on the Caribbean island. This first crop of medals may, however, only be the tip of the iceberg.

The Marine Corps, the navy, and the air force have begun issuing or taking applications for their own medals. In addition, the Pentagon is expected to issue an armed forces expeditionary medal to all the men and women on or near Grenada during the course of the invasion, including an estimated 10,000 sailors and officers who sat on ships arrayed around the island. This could result in the issue of a further 19,600 medals.

This orgy of award giving seems to reflect a deep-seated need

A Special relationship

27 October, 1983

within the American military to laud its success in the Caribbean
after a series of setbacks in Vietnam, the Iranian desert, and
most recently at Beirut international airport.

Among those who have been given medals for their part in the
Grenada invasion are about 50 Defence Department officials
who got no closer to the Caribbean than the Pentagon building
just south of the Potomac. Awards have also been given to staff
and rear support troops at Fort Bragg in North Carolina – the
home of the 82nd Airborne Division; at Fort Stewart in Georgia
and Fort Lewis in Washington which are homes to the Army
Rangers and the headquarters of the army's Forces Command in
Atlanta.

The army explains it decided to award the medals as a
'valuable and effective leadership tool to build unit morale and
esprit'. The Grenada invasion began on October 25 with land-
ings by the marines and Army Rangers. The fighting was
declared over on November 2 with 18 American servicemen
dead. Several of these died when two helicopters collided while
taking Point Calvigny in the south early in the campaign.

The army awards include 275 decorations for valour, for combat deaths, and wounds. The other 8,337 medals were for 'individual performance'.

31 March, 1984   **Alex Brummer**

Grandfather's Godfather

On the long flight to Japan, I read for the first time my grandfather's posthumously published book, *Choose Life—A Dialogue*, a discussion between himself and a Japanese Buddhist leader called Daisaku Ikeda. My grandfather, the historian Arnold Toynbee, was 85 when the dialogue was recorded, a short time before his final incapacitating stroke. It is probably the book among his works most kindly left forgotten—being a long discursive ramble between the two men over topics from sex education to pollution and war.

A few months earlier, I had received a telephone call out of the blue from Mr Ikeda's London representative: Mr Ikeda was inviting my husband and myself to Japan, in memory of, and in gratitude to, my grandfather. We were puzzled at this—eight years after his death. But perhaps it was some inexplicably Japanese sense of obligation and family, beyond Western understanding. Try as we might, we could elicit no further explanation—though by the end of our trip some much clearer motives were to emerge. As it turned out, we were to see a rather different side of Japan from the view usually afforded to Western visitors.

We arrived at Tokyo airport, and at least 10 people were there to greet us, with a huge bouquet each for myself and for Milly, my astounded twelve-year-old daughter. A long solemn message of welcome from Mr Ikeda was read out, and we were driven away in a vast black limousine with electric darkened windows and Mr Ikeda's emblem emblazoned on the carpet in gold thread. Walkie-talkies between the vehicles of the motorcade to the hotel relayed further messages from our mysterious host. The scale of his operation was soon made clear.

Two representatives from the English branch of Mr Ikeda's movement had accompanied us all the way from London and were scarcely to leave our side, together with a phalanx of interpreters, drivers and aides of all kinds. 'Mr Ikeda wishes you to feel entirely at home,' and 'Mr Ikeda wishes you to make every use of the hotel's services and 36 restaurants' came the messages at regular intervals, as we gazed down out of our fourteenth floor window on to the hotel garden—full of waterfalls, bridges and carp, squeezed, like everything in Tokyo, between intersecting flyovers.

Several days passed before we were to meet our mysterious host, time in which we learned more about Mr Ikeda and his Soka Gakkai movement. One thing above all others was made clear: this was an organisation of immense wealth, power and political influence. One book on the sect declares that 'no understanding of postwar Japan is complete without some knowledge of this potent religio-political movement.' Its influence strikes deep into every aspect of Japanese life. Among its many publications is a newspaper with a circulation of over 4 million. It has the third largest political party in the country. It has a membership of 10 million, still growing. It has a university with 7,000 students, schools, an art gallery—and more.

Mr Ikeda is the third leader of the movement since it started in the thirties. But it is under him that the thing has taken off and become so powerful. He is the relatively uneducated son of a laver seller from Omori, who succeeded to the leadership at the age of 36, when he was head of the Young Men's Division of the Soka Gakkai. It is mainly a lower middle class movement, gathering up those uprooted from old communities, and binding them very tightly to its strong cell-structure.

Night and day, surrounded by his aides, we heard his name mentioned in tones of reverential awe. The head of the British section (an English retired businessman) told us that Ikeda was 'A man who has made the revolution in himself.' Others testified to the greatness of his writing, his mind, his poetry, his spirit, even his photography. (Later we caught a glimpse of his photographic methods when we watched as an aide handed him a loaded camera. He held it out at arm's length and clicked it randomly without bothering to look in the viewfinder. 'He takes photographs with his mind, not with his eye,' murmured an aid on enquiry.)

The evening came when we were at last to meet him. The great black limousine pulled into the palatial headquarters. The doorway was flood-lit with camera lights, and there stood Mr and Mrs Ikeda surrounded by bowing aides and followers. Dazed and dazzled by this unexpected reception committee, we were led up to him to shake the small, plump hand. There he stood, a short, round man with slicked down hair, wearing a sharp Western suit. Camera bulbs flashed, movie cameras closed in, and we were carried away with the throng, past corridors of bowing girls dressed in white to an enormous room.

Vast white armchairs were arrayed in a huge square and we were ushered to a throne-like set of three chairs at the head of the room, one for each of us and one for Mr Ikeda. He speaks no English, so behind us sat his beautiful young interpreter who accompanies him around the world. She sat at a microphone, so all our words could be heard clearly echoing round the room by all the aides and followers, who had taken to their rows of armchairs in strict order of precedence.

We sat there awed, appalled, intimidated, while royal courtesies flowed. 'I want you to feel absolutely at home this evening,' said Mr Ikeda, as we felt about as far from home as it is possible to be. 'Just enjoy yourselves on this very informal occasion,' he said. What would a formal meeting have been like?

We talked of the weather in London and Japan, the city, the sights—desperate small talk, conducted in public for half an hour, balancing champagne glass and smoked salmon plate, while the aides round the room nodded solemnly. Our host's style of conversation was imperious and alarming—he led and others followed.

Any unexpected or unconventional remark was greeted with a stern fixed look in the eye, incomprehension, and a warning frostiness.

As we took it in turn to sally forth in this game of verbal royal tennis, we each had time to study the man. Worldly, he seemed, down to the tip of his hand-made shoes, earthy almost, without a whiff of even artificial spirituality. Asked to hazard a guess at his occupation, few would have selected him as a religious figure. I have met many powerful men—prime ministers, leaders of all kinds—but I have never in my life met anyone who exuded such an aura of absolute power as Mr Ikeda. He seems like a man who for many years has had his every whim gratified, his every order obeyed, a man protected from contradiction or conflict. I am not easily frightened, but something in him struck a chill down the spine.

Dinner was an ordeal. We were ushered into the traditional Japanese dining room, where we sat at cushions on tatami mats at low tables, around our host. The cook crouched in the middle of the table, serving tempura from a vat of boiling oil. 'No serious talk tonight. Only pleasure,' Mr Ikeda ordained. Our hearts sank. That meant more excruciating small talk.

He turned eventually to reminiscences of my grandfather and their meeting in London. I could hardly imagine the incongruity of this small stout ball of power clanking up the creaky lift to my grandfather's dark and sparse flat. I wondered what meals he had been served—a slice of spam and a lettuce leaf being a typical meal there. 'He was a very, very great man,' Ikeda said, leaning towards me, and staring me in the eye. 'The greatest scholar in the world!' I pondered on some irreverent family stories, but hastily tucked them away.

'It is my mission in life to see that his work is read by everyone. You will support me in this?' I could hardly say no. 'You promise? I have your promise?' I felt uneasy at what exactly was expected of me. Then he suddenly mentioned the fact that there are in existence some more parts to the Toynbee/Ikeda Dialogue, as yet unpublished, which he would like to be able to publish soon. A part of our reason for this journey fell neatly into place. Later I was to find out more.

There was one sticky moment in the course of the meal. He asked us what we thought my grandfather's last word of warning to him had been as they parted. We racked our brains until, in desperation, my husband ill-advisedly answered, 'Greed.' An icy look passed across Mr Ikeda's ample features. He looked as if he might summon a squad of husky samurai to haul us away. I hastened to explain that Peter meant the greed of mankind, of course, as referred to frequently in the *Dialogue* —man's grasping selfishness and so on. He looked not entirely mollified and the moment passed.

After dinner we returned to the room of the great armchairs, and lavish present-giving followed—a giant doll and a calculator for Milly, pearls, a record album of the Toynbee/Ikeda Dialogue, a personally signed copy of the Toynbee/Ikeda book. At last the nerve-racking evening was over, our cheeks cracked from smiling, our minds drained of all ingenuity in small talk and pleasantry. We were swept past the bowing girls in white and the movie cameras—and away off in the limousine.

Next day our photographs appeared on the front page of Ikeda's multi-million circulation daily, the *Seikyo Press*, with a record of our dinner table conversation. No-one told us it was on the record—but it didn't matter, since it was the words, mainly of Mr Ikeda, that went reported, and little of us beyond our presence as his audience.

We departed for a brief trip to Kyoto and Hiroshima, only to be greeted again by more bouquets, banquets, black limousines and local Soka Gakkai groups.

Hiroshima is an uncomfortable place—the shrine of Japan's post-war peace mission. 'What do you think of Hiroshima? Have you a few words to say about Hiroshima?' we were asked continually. The exhibits shock and stun, but words fail. After the first blast of horror, something else creeps in. Here is a national shrine to Peace and Never Again, telling the story of the sunny day the bomb dropped out of the blue sky, telling the story of what the world did to Japan. But there is not a word, not a thought, not a hint of anything Japan might have done. Hiroshima was one of the main military bases from which went out the marauding forces to Burma, Singapore, China, Korea—countries who still find it hard to link Japan and peace in the same breath. But Hiroshima is the shrine of Japan's innocence.

One night we were shown a film of Ikeda's triumphal tour round America, at massed rallies in stadiums from Dallas to San Diego. Formation teams of majorettes and baton twirlers spelled the words SOKA and PEACE in great waves of thousands of human bodies and Ikeda, spot-lit and mobbed by screaming fans, delivered his usual speeches on peace—always peace. It is one of the Soka Gakkai's themes, peace in men's hearts, peace across the nations, the brotherhood of mankind and so on. The effect was somewhat spoiled when the stadium hushed reverently as a message from President Reagan himself was read out—sending a sincere message of good-will, peace and greeting to the Soka Gakkai and Mr Ikeda. The stadium burst out in delirious applause.

The Soka Gakkai takes its peace mission round the world, often accompanied by an exhibition of horrific photographs from Hiroshima, which is used as a powerful recruiting aid. What were they doing, we asked, preaching peace and accepting messages of support from Reagan in the same breath? 'We do not think there is anything incompatible in voting for President Reagan and being a member of the Soka Gakkai,' Ikeda's usually silent male secretary said. The English Soka Gakkai head hastened to add, 'We believe every man can change, and when President Reagan sent us that message, it showed that he too is capable of change in his heart.'

It was then, at yet another banquet in Hiroshima, that we lost our temper. We told them what we felt about the Soka Gakkai and Mr Ikeda's style of leadership. Our hosts were horrified and tried to smooth it all over and pretend the words had never been uttered.

We asked for a proper, serious interview with Ikeda, but later we doubted if anyone had dared relay our comments or our request.

The last time we saw him, not a flicker crossed his face to suggest that he had heard of our outburst, or our request. It was at Soka Gakkai's founder's day, with the same kind of mass rally of 6000 majorettes we had seen on the film, to the theme tunes of *Dallas* and *The Sound of Music*. After the finale Ikeda took a lap of honour round the stadium, while carefully re-hearsed groups of girls, shrieking with adulation, pealed away towards him.

We didn't see him again, but we reckoned his final gift showed that no-one had recounted our outburst to him. He sent us yet another silk-bound tome, in which there was no text, but only 296 huge full-page photographs of himself and his family—a book of colossal narcissism.

What had the whole trip been for? By the time we left, it all became clear. We had been taken to be interviewed by newspapers and television—Peter about international affairs, I about my grandfather. Each interview in which we appeared bound Ikeda and Arnold Toynbee closer together in the public eye. Ikeda was making a firm bid to become the chief official Toynbee friend and spokesman.

I had no idea of the extent of my grandfather's fame and importance in Japan. He was awarded the Order of the Rising Sun, and his work is compulsory reading in all universities. As the prophet of the rise of the East and the decline of the West, he has long been a hero in Japan. There is a Toynbee Society, run by distinguished academics, some of whom knew my grandfather well for many years, and they print a quarterly journal.

My grandfather never met Ikeda on his visits to Japan. His old Japanese friends were clearly less than delighted with Ikeda's grandiose appropriation of his memory, on the basis of a handful of rather vague interviews in extreme old age.

Soka Gakkai is the most powerful of Japan's 'New Religions' which have sprung up since the war, collecting together an uprooted urban people lacking an identity in a society that puts a high premium on belonging to groups. Soka Gakkai means Value-Creating Society, and it is based on the teachings of a thirteenth-century monk, Nichiren Shoshu, a militant national-ist who promised worldly rewards to his followers. It is rigidly hierarchical, with no democratic elements, and absolute power in Ikeda's hands. It imposes few religious or moral duties, beyond chanting twice a day, but it expects a high degree of obedient social participation in its organisation.

When Ikeda founded the movement's political party, Komeito, there began to be some alarm as to how he would use this power. This alarm has led the party to officially separate itself from Soka Gakkai, though all its leaders remain Gakkai members. The Komeito (Clean Government) Party is the third largest party in the mysterious and labyrinthine shifting factions of Japanese politics. It is called a centre party, but such labels mean little in a country where a huge consensus agrees broadly on defence and foreign relations, and approves the absence of a welfare state. With the same party in power for 25 years, it is the factions that count, and Komeito, Clean Government or not, has often helped Tanaka faction candidates, in exchange for Tanaka having helped them over a scandal.

To call Soka Gakkai and its Komeito party 'fascist' is to misunderstand Japanese politics. Certainly the movement is run on rigid anti-democratic lines, demanding absolute obedience. It is partly nationalistic, but also highly Americanised in taste and culture.

But it is a supporter of the Peace Constitution and it is not in favour of Japan rearming. Politically, like most of the other parties, it is mostly in favour of being in power.

Soka Gakkai has non-governmental organisation status at the United Nations, a fact used much by Ikeda, as it establishes them as a world-wide 'peace movement' and helps to give Ikeda access to heads of states around the globe. At Soka Gakkai's founder's day, we found representatives of many foreign embassies, and the French Ambassador was the guest of honour. People who seek influence in Japan cannot afford to ignore Ikeda, and indeed his own books sport hundreds of pictures of himself meeting people like Edward Kennedy, John Galbraith, and Presidents from every continent.

As we were leaving, Ikeda's secretary took us aside and asked if we could help with the publication of a second batch of Ikeda/Toynbee Dialogues, left over from the first book. There were, it appeared, problems with executors and rights. Also it was hinted that in Ikeda's forthcoming tour of Britain in June 1985, we might be of some assistance. Exactly what was unspecified, but the marker was put down.

Back in England I telephoned a few people round the world who had been guests of, or who had been visited by Ikeda. There was a certain amount of discomfort at being asked, and an admission by several that they felt they had been drawn into endorsing him. A silken web is easily woven, a photograph taken, a brief polite conversation published as if it were some important encounter.

I talked to the Oxford University Press, my grandfather's

publishers. They said they had firmly turned down the Toynbee/Ikeda Dialogues, which were being heavily promoted by Ikeda after my grandfather's death. It would have been better if they had stuck to that decision. But Ikeda succeeded in getting it published in New York and the OUP felt obliged to follow suit. In the file lies a later letter referring to the possibility of a second batch of dialogues being published.

A reply from OUP tells inquirers that the manuscript can now only be obtained with the permission of the literary executors. The papers are stored, unsorted, in the Bodleian Library in Oxford. It emerged that even while we were in Japan, Ikeda's representatives had been making discreet calls to England about the Toynbee papers. That in the end, I suspect, was the purpose of our trip—but from the present firm attitude of the OUP it is highly unlikely that further Toynbee/Ikeda material will appear.

I like to think that if my grandfather had not been so old, or if he had met Ikeda in his own bizarre surroundings, he would not have lent himself to this process of endorsement. He was a frail man at the time, and by nature trusting. If our trip to Japan was intended to bind him yet more tightly to Ikeda, I hope the effect will have been the reverse.

19 May, 1984   **Polly Toynbee**

A carnival of cadavers

Painting the corpses of the recently dead is common enough in Flemish art. James Ensor took it into the macabre: he painted his father on his death bed and then a few years later his dead mother. True enough, the picture of his father looks like an exercise in filial piety; but the painting of his mother is self-flagellation.

Her white, wasted profile, jaw locked open in rigor mortis, testify to Ensor's will to stare death out. In other paintings, Ensor himself is on the cross: portrait of the artist as Jesus Christ. In another, skeletons brawl over a hanged man, black tongue protruding a foot long from his mouth. And the figure of a skeleton wielding a scythe, the Grim Reaper, was so prevalent in his work that Ensor was given that nickname: Pietje de dood, in the leaden-sounding Flemish.

So much is known, if not with much familiarity, in Britain. But the huge exhibition currently in Antwerp shows that he was a painter in the direct tradition of Netherlands realism as various as Rembrandt and Vermeer and Brueghel, a painter of visions as singular as those of Hieronymus Bosch. If some British institution like the Arts Council or the Royal Academy or the Tate could pick up less than a quarter of the four hundred works here on show – mostly owned by Belgian public collections – for, say, a 125th anniversary exhibition in a couple of years, it could have a great impact in a nation which regards Ensor as a local phenomenon, like a Belgian Stanley Spencer.

Ensor was born in 1860 and lived until 1949, and although his skills never really declined, his years of great development lay between the ages of 20 and 40. Ensor's father was English, his mother Flemish. They ran a souvenir shop for tourists in Ostend, where Ensor would live out his life apart from art-school years in Brussels. At the age of 17 he painted a picture of a small bathing hut on the beach: just the hut, the beach, massed clouds, and a plume of smoke out at sea. It could be a little Boudin, but brooding.

There are other seascapes and townscapes of Ostend preferably in fog or under snow: the nearest Ensor can come to turning the outdoors into indoors. For it is the interiors in his early work that carry the full weight of his sensibility. Light filters through net curtains and between heavy drapes with great tassels, falls on the polished wood of piano and table, across the corner of a white marble mantelpiece, and on to the shawls and hats and suits of the comfortably-off people sitting edgily, on their best behaviour. The genre description for many of these canvases is conversation piece, except that a heavy silence hangs over them.

He felt the weight of everything. An oarsman rows a boat through water stiff as treacle. And never was a still life – nature morte, in the descriptive French – more still than in Ensor's painting of a dead duck with the pendulum of its hanging head stretching the long neck taut over the edge of a table.

Then he painted 'Woman Eating Oysters'. It scandalised his

contemporaries and was refused by the Antwerp Salon of 1882. Maybe this was because of the informality of the piece, like a composition painted by Courbet but conceived by Vuillard. The sleek plumpness of the face and hands of the diner, reaching for the first oyster in a huge dish, uncut lemon lying ready, a roll of bread, a bottle of wine, a flask of water, the whole table laid for one woman's satisfaction: the gluttony carries an implied sense of unease as though Ensor detested what he was painting and as though this painting summed up all those other proper, bourgeois interiors in his past.

But hindsight helps this reading, because the colours are suddenly high-keyed, crimsons, yellows, acid greens, starchy whites, and these colours, slightly turned, become in the masques of later the same decade lacerated reds and greens and yellows slashed across garish whites: paint whipped to the raw. Life is nasty, brutish, and short; Ensor paints it as a carnival or as a perpetual Hallowe'en, with death as the life and soul of the party.

From being a great painter of the substance of life, he becomes obsessed with flux, with incorporeality. There is a drawing of the Battle of Waterloo, with the French cavalry and arabesques of artillery smoke eddying hectically around and above the red-coated square of British infantry – by now Ensor had seen the late paintings of Turner, but where Turner would paint a storm as the apotheosis of all storms, Ensor turns it into the expulsion of the rebel angels from heaven or the flight of Adam and Eve from Eden with the avenging angel, eyes two points of glowing ochre, part human form, part storm and lightning.

Ensor poured out drawings covered with figures lost in ant-like industry, paintings of people with eyes glowing feverishly, or those transfixed masks caricaturing the senseless whirligig of life. And in that painting of his dead mother, he works into the finished painting, unlike the pencil studies, a row of medicine bottles in the foreground, precisely because, though they are transparent, he can make them more substantial than the white cadaver.

Ironically for an artist so obsessed with death, he lived until his ninetieth year, created a baron by Albert I, honoured by retrospectives in Paris and Brussels, photographed with his friends, the solid burghers of Ostend, and as a white-bearded, rheumy-eyed old man, playing the harmonium in his parlour before the massive painting of 'The Entry of Christ into Brussels' (in which Christ on the donkey is, again, the young Ensor). This was only the most famous of the paintings which was to shock his contemporaries in the 1880s and be rejected by them.

28 September, 1983   **Michael McNay**

Stepping away from a miracle

To the astonishment of nuns and staff in the Vatican, a British pilgrim climbed out of his wheelchair, neatly folded it and carried it away, shortly after being given a blessing by Pope John Paul II.

'I heard someone saying: "It must be a miracle," ' said Dr Jan Lavric, a South Yorkshire GP who was in Rome with a party of disabled people from Cheshire and Sue Ryder homes. The doctor, who is actually able-bodied and a keep-fit enthusiast, found himself caught in a classic misunderstanding when he arrived late for the blessing ceremony.

'Everyone was sitting in the audience chamber except for me,' he said. 'I looked around and I noticed this empty wheelchair.' Shortly afterwards, a Swiss guard arrived, unhitched the brake and began to wheel Dr Lavric forward at the head of a procession of disabled pilgrims. 'I tried to stop him. I said: "No, please, don't," but he carefully pushed me back and said: "Don't exert yourself," ' said Dr Lavric.

'What was I to do? What would you have done? I didn't see how I could jump up and run away without making things worse, so I just kept quiet.'

The Pope looked puzzled when he came to the doctor, noticing his identity tag which clearly marked him out as a medical helper.

'He didn't know what to do and to be honest, neither did I,' said Dr Lavric, who is in his sixties and lives in Clayton, near Doncaster. 'But he gave me his hand to kiss and then moved on.'

Dr Lavric did not make his escape until after the Pope had gone, by which time a nun had obligingly turned his wheelchair round to let him see the others being blessed. 'I tried to stop her as well but it had the same lack of effect as it did on the Vatican guard,' he said. 'Then I got up and folded up the wheelchair. I must say, they were all very surprised.'

Dr Lavric, who is medical adviser to the Sue Ryder home at Hickleton, Lord Halifax's former home near Doncaster, was anxious that the escapade last month should not spoil the solemnity of the occasion. But once everyone realised what had happened, they took it in good part.

'After all, it was one of the happiest moments of my life,' he said. 'We all had a tremendous impression of a man who gives happiness and peace.'

2 May, 1984   **Martin Wainwright**

Real toads, imaginary gardens

Poets don't, on the whole write about places other than those they know. There may seem to be good exceptions, like the opiate crystal palace at Xanadu of Samuel Taylor Coleridge. But even Coleridge had seen his dome at the pleasure-grounds in Vauxhall Gardens, and a few deft kneadings could mould it up to an oriental dream-house.

And Keats, too, had seen his 'magic casements, opening on the foam. Of perilous seas, in faery lands forlorn.' They used to open on the back-street slums of Whitechapel, where sash-windows were still a rarity, and where buckets of dirty suds gleamed like rainbows in the occasional sunshine, as their emptiers-out shouted vociferously 'gardez-loo'.

Romance was added, yes. That mysterious ingredient x that made the zip in lines that might otherwise have languished like the dullest of Akenside. It was imagination that put the magic gardens round Marianne Moore's real toads. Nevertheless, there were always real toads there, and it was often their flaccid and heaving skins that gave the blush of reality to the aery fancies of the Romantic poets.

Toads, yes—the killer-infested acres of Hampstead Heath, from whose brakes the nightingale rose to sing, the scrubby hillsides of the Lake District, where perpetual rain lashed down on Wordsworth's glorious grass. These were the warty places underneath the silken glitter.

They always are. If the 20th century had tended to emphasise the banal, the grit and the splutter, the street-lamps muttering in Eliot, and the slaughtermen wielding their bloody axes in Carl Sandburg, these are the inevitable excesses of an American hegemony, of an age that has burned trees down across Vietnam, and set artificial cocks to crow in clockwork cages, the puppet heirs of Yeats's Byzantium.

No, the toads, the true places, the kernels of what we know and can see and touch—where we have been, and what we heard there—these are the daily bread of English poetry. Take any lines by Housman at his most up-high, when the great gale is making the shutters shake in Wadham, and we look out over the University Parks and see the flower of sinner's rue blooming by Carfax, and the blood of beeches that 'stain the wind with leaves,' and there will still be those dumpy hills behind Ludlow and real subalterns in their mess dress.

Many a poem of place has roused its lethargic limbs from the stews of Cheapside, or the perfumed elegance of a boudoir cushioned with Boucher. Shakespeare himself, we are told, loved boys, and turned them into women. Since then, he has had his school. More to the point, perhaps, he has had his opponents. There are those who have laid—and exploited—their plough-girls in the landscape of a pastoral England—or even a Lowland Scotland—long since carbonised from the sunny fields of Arcady. Theocritus had nothing on Spenser. Burns lets massive feeling emerge out of unconvincing thistles.

But love in the countryside is usually a poor theme. Where in poetry can we find a ruddy-cheeked maid to equal the solid charms of Tess? Not in Hardy's own wry verses, for sure, where the drooping waves and the beetling crags of Beeny make more impression than the thin image of the young wife in her 'air-blue' gown. It isn't the human foreground that enlivens the rural scene in Cowper or Cotton, Cromarty or Cragside (there must be one called Cragside).

No, not that. The milk-white kine in the meadows, the wine-dark sea, these are the elements that grip and change. Love and patriotism, rape and revenge, criminality and grief are often the themes that boil and simmer in the over-heated souls of those poets who dip their pens in chlorophyll, to trace the merits and the beauties of the countryside. But the plots and tergiversations—whether shepherds carousing or Renaissance princes beheading daffodils with their canes—are never so commanding or memorable as those background vignettes thrown off to brighten a corner or balance the reds of the foreground. The best of Webster and Byron in this kind comes out when the action is at its swiftest.

Nowadays, and by this I mean since the death of Swinburne in 1909, when 'Who's for croquet?' was already becoming an anachronism, our critics tend to ask for a more isolating, a less diversified, poetry of place. The holocaust of Paschendaele was too extreme to be filtered through the gentle sieve of John Masefields's postwar stanzas. Georgian verse grew local in the wake of Squire, all cricket and churchwardens.

War poetry (an intense *genre*) meant Wilfred Owen, and the pyrotechnics of the Light Brigade were gone for ever. Imagination was out. If you knew about mud and rats, then you wrote about mud and rats. In with Rosenberg, out with Henry Newbolt. The motion that our most profound—because most permeated and subtle—war poets were Edward Thomas and Edmund Blunden would receive a poor hearing from our dour and passionate advocates of unmitigated horror.

Where is the pure poetry of place to be found? It may be that the answer is to be found in the concept of 'going abroad', the vitality of what, for want of a better word, I dub the tourist tradition in English verse. It began early, with Chaucer (cheap fares to Canterbury) and by the time of Bishop Corbet, horsing his way through the Midlands with three friends from Oxford, the tone and style—a bit of bawdy, a bit of politics, a bit of description—was already well established. The Romantic Movement, inheriting the rigours and the splendours of the Grand Tour, which was more a matter of snapping up unconsidered marbles, launched a thousand pens on to a sea of scribbled snapshots.

Even Shelley, that most ethereal of men, could lay out a few misty views of the Abruzzi and the glories of Imperial Rome. Byron went further, to Greece and Turkey, and you could still use bits of *Don Juan* to find your way in Constantinople. But the doyen of everything in this kind was, of course, that genial and cautious man, Samuel Rogers. His book, *Italy*, remains a wonderous farrago of prose and verse, verse in prose and prose in verse, with gripping narratives to fill in the spaces between the mountains and the fallen columns.

Who are the modern heirs of this? Well, who are not? Alan Ross has carried his bat, and twiddled his Pentel, through half the great cities in the globe. (And like Blunden he, too, could tell a tale or two about the horrors of war, if he chose.) As for our laureates, Cecil Day Lewis followed Clough and Rogers around the Latin circuit, and with some credit. And, if one turns to the present incumbent, where has he not been? By a splendid confining to his own country—with an occasional voyage to Ireland—John Betjeman has brought most counties in England to brilliant if suburban life. Cornwall to Norfolk, Highgate to Dore and Totley, they're all there, and speckled with as many golf balls as plovers' eggs.

The landscape was always thus. Not just a matter of roses and skylarks, but a solemn, mixed affair, 'a serious house on serious earth' as Larkin called the church, and yes, to end with, a good deal of our best poetry of place has that there too, the original, ivy-wrapped, yew-ringed Anglican church, the village centred on God, and the lands laid round in the orthodoxies of parson and squire.

The poetry of place may often, still, be the poetry of keeping things in their place. But the harm in that may be less than it seems. Cruise missiles won't look at all well in the dank fens. British soldiers in masks and khaki are hardly the ideal inhabitants for the hills of Armagh or the back streets of Belfast. Ducks on a pond, cows in a field, these may be banal images, but they feel right. Even so bizarre a talent as Craig Raine has the wit to know what putting a kettle on an octopus really means. It means a world of peace with courtesy, and of courtesy with peace.

17 December, 1983   **George MacBeth**

Take it or Leavis

'Morals? Can't afford 'em, guv,' says Shaw's Alfred Doolittle. But his plight is no worse than that of the Cambridge literati who make up the cast of Simon Gray's new play, *The Common Pursuit*, who can afford ideals but seem unable to fulfil them. In a sense, the play is an elegy to lost literary dreams; and, while I found it consistently absorbing, it never persuaded me that major talents were being muddied by the market-place.

Mr Gray's play spans 15 years; and, starting at a Trinity College, Cambridge, party in 1964, it pursues the interwoven lives of six characters. Stuart, who convenes the party to launch a literary review, goes on to marry his undergraduate love, Marigold, and become an impecunious editor and uncompromising taste-maker. His smooth friend, Martin, meanwhile bankrolls him and sucks him into his coffee-table book publishing firm. Of the others, Nick, a putative undergraduate Tynan, turns into a chain-smoking media hustler. Peter becomes a lecherous don churning out instant books to finance his voracious family, and Humphry, a North-country homosexual philosopher, never publishes but is still ultimately damned.

Obviously Mr Gray knows intimately the literary-academic world and he pins down its bitcheries and treacheries with the care of a lepidopterist. One has met (all too often) people like Peter who pour their energy into adultery and their slender talent into slim books on The Great Religious Leaders of the World. And one can recognise, without too much difficulty, the media pusher who offers the same article to two magazines simultaneously and the fastidious academic who labours on a mighty project (in this case a Wagner book) and backs off from publication.

The surface detail, the pressure of time on old friendships, the in-jokery that makes up a lot of English conversation are all caught with absolute accuracy. What the play doesn't do is convince me there is anything uniquely tragic about the compromise these characters undergo. Mr Gray comes close to suggesting that you have to choose between life and literature and that most people cravenly opt for the former. But Cyril Connolly many years ago pinned down the pram in the hallway as one of the enemies of promise; and anyway nothing in the play suggests that any of these characters (except possibly Humphrey) has the capacity to be a first-rate writer. What one has here is an astute portrayal of the literary world but hardly the feeling that the pursuit of letters has been dealt a death-blow.

But it is at least something to find a play that confronts opportunism with literary idealism (Take It or Leavis might be the sub-title); and Harold Pinter has come up with a typically scrupulous production that mines the text for every nuance. Not surprisingly, the best-written characters yield the best performances and Clive Francis is outstanding as the hunched-shouldered, flat-haired, flat-vowelled, truth-telling Northerner.

Nicholas Le Prevost gives the uncompromising Stuart an accosting profile and strong sense of refined sensibility. Ian Ogilvy as the smooth publisher also carries with him the unmistakable aura of expensive Soho lunches.

In the end, however, it is a good, intelligent play that makes one wish it were that much better. Mr Gray has the capacity to handle a big theme. I wish he would not disfigure his own talent making easy gibes against instantly recognisable figures.
5 July, 1984   **Michael Billington**

The celluloid surrealist

Luis Buñuel was brought up in that part of Spain where the Middle Ages lasted until the First World War. He was taught by priests to believe that babies arrived by car or train from Paris. He was also taught how to refute Kant in two minutes. Hence, he says, there is in his work a feeling for sin which is positively voluptuous, and in this, his posthumous autobiography* which he dictated to Jean-Claude Carrière, there is a notable feeling for religious simile.

*My Last Breath, by Luis Buñuel (London, 1984).

He sits in a bar 'like Simon Stylites perched on his pillar talking to God'. A Dry Martini resembles the Immaculate Conception, for sunlight should pass through a bottle of Noilly Prat before hitting a glass of pure gin, in exactly the way that St Thomas Aquinas tells us the Holy Ghost pierced the Virgin's hymen: 'like a ray of sunlight through a window – leaving it unbroken.' During Prohibition, by the way, he discovered that real gin bubbles when you shake it.

A boy who made deliberate mistakes in his exams in order to avoid the embarrassment of winning all the prizes, he was nevertheless 45 years old before he was allowed to make films on anything like a regular basis, and then in Mexico under conditions and on budgets at which most film-makers would have laughed. The greatness of an artist, Buñuel says, is often confused with the power of the country he lives in. Steinbeck is overrated because he is American. Because he is Spanish, Galdos is not read.

Buñuel learnt about poetry from Lorca, and about the need to disrupt our view of life from the Surrealists, whose successes were in an artistic world which was of no declared interest to them. Their impact on the real world was non-existent.

His first play which he both wrote and directed was called *Hamlet*. In Paris he performed various low tasks on the kind of films for which Josephine Baker would turn up eight hours late, throwing her make-up bottles against the wall, on the grounds that her dog was feeling unwell. *Un Chien Andalou* was meanwhile filmed in two weeks. At the première he hid behind the screen working the gramophone, alternating Argentinian tangos with *Tristan and Isolde*. He had first taken the precaution of filling his pockets with stones in case the audience turned nasty.

A visit to America. supposedly to work in the studios, left him with nothing but the ability to predict the plot of any Hollywood film, by means of a synoptic table he kept on the wall. As soon as he saw Dietrich appear as a whore in pre-war Vienna, he knew she would be shot.

Digression is to Buñuel the natural way of telling a story. His account of the Spanish Civil War gains by the tension between 'my intellectual attraction to anarchy and my fundamental need for order and peace'. At a time when it was dangerous to stick your hand out of your car to turn right, for fear it would be taken as a fascist salute and met by a hail of bullets, Buñuel was repelled by the needless cruelty of the Anarchists. He admired the group of workers who went with a full-scale firing squad to execute a statue of Christ. But in the hysteria of settled scores they forgot what they were fighting the war for.

In much of what he says about both his life and his work, which happily remained controversial to the end, there is the ambivalence of a highly intelligent man who finds this century's claims to progress to be bogus, and yet who delights in seeing authority destroyed. Chance rules everything. Our dreams are as real as our waking lives. Work is deadening and unnecessary. Buñuel takes the pokerwork mottoes of surrealism and by his freshness and humour makes them live. Typically he remembers a notice he found on a convent door: 'Traveller, if your conscience is troubling you, knock and we shall open. No women.'

26 January, 1984   **David Hare**

Tales from the Vienna Woods

She says that she only wanted to practise psychoanalysis until she had learnt enough about people. She stopped taking new patients after seven years and if you think that means she was pretty quick at getting to know about people, you are probably right. She had to be.

As a young woman studying in Vienna in the thirties, Dr Muriel Gardiner was a courier for the underground Socialist opposition. She sheltered Jews and Socialists trying to escape, she smuggled money and forged passports and knew what it was like to be woken at six a.m. with the Austrian equivalent of the Gestapo hammering on her door.

Many people think, though Dr Gardiner herself has never claimed this, that she is the person called Julia in Lillian Hellman's book *Pentimento*, the character played by Vanessa Redgrave in the film *Julia*. Earlier this year, she published her own account of her Vienna years, *Code Name Mary* (Yale

University Press), and last week she was in England to be honoured by fellow analysts at Oxford.

In the beginning she never wanted to be an analyst. She wanted to be a teacher. She comes of a rich American family, went to Wellesley College and Oxford, and then studied in Italy just as Mussolini was coming to power. But she suffered some personal difficulties that she does not specify, and some neurotic symptoms, and she thought being psychoanalysed might help.

So in 1926 she went to Vienna and wrote to Freud asking him to take her on as a patient. But his couch was a little overcrowded at the time and he recommended to her an American woman analyst who was also practising in Vienna, Dr Ruth Mack. Muriel Morris went into analysis, her symptoms improved, and she came out of analysis. She met and married an Englishman and became Muriel Gardiner, and she had a daughter. Then she went back into analysis.

She was with her analyst on February 12, 1934, when the army and police, under orders from Austria's Fascist leader Dollfuss, opened fire on the workers' flats in Vienna, the Karl Marx Hof. It is one of the famous moments of recent history, the beginning and very quickly the end of Socialist resistance to Dollfuss, leaving the way open to the Anschluss and Hitler's first conquest.

Muriel Gardiner had been contemplating a return to the US. Until then, her socialist credentials, such as they were, consisted of a grumbling unease about her wealth and open support for Sacco and Vanzetti. But on that February day, she decided to stay in Vienna, and soon she had contacted the Socialists who had now been forced underground.

She had not only a flat in Vienna, but a cottage specially built for her in the Vienna Woods, and both were used as safe houses by the underground. Because she was an American, she was less likely to be suspected. She carried messages, and orders from Joe Buttinger, then chairman of the central committee of the Socialist underground.

By now she had decided to become an analyst herself, and she was doing her medical training. She had a brief love affair with a young visiting English poet and journalist, Stephen Spender –

188

she appears in his autobiography *World within World*, as 'Elizabeth'. But later, Buttinger displaced Spender in her affections. Later still, when they were about to flee from France in 1939, she and Buttinger married. They are still married, though Joe is in a nursing home now, his memory totally gone.

In those middle years of the thirties she was both in the secret world, where every instinct is to conceal, and in analysis, where everything should be revealed. Yet she says she never felt any conflict, though it's a question other analysts often raise with her.

'Analysts then told you a little more about themselves than they do now. I knew she was the daughter of Judge Mack, the judge of the first juvenile court in the world. She was from Chicago, I was from Chicago. I knew she was a little left of centre, I knew she was 100 per cent on my side.'

Besides, for Freud and his followers, analysis bore the seal of the confessional. 'Anna Freud said to me once, "Why are so many young men today trying to discover who particular patients of Freud's really were, when he did everything he could to keep their identities secret?"'

Muriel Gardiner did know some of these secrets. She knew, for instance, one of Freud's most famous patients, the Wolf Man – she took Russian lessons from him. Later, she met him just after the Nazis had taken over, and the Wolf Man's wife had committed suicide. He was in a bad way, and she arranged invitations for him to visit England and France.

Did she give him money too? 'I gave him money for his journey, because you couldn't use Austrian money for trips beyond the border.' Her money would – as she puts it – just have been piling up at home, so she used it, both directly, and by guaranteeing people that she got out of Austria against becoming a charge on the public purse of Uncle Sam, one of the conditions of immigration to the US. 'I had plenty of money, and everything in Austria was very cheap, the money was very devalued.'

She had two passports, both legal, US and British, which reduced the risk of raising suspicion by her frequent trips across the frontier. One of her scariest moments was when she was carrying five forged passports back to Austria in order to get another batch of people out. She wore them strapped to her body, under a thick, bony corset.

When they got to the Austrian frontier, all the passengers were ordered off the train, to line up at passport control and customs. She then realised they were searching people. It was only when she got to the head of the queue that she saw that they were searching only one in three. She was not the one.

There is a very similar scene in Hellman's *Pentimento*, when Lillian is smuggling money into Austria for Julia. There are a whole lot of other parallels, though Julia loses a leg in the Karl Marx Hof attack, later is caught and murdered. Muriel Gardiner Buttinger is 81, a bit stiff from a back injury, a bit deaf but an imposing figure in plum velvet trouser suit and very much alive.

When *Pentimento* was published in 1973, Muriel's friends started to phone up pointing out the similarities between her life and Julia's. And before Muriel Gardiner's book was published here this spring, one Sunday newspaper ran a story claiming she had said she was Julia. Not only that, it claimed that Dr Herbert Steiner, Director of the Documentation Archives of the Austrian Resistance, had also said she was Julia. She insists that Dr Steiner had only said that he had asked many former Austrian resistance workers if they had known any American women involved in the resistance at that time, and they had told him 'Only Mary,' Muriel's code name.

'I was very distressed by the misunderstanding of thinking that I claimed – and that even Dr Steiner claimed – that I was Julia. Neither of us ever made such a claim.'

I doubt that she would want to be Julia, for her own life is remarkable enough, her identity certain. She says she is thinking of having, for the first time, some visiting cards printed. Dr Muriel Buttinger. Occupation: pleasure. Address: travelling. When we met she was about to travel to Oxford, because she had been asked to give the inaugural lecture to a new group of psychoanalysts formed there. When she was a girl at Oxford in the twenties, she felt unwanted, penalised for being a woman. Maybe some kind of justice is being done.

14 October, 1983   **Hugh Hebert**

The lost souls of Hollywood

Los Angeles was a terrible shock to the war emigrés who washed up in Hollywood in the 1940s. They, who had endured Gestapo persecution and last-minute escapes, often failed to survive in the new, seemingly benign culture which held so many hidden terrors. Bertold Brecht, Heinrich and Thomas Mann, Feuchtwanger, Alfred Doeblin and Leonhard Frank – their spiritual homes were Berlin, Vienna, and Paris. They hated a city without theatres or cafés or coffee table talk. And they were a horribly unmechanical lot. What kind of place was this Los Angeles where you had to drive a car to see your closest friend?

LA's everlasting sun, inescapable blandness, chronic suburbanity and mind-stunning domesticity did a job on many central European refugees that the SS had not been able to. A few prospered. The rest withdrew into a kind of puzzled insularity, a pained and superior provincialism to rival any they found in California. And their creative hearts withered. There was a moment when some hoped to make a 'New Weimar' in LA. But as Christopher Hampton poignantly shows in *Tales from Hollywood*, his play about refugee talent in wartime Los Angeles which opens at the National Theatre next week, most failed utterly.

It wasn't that Hollywood turned an obviously cold shoulder to the newcomers. The film community embraced the foreigners socially – but closed doors to work. Oh yes, parties were thrown, dinners given. A few studios were cajoled into handing out charity jobs. Briefly, Heinrich Mann, Brecht, and a few others were hired as screenwriters. But mutual awe – and snobbery – killed off most of these experiments.

Resident Hollywood was intimidated by the emigrés' intellectual brilliance, the refugees were amazed and disturbed by the power of money in screenland. Gradually, since only status or money 'talks' in Hollywood, the refugees were seen as losers carrying a plague of failure that it was best not to associate with.

As a reaction of, or perhaps spontaneously from the depths of their *Mitteleuropa* souls, the exiles looked down on Hollywood as irredeemably philistine, not worth the effort. Initial enthusiasm and sympathy on both sides degenerated into total boredom with each other.

My personal memories of this era, jogged by Hampton's sadly funny play and also by John Russell Taylor's *Strangers in Paradise*, a study of the Hollywood emigres from 1933–1950, are bizarre footnotes to cultural history.

In 1947, when many of the Hollywood emigrés were struggling to return to post-war Europe or to stay alive in the unfriendly job market, I was enrolled at the University of California as an ex-GI student. Among my classmates were Deanna Durbin's stepson (his father was the writer Felix Joachimson, soon Jackson), the German actor Fritz Kortner's son Peter, and the sons of two leftwing screenwriters, John Howard Lawson and Donald Ogden Stewart. My girlfriend was Tarzan's current 'Jane' at MGM, alias Vanessa Brown a.k.a. Smylla Brind of Viennese parentage.

Hanging out with Jeff Lawson and Ames Stewart and Smylla-Vanessa-Jane brought me into social contact with Brecht and the Manns and their hostess, Garbo's favourite scriptwriter, Salka Viertel (whose son Tom was also a chum).

For good reason, the emigrés hardly noticed me. I was a brash, movie-mad kid infinitely more turned on by my occasional encounters with 'real' stars like Peter Lawford or Elizabeth Taylor than by this slightly seedy assortment of bit players left over from the European wartime drama. I mainly registered actors like Conrad Veidt and Otto Preminger as the Nazis they usually played on screen. Not until a long time later did I grasp who I was meeting. Today I could kick myself.

Brecht I met at a party at Salka Viertel's house on Mabery Road in Santa Monica. Most of the others present were German or Austrian emigrés floundering in the half-world of 'spec' (speculative) writing for the movies. Brecht, bristling and uncomfortably warm in a rumpled wool suit, looked like an illegal bookie for whom I'd once worked as a messenger boy in Chicago.

Brecht was delighted by this comparison, even more so when

192

I explained one of my childhood tasks was to drop a weekly bribe in a sealed envelope on the desk of the local police captain. 'Yes, I wrote a play on this very idea,' Brecht agreed in his almost impenetrable accent. Then he tapped his close-cropped head. 'You see, I am from Chicago up here even if I have not been there.'

I did not see, partly because I found his gutturals hard to follow. He told me the plot of the 'western cowboy' film he was trying to write for Columbia (Brecht had collaborated with Fritz Lang at this studio on *Hangmen Also Die*). His story was suicidally convoluted and 'Brechtian', a real contract breaker.

Soon I began edging away from this garrulous, cigar-chomping, sweating German who blazed with a kind of saturnine energy. But not before we quarrelled over the role of the Hero in westerns. He insisted that my boyhood idols, from Buck Jones to Gary Cooper, had 'fascisized' my psyche as Karl May's mythical cowboys had helped prepare the German mass mind for Hitler. The true frontier heroes were not 'imperialist predators' like Kit Carson but the defiant, defeated Indians. (Brecht's box-office timing was not that awry: this immediately preceded Hollywood's liberal cycle of pro-Indian movies like *Broken Arrow*.) I left Brecht as one shrugs off a bothersome panhandler.

Some months later Smylla took me up to Thomas Mann's comfortable home in Pacific Palisades. The 'Weimar gang' was there, including Heinrich and his lovely wife Nelly (who committed suicide later in LA). Having devoured *The Magic Mountain*, I was eager to impress Thomas Mann who had just published *Dr Faustus* to great acclaim.

Remote and inflexible, he sat absolutely silent all through dinner, frowning at my nervous smiles and feeble attempts to strike up a literary conversation. He radiated moral disapproval as a general principle.

While loudly boasting of my contempt for the professors on my campus who had bowed to authority by signing the University of California's notorious loyalty oath, I called them 'good Germans'. Smylla stared daggers at me. I wanted the earth to swallow me up. After all, Thomas Mann was the most famous representative in the USA of the truly good German. I apolo-

193

gised to Mann for the slip. He spoke to me only once, frostily. 'Apologise to your teachers, not to me.' End of conversation.

After graduating from UCLA I worked in 'the industry.' At Columbia, Warners and Universal I had ample opportunity to deal with the pre-war emigrés who had struck gold in Hollywood. Fritz Lang, Henry Blanke, Otto and Ingo Preminger, John Brahm, Michael Curtiz, Bill Dieterle, Hugo Haas, Paul Kohner, Henry Koster, Anatole Litvak, Joe Pasternak, the Siodmak brothers, Edgar Ulmer, Fred Zinnemann – all were as middle-European as the later political refugees who had failed so stupendously in movies. What was the big difference?

Timing was crucial. It was one thing to arrive in Hollywood in early thirties splendour after having been recruited as a hot property specifically for your foreign touch. You might privately scorn Hollywood but also you understood how to exploit your 'Europeanness'. Assimilation meant being one of the boys, making yourself a saleable commodity that was both acceptable and acceptably exotic. As a producer at Universal told me, 'Dougie Sirk is a Kraut down to his Prussian instep. But he knows how to make *American* movies.'

But many of the post-Reichstag Fire exiles not only refused to compromise artistically – they really didn't want to be in America at all. And they did their best to pretend they weren't there. They clustered in national communities speaking only the home-tongue.

It's possible that Brecht and the others understood all too clearly the lesson taught by Peter Lorre's career. Lorre too had escaped from Germany after Hitler. He soon got side-tracked playing comically eccentric villains in B features such as the Mr Moto series. Not even his brilliant Joel Cairo in John Huston's *The Maltese Falcon* rescued him from absurd caricatures.

In the mid-fifties, when I was briefly his agent, he begged me to remind producers of his deeper talents. 'They just want this crazy man I've been ever since M. Sometimes I curse that picture. I am one of the sanest and gentlest men I know, don't you agree, Clancy?'

Suddenly, at the end of one lunch in Frascati's on Sunset Boulevard, he flung himself upward out of his chair. To the delighted consternation of the other patrons he went into his

'The Beast With Five Fingers bit' (as he called it), all sinister sneer and eye-rolling rage. It was a comment on his career, his idea of self-torturing irony. But, by then fat and under-used, he simply looked like a bad night club comedian's imitation of Peter Lorre.

Brecht and the others may have preferred failure in America to a success like Peter Lorre's.

26 August, 1983   **Clancy Sigal**

The golden boy of the West

San Francisco must be the most opera-conscious city in the world. When Carlo Cossutta, the tenor scheduled to open the season last week as Verdi's Otello, awoke on the morning of the première to find himself voiceless, the news quickly spread all over town. As did the decision of the opera company's general manager, Terence McEwen, who decided to go ahead with the performance and immediately set out to track down a substitute Otello – undaunted by the fact that first-rate exponents of this notoriously difficult role are among the rarest of operatic species.

Nevertheless, within the hour, McEwen, who is known to enjoy exceptionally good relations with singers, had somehow managed to persuade no less a star than Placido Domingo to take on the role. The only trouble was that Domingo was 3,000 miles away, having just arrived in New York to start rehearsals for this season's opening production of *Les Troyens* at the Met. However, the three-hour time difference between the West and East coasts was in McEwen's favour.

All through the day San Francisco's radio and television stations kept the city apprised of the latest developments in the drama. Domingo was being taken by helicopter to an airfield in New Jersey. An anonymous friend of the San Francisco Opera was lending Domingo his private jet. The jet was on its way. The jet had run into strong head winds and had landed in Colorado to refuel. Domingo had just telephoned to say he would be there as soon as possible. The jet was racing on. Domingo expected to be in San Francisco by eight o'clock. The performance, scheduled to start at seven, would be delayed two hours.

In the event, the head winds proved more of a deterrent than expected and Domingo did not arrive until after nine. Accompanied by a police escort that cleared the highway he was rushed to the opera house and at 10 McEwen stepped out to announce the impending rise of the curtain. Half an hour later, just before 10.30, the performance began.

Though many in the house had paid several hundred dollars for the privilege of attending the opening night gala, the audience, far from being put out of humour by the three-and-a-half-hour delay, seemed to be enjoying itself immensely. There were good-natured cheers when the houselights went down and a rousing ovation when the conductor, Marek Janowski, took his place. Most of the audience even stayed the course, though by 2 a.m., when the last curtain fell, about a quarter of the stalls were, understandably, empty.

But the most notable thing about Domingo's appearance was not his gameness but his brilliance. By any standards of back-stage drama, his Otello was unforgettable. By the standards of art it was memorable. After a moment of discomposure in the Esultate! of Act One, he sang with a richness of tone, a command of shading and a nobility of manner that are without peer in this role today. During Otello's ungovernable outbursts of rage in Act Three he was like a destructive force of nature. No wonder the audience stayed on until well after two o'clock to cheer him on his way.

For Domingo, who was still on Barcelona time, the perform-ance ended at 10 in the morning. Yet he was by far the freshest member of the cast, and certainly the most vibrant. No doubt it is impossible to judge the true capacities of Margaret Price as Desdemona and Silvano Carroli as Iago from their showing under such extraordinary circumstances but next to Domingo it was clear that the former lacked warmth and the latter subtlety. As for Janowski, he seemed to be half asleep during the slow passages and frantically fast during the rest – as if he were dropping off and suddenly waking up.

As if the tale of Domingo's San Francisco Otello were not already extraordinary enough, there is an amazing coda. Opera stars at the height of their fame are indeed in a class of their own but, so grateful was San Francisco to the Spanish tenor for getting its opera season out of a hole, that last Wednesday was declared Placido Domingo Day by the Mayor of San Francisco. And the mayor himself flew off to New York, there to confer on the tenor the freedom of the city. Who says music does not count?

19 September, 1983   **Dale Harris**

The world America has lost

Riverhead is an old town, almost at the tip of Long Island. Small blue plaques all around Main Street celebrate the history of its early settlers in the 1600s and there is a move afoot at last to renovate some of its fine old buildings.

It used to be a prosperous market town, at the head of a small river, between the north and south forks of the island, surrounded by rich agricultural land; its lovely clapboard colonial houses bearing witness to a time of greater wealth and style. It is said that Riverhead went down when 'they' let the welfare types in: the truth is that it was nearly left behind. Its shabby old-fashioned shops in the town centre seem to come from another age. It was a functional town then, an embarrassment, clearly, in the midst of all the resort developments that grew up along the nearby shores of the Atlantic and became the Hamptons.

In Riverhead, there is Swesbey's department store with its undergarments and talk of girdle support and madame's fullness across the back. In West Hampton Beach, there is The Intimate Boutique – silk, froth, and Dior satin for night dalliance. The Woolworths in Riverhead still has that spell of long ago – wooden floors, pine disinfectant, slight must and mothballs. There are hair nets, cheap plastic 20 cent toys, and sympathy cards with rabbits, flowers and long, silver-inscribed verses of comfort. In the Five and Ten Cent at West Hampton, there is a complete line of coordinated, almond-shaped kitchen plastics, snow-shovels, hammocks and running shoes.

197

It was only a question of time before Riverhead acquired its own nostalgic appeal. They come now from all over the Hamptons to wander up and down Main Street, browsing in windows of discount shoe shops, rummaging among the nylon pillow slips and handy pink cardigans for that one simple bargain to cart home with pride. On the corner by the bank, there is a large, old jewellery store, which trades mostly in repairing clocks and watches. Only the very poor or the very rich can support a watch-repairing service: disposables must suffice for most people nowadays.

Further along on the same side, there is even a fix-it shop. There is always a wireless or steam iron, a kettle or toaster awaiting collection on display in the window. The fix-it shop, it is largely believed, survives only on *Sesame Street* as an ideal not meant to be taken seriously by young viewers. The rest of the world has learned to take out insurance for servicing or indeed to buy something new when the old goes wrong. But in this fix-it shop, there are quite a lot of old portable washing tubs waiting their turn for repair – old-style tube vacuum cleaners too. There are always two or three people peering at them through the window, lost in their memories.

It is hard for an English person to comprehend how inaccessible to an American is even this most recent past. The English landscape is the work of many generations and their effort has marked the land indelibly. Villages, stonework, ditches, railway tunnels and bridges: all these products of man's own hand remain in place, touchstones of the past. In America, everything vanishes – the present is all of it. No winding roads to tell of other parishes, no need to make do with what is outmoded or merely inconvenient. Everything that can be improved will be.

And in the middle of this busy progress, Riverhead was simply left out. There was no reason to knock most of it down. There was no money to buy all that the bigger and better could offer. The dingy furniture shop with its range of marquette and imitation oak was in itself way above the dreams of most who live here. Of course, there is a military recruiting shop in the middle of Main Street. How else would a local boy find work?

Along the road from the posters of confident and beaming soldiers there is another kind of army: the Salvation Army, in its huge new thrift shop. This store, among the biggest in River-head, has become something of a find for smart Hamptonites, all of whom doubtless imagine themselves to be the only ones in the know. Carefully arranged in the window are the special objects of the day: an ornate brocade love-seat with curling wooden frame, a girl's red velvety hooded coat, an end table or two with gold embellishment around the leg.

Behind the cash register, the manager, Mrs Lois Hazk, Riverhead born and bred, keeps a knowing eye out for the needy who come in with no money to buy. Her dainty, white-haired charm could offend no-one. She knows so well how to offer a coat, a sweater, or whatever seems right, without being mis-understood. 'We would never refuse anyone who couldn't afford it,' she says. 'Some people are dreadfully poor and they can't pay, others pay what they can.'

Three-quarters of her customers, or so she records, are known to her. They come in every day, hunting for that particular bargain. The rails of clothes are arranged with care: every size or colour is placed exactly so. Fur coats for $20, suits for $10, evening frocks for $3: Mrs Hazk's regulars know just where to hunt for them.

And now there are these other strangers: In their Loden coats and French scarves, the four-wheel drives parked outside on five-cent meters, they come to unearth their part of bounty of the past and some, after a while, just stand there as the meaning of it all begins to make itself clear. All around them is the world of their parents and grandparents, totally lost to them until now.

It is always clear who has been touched this way by the Sally Army shops; they're the ones who come back the next day bearing big sacks of expensive children's toys, beautiful woollen jumpers, men's camel-hair coats – their private offerings of thanks. They never quite forget of course, to ask for their signed receipt of listed articles deductible for income tax purposes according to Publication 526 of the Internal Revenue Service.

'Valuation of gifts in kind are the privilege and responsibility of the donor' it says on the Salvation Army adult rehabilitation form. What price charity? Is it simply an old camel-hair coat?

4 January, 1984   **Linda Blandford**

199

A good guy at heart

Katherine Hepburn once stared Robert Mitchum in the face at the beginning of a movie they were in and commented: 'You know you can't act and if you hadn't been good-looking you wouldn't have gotten the picture. I'm tired of playing with people who have nothing to offer.'

The picture was Vincente Minneli's *Undercurrent* and the outburst was said to have been caused by Mitchum's attempt to break the ice with a few jokes. At the time, he was working on *Undercurrent* in the morning, on John Brahm's *The Locket* in the evening, and on *Desire Me* in the afternoon. Those were the days, in the Forties, when he was RKO's workhorse leading man, contracted out to MGM as well.

No one in their right minds today would say that Mitchum can't act. Not after Charles Laughton's *The Night of the Hunter*, for which he should have got an Oscar as the evil preacher with Love and Hate tattooed on the fingers of his hands. John Huston, in fact, has compared him with Brando, Burton and even Olivier. And almost all his directors have praised him as an ace professional with a towering screen presence and far more ability that he gives himself credit for.

He arrived in London this week to give a *Guardian* lecture tomorrow at the National Film Theatre in conjunction with a season of his films, and those fortunate enough to have a ticket for the lecture are likely to hear some very good stories, one or two of them unprintable. But it might be difficult to get much out of him about himself because he's one of the very few Hollywood stars who doesn't appear very interested in that subject.

Nor, I'm happy to say, since I'm interviewing him, is there likely to be a riot. The reputation that's followed him around on that score may or may not be deserved. But in person Mitchum seems the opposite of aggressive, and a great deal more intelligent than some to the past headlines about him suggest.

The modesty, and the politeness, do not seem fake. And he gives a quick example of how he had been misinterpreted. He says he was once asked by a reporter what he thought of London. He replied that he loved it. It was better than almost any place he had come from to get there. But, said the reporter, is there anything you don't like?

Well, he said, he sometimes wished the airport was a bit nearer so that he could get to enjoy the place quicker once off the plane. When the interview was printed, it said that Robert Mitchum 'wanted the dump moved nearer the airport.'

He says this sort of thing has happened to him for most of his Hollywood life. And since he's been a star for about 40 years, that must mean a lot of times. It gets, he would like to tell you, a little tiring at times.

But even he would have to admit that he's had a pretty rumbustious life, though still married to the same Dorothy he first met way back in the years of the New Deal in America when she was a brown-haired girl of about 14. I forgot to inquire whether he really made the proposal that's regularly ascribed to him: 'Marry me, and you'll be farting through silk.' But if he did—and we really must find out the truth tomorrow —Dorothy must have taken leave to doubt it. Though now reported to be a very wealthy man, he hadn't a bean when he popped the question.

In fact Mitchum was digging ditches and planting trees on a soil reclamation project with the Civilian Conservation Corps, when he wasn't making a few dollars from casual labouring or dish-washing. It was just before his sixteenth birthday that he had the first of quite a few brushes with the police, who picked him up on a vagrancy charge in Savannah, Georgia, and accused him of burglary.

'They looked at your hands down South in those days. If they were calloused, you might be okay. If they weren't you were a thief,' he recalls. Acquitted of the burglary charge, he was sent as a vagrant to work in the Chatham County chain gang, shackled by the ankles and chained to those on either side of him.

He escaped after a week and by nightfall reached a swamp which he had to wade through to reach South Carolina and safety. He hitched his way back to his home in Delaware, sleeping in ditches, treating his swollen ankles with drug-store remedies and cooking raw vegetables stolen from the fields over a campfire.

When he finally got home, his family found him pinched and wasted. His left leg was swollen to almost twice its normal size and he had Black Tongue Fever—the deficiency disease of pellagra. The doctor thought about an amputation but his mother poulticed the leg with herbs from the garden, drawing out pints of poison. He wouldn't have been much good as a one-legged star, even to Howard Hughes at RKO.

Mitchum's wandering youth on the freight trains may not have prepared him for cinema stardom, but it certainly gave him a good idea of how to look after himself. He was a heavyweight boxer for a spell, fighting for a few dollars until he broke his nose and decided enough was enough. There have been one or two less orthodox fist-fights since.

He found work at Lockheed when America entered the war, next in line to a gentleman called James Dougherty who showed him a picture of a girl he'd just married called Norma Jean. She later became Marilyn Monroe, and starred with Mitchum in *River of No Return*.

To cut a slightly longer story short, it was his mother who persuaded him to go into movies with the simple observation that if all those other idiots could get away with it, so could he.

He borrowed $55 from his grandmother's funeral fund to pay his union dues, and replaced an actor by the name of Charlie Murphy in a Hopalong Cassidy movie. Seven more Hopalongs followed with William Boyd in the lead and Mitchum usually cast as the heavy. That was the beginning of a career that is still going strong today, and has easily survived his famous gaol sentence for smoking pot which caused headlines all over the world.

Howard Hughes, who owned RKO, brought him candy and nut bars in prison which Mitchum described as 'just like Palm Springs without the flotsam.' And by the time he came out it was clear that his fans, if they ever felt disappointed in him, had forgiven him. Later, incidentally, he was officially exonerated and the verdict of guilty set aside.

Now, he says, it's cocaine sniffing that's the major business in movies. And no, he doesn't touch it, but he could tell you one or two who do. He recalls the story of one Hollywood alumnus who woke up one morning complaining that he felt as if he had a hole in his head. He went to the doctor, and found that he had. 'If that's what it does to you, I think I'll stick to cigarettes.'

He grumbles a bit about getting old and falling gradually apart—he's well into his sixties, just out of hospital, and says that it is not worth trying too hard to get past 50. And yes, he's definitely going to retire tomorrow. Or possibly the next day.

Then he cheers up and launches into a perfect imitation of Michael Winner making a picture, telling a henchman not to worry about a tankful of spilt petrol, throwing a match on it to prove his point, and blowing up the whole set.

Which is instantly followed by another of Lord Olivier complaining of a pet dog brought on set by a certain lady star we all know and love: 'But, my dear, it hasn't an ounce of acting talent in its entire body.' And then he does an excellent parody of the Indian Prime Minister who, asked on American television how he kept so fit, said that he walked everywhere, ate sparingly—and drank his own piss.

Finally, he gives an hilarious approximation of the look on the interviewer's face when the last part of the remark is made. It's great acting all right, but what's endearing about it is that it doesn't seem in the least malicious.

'You really don't give a damn, do you?' Howard Hughes once told him. Actually, he does. But not an awful lot about himself. Which is probably why his legions of fans, once called the Mitchum Droolettes, still care so deeply about him.

23 June, 1984   **Derek Malcolm**

Qadir, the master of disguise

Nothing can be happier, healthier or more entertaining for cricket than the fact that Abdul Qadir has replaced Dennis Lillee as the cult figure of the game. His bowling is almost as hypnotically baffling to the spectator or the television watcher as to the batsman. Even from the almost perfect position of the television camera, where everything might be revealed, nothing is; the harder he is studied the more impossible it becomes to 'read' him. Therein lies much of his entertainment value – though not for batsmen.

Abdul Qadir was only 23 when he was brought into the Pakistan team for the second of the three Tests against England in 1982–3. At once he took six for 44 to play a major part in dismissing Mike Brearley's side for 191, and finished with top Pakistani bowling figures for the series of 12 wickets at 25.41. Even so, his Test place was rarely a foregone conclusion, although Pakistan cricket has never turned its back on wrist spinners in the English fashion, they have grown accustomed to their being measurable batsmen, in the fashion of Mushtaq and Sadiq Mohammad and Wasim Raja.

Abdul Qadir's arrival in England with the touring side of 1980 aroused much interest, but a shoulder injury which dogs so many wrist spinners reduced him to six wickets on the tour. When he returned in 1982 he posed an altogether greater problem. The experts who studied him closely – but by no means infallibly – came up with variants of the theory that, as embellishments of his leg break – delivered with two different hand actions – he employed a googly, a Grimmett-style 'flipper' and, as one senior wrangler staunchly asserted, two different top spinners, one of which looked like a googly.

Whatever may be the truth of that abstruse matter, Abdul Qadir savagely tormented normally good English batsmen inexperienced to the point of ignorance in wrist spin. He took 57 wickets, but only 10 of them in Tests, where on slow pitches he reaped less than his due. As one old player put it, 'They didn't bat well enough to get out.'

Returning home, he played in the three Tests against the Australians, reputedly the masters of this type of bowling, and took 22 wickets – nine more than any other bowler on either side. In combination with Imran Khan, he was largely responsible for Pakistan's historic 3–0 win. He was less successful in the following rubber against India, but was twice Man of the Match with decisive bowling performances in last summer's World Cup.

He is a serviceable right-hand bat – indeed he scored a century in only his second first-class match – but his major contribution to cricket is as a bowler. His unique approach is indelibly printed on many memories. He walks to the end of his run, stands for a moment, takes half a stride backwards, suddenly spins the ball across from right hand to left, peering along his knuckles as if he were 'drawing a bead' on the batsman, then shows him the ball and, in the course of four walking steps, pushes it back into his right hand then, taut as a coiled spring, bounds in four more strides, releases it in a wickedly spin-curved arc and seems only partly to check the urge to leap after it.

He had an unprofitable tour of Australia this winter, taking only 12 wickets at 61.08, for a well-beaten side, but seven of those wickets – including Greg Chappell twice – were in the first six of the order. That last fact indicates that he still has not been truly mastered. He still bowls so joyously and well that he must continue to surprise and delight.

He might have done more than that for English cricket, which must hark back to 1928 to find 'Tich' Freeman, of Kent, taking 304 wickets in a single season with leg-breaks. In the less distant past, England included four wrist spinners in the second Test of 1946–47 in Australia, and they all bowled. Since then, too, the Australians Jack Walsh, George Tribe, Colin McCool and Bruce Dooland have practised the craft with considerable success in this country. English cricket, however, allowed it to die in 1980, when Robin Hobbs, the last true leg-spinner to play for England, was allowed to go out of the game.

It is sad that in the season of 1983 only three wickets were taken by English-born wrist spinners. Certainly it was possible to watch Nasir Zaidi perform zestfully in that vein for Lancashire, but even he took only 16 of the season's total of 20. The solitary Englishman to make his mark was Derek Aslett of Kent, who captured all three of those English-claimed wickets, and needless to say, he is employed as a batsman.

After the 1982 season Kent negotiated with Abdul Qadir to join them. What he might have done for young Aslett and English cricket can hardly be guessed. This summer though, in the event of their permitted one overseas player, medium-pacer

Eldine Baptiste being wanted for the West Indian tour, Kent have taken an option on replacing him with Terry Alderman, an Australian of similar pace.

17 April, 1984   **John Arlott**

Life with Father

When their mother left, the boys were fifteen, five and three and we sat around for a long time just as if matron's eyes were still upon us. Then one fine day I said:

'Kids, put the sauce bottle back on the table. Put all the sauce bottles on the table. Boys, in fact, put your feet on the table, from here on in, this is liberty hall.'

Whenever the one-parent chaps get to whingeing about their baby leaving town they always seem to forget just what absolute bliss, what a pleasure it is to get up in the morning and get into a bath, light up a cigar and drink some beer.

That is inside the house. Outside the house is different. Outside the house Motherhood still reigns supreme and a man alone ain't got no chance at all for he is merely a father.

I don't know why they think so little of fatherhood. God is God the father. He was God the father for thousands of years. But that wasn't good enough. They had to write Mary the Mother of God into the script. And not just any old mother, a Jewish mother at that, just like poor Portnoy. At least Jesus had the right idea about motherhood. 'Woman, do you know not that I must be about my father's business?' And what did Mary say to that? 'Twelve years old and already he's talking like a *goyischer!* What a way for a boy to talk to his mother!' Hamlet had the right idea too.

The next thing I did was get out of the bath and redecorate the house, singing: 'Since my baby left me, I found a new place to dwell', with Bro, the oldest and a handyman, turning the front hall into a sort of a cross between the cricket pavilion at Hove and El Vino's, with cricket prints and turkey red carpet, stud marks on the places where the floorboards showed, until it was the sort of front hall a man would be proud to fall down dead drunk in; and then we went on like that from there until we got

206

to the kitchen which might have been made for Zorba the Greek; Zorba who said, 'What is life, boss, but taking off your belt and taking a chance?'

George Orwell was a one-parent family. F. Scott-Fitzgerald was a one-parent family.

Lying in the bath, smoking an El Rope-O cheapo see-gar and drinking beer. 'Say, dad just where are you from?' 'West Texas, keed, back in the hills, same as everyone else.' 'Wow Dad.' 'You said it, kid, ain't life grand!'

Personally I wish I'd never been defrosted.

19 July, 1984

One kid kept putting jam in the other kid's bed. The other kid retaliated by giving the first kid cups of piss to drink. 'Oh, Sandy, I've got a nice drink for you!' Every night one kid cried for his mother.

'And oh, Mr Reynolds, what did you do to comfort that

weeping child?' asked the Court Welfare Officer, because it came to that, when, after nearly eight years, the mother wanted them back because she could not stand the idea of her children going to an English public school. Living with a loud-mouth, cheap-jack, layabout, drunken, greasy-haired, pig, great, grey slug, monster parasite of the world was OK but not an English public school.

'Every night, lady, I had to slap that kid to sleep.'

'Only sissies got mummies, kid,' I told him. 'John Wayne, you think John Wayne's got a mummy?'

We are the poor, battling bastards of Bataan.

I taught the boys to sing.

Got no momma, got no poppa, got no Uncle Sam.

'But we got a poppa, Dad.'

'How many Japs you kill in the Korean War, Dad?'

'Lots.'

'With your bare hands? And you were strangling them and their eyes went *pop*, Dad?' And you said, "Okay, popeye, take that, sucker!"'

'You must have second sight, kid, that's just what I always said when, of course, I wasn't throwing grenades at them shouting, "Eat death, yellow dwarfs!"'

'Gosh, Dad.'

'It wasn't anything, kids, now go to sleep.'

That's inside. Outside, down at the supermarket, the old crones are clicking their tongues over their plastic teeth, saying, 'It's them kiddies I feel sorry for. Those motherless kiddies.'

'Hey, lady, yeah you, with the hair on your chinny chin chin, how's your son? Out of Walton gaol yet?'

The great, gooey, sentimental chip shop heart of England opens up to motherless children. Or does it? This is a country where children are beaten to death. Actually tortured to death. The only country in the world where they have to have an organisation to keep people from mistreating children.

Suspicious and insular, the British, watchful of foreigners, and I am a tall, dark stranger speaking in an outlandish tongue, laughing with my sons on the rain-washed streets. What do they have to laugh about?

Ain't no use in marching fast, we sing coming home all laden down from the supermarket, walking in a string up the street.

Because third platoon is draggin' ass.

'How terrible it is, a man bringing up children like that,' says a hunched-shouldered ex-scrubber, ciggie poking out of her dirty-finger-nailed hands. *Cough Cough* goes her own kid, a real snotnosed kid, with a cough like sixty Woodies a day, but brought up with a mother's love, the love that only a mother can give. *Swat* goes the back of the hand round the kid's ear hole. 'Trevor,' she screams, 'I'll never take you out wit' me no more.' She will never say 'hit', but always something like 'I chastised him one.' That's what those heavy-handed mothers say. The ones who never say 'hit' are the real heavy-handed ones. They are watching me, but I am watching them as well. And I know.

I know the secret of their miserable lives, the former scrubbers and the bourgeois housewives too. I know they are hanging on to the symbol of sacred Motherhood because it alone will explain their failure, their grossly wasted lives. I know their lives would be wasted anyway, without any children. That is the secret I know. Hang on they must to Motherhood; and at that, too, are they also failures: their children are unhealthy, full of nervous tics and little mannerisms, badly behaved and uneducated because they are reared, all of them, in the dreadful shadow of the perverted idea of Motherhood.

'I suppose it's all chips from the chippie for you lads, eh?' says one of them, a friendly one this one, almost. She is a school teacher and I spend more in a week on food than she earns and I cook it, up in the morning doing black pudding, the real thing, and pancakes, flipping them in the air, steak, roast beef, the serious business of meat, roast lamb, lamb chops, roast pork, roast turkey, chicken, pheasant, partridge, haunch of venison (a failure); tea and crumpets, muffins, scones on a winter afternoon, cozy by the cozy, hissing gas fire in the cozy sitting-room after school, all cozy.

And lots of noise. Wild sounds from Bro and the teenagers upstairs, writing songs . . . 'Lilly's off to Paris with fifty pee and a hot sausage roll/Everyone goes to Paris when they're on the dole . . .' 'Hey listen to this one,' says Dave Knopov, bright eyes gleaming, eager, keen, non-stop talking now when once, when he first came, he was too shy to say a word: 'Plastic bag, plastic bag, plastic bag . . .' Plastic bag, he says, repeated 76 times, count 'em '. . . killed my granny with a plastic bag . . .' And a kid called AWOL because he was always sagging off school, sitting in the morning-room all day and all night making a white-noise machine, a brilliant kid but he didn't like going to school. AWOL, Dave, Sharon and Suzie, big brothers and sisters for the little ones.

Outside, there in the dim mentality of surrounding suburbia I know they are thinking, 'That Yank over there, he's selling DRUGS to the KIDS!'

One fine day, early in the morning, you wake and hear the children singing and it is a long time before you remember that you have a broken heart. Getting up, singing 'Free man in the morning . . . Free man in the morning' all the way out of the door and into the car because it is Saturday morning and you are going out on The Ha Ha Ha. Legless.

It's those children, those kids, those kiddies, those kid-diewinkies they feel sorry for, these neighbours as they sit in their buttoned-up suburban misery, Mum, Dad and Tina.

Now they must try a different tack, these ladies at the supermarket and launderette, the female social workers with their complexions full of bad food and their minds full of evil thoughts: the children are not starving to death: they must work on me – I must be made a *victim* like them. Good Christ, they want me to join them, in Motherhood!

'But how do you get any work done?' they ask and answer it themselves, not waiting for an answer: 'You can't get your work done, not with the kiddies. A pity. A shame. Such a shame.'

Ah these women, these Mothers, but for the children what worlds they would have conquered, or, at least, nagged to death. Sacrificed, all of it, to Motherhood.

'That's true, that's true, you are right,' I say. 'I can get no work done at all, hardly.'

What with the kids, the kiddies, I was only able in those eight years to write just over a million words. Well, a lot over a million. 1,197,550 to be exact. 416,000 words for the *Guardian*; 373,000 words for the *Manchester Evening News*; 283,750 words for *Punch* and 124,800 words for *The Times*. That's the equivalent of doing *War And Peace* or writing James Joyce's *Ulysses twice*. And that was just the regular work. I wrote 30 songs, half of them for marvellous Julie Walters; two and one half plays, one TV script, lots of incidental journalism plus several hundred pages of yet another half assed attempt at a novel . . . in between cooking and cleaning, and mopping up the blood and, of course, being the lazy, idle, drunken layabout which the wife left and which is practically a full time job in itself.

ᴮut in the end Motherhood was too strong for me. After eight years I lost custody of the children in that most peculiar matter of the public school. How could an English judge take English children out of an English public school? Because he was an English judge and he had a mother, and of course he knew a father's place was not in the home, you bet. One boy liked the school and he is still there. I still see them sometimes. They are not called Sandy and Buck any more; and Bro is going to make me a grandfather. He is, he says, looking forward to fatherhood. I wonder why?

15 March, 1984   **Stanley Reynolds**

Setting his cap at the world

Today's national club gala at Leeds represents the British swimmers' opening plunge in the six-month run-up to the Olympic Games. The endless shuttle length-upon-length of bleary, dreary dip at dawn, is nearly over for the children. Their parents can now summon just one last fierce, despairing shove, then it is up to the selectors.

Some of the toddling dolphins will sink without trace and with a sigh. It will be a crowded plughole. Those who remain afloat guarantee us months and months of fast moving froth all the way to LA. Red-eyed, teeth chattering little mites who might. In TV terms we are in for weeks and weeks of Weeks.

At the Leeds poolside today, watch out for one ex-mite who did. You cannot miss Duncan Goodhew. He's the one in the city suit and without a hair on his head. He won the Olympic Gold Medal in Moscow in 1980. Today he will only be wearing a cap, not *the* cap.

The engaging enthusiast, Goodhew, resents my dismissive tease of 'moving froth'. He says: 'Competitive swimming is unique. It is the most "psychological" physical sport known to mankind. You dive into an alien environment; you can't hear anything, you can't see anything, you are all alone. In athletics Coe can see and hear Ovett on his shoulder: he can react. Swimmers have no such audio-visual awareness for the challenge. It is eerie. It is tremendous sport.'

Goodhew, now 26, is a remarkable young man. Since larking about at five with his flippers in the family pool in Sussex, there has been more than water pressing down on his shoulders. He was dyslexic and, as a presumed dimwit, the butt of every school joke – far more so when, after Tarzan-tumbling from a tree at 10, all his hair fell out inside a year.

Only his eyelashes have grown back. 'Wonderful incredible things are eyelashes. I can't tell you how vital they are: they field every bit of fluff, dust and sweat. I used to see flies coming straight at me, straight at my eyeballs and couldn't do a thing to stop them. Terrible.'

The wretched, sorry-for-himself, over-aggressive oddball at whom they jeered 'Kojak', supposes he must have found some sort of lonely solace in swimming. It helped him get to Millfield. 'I suppose I had a raw talent – like two arms and two legs.' Millfield was co-ed. 'I'd arrived there as a broken person. They helped put the pieces together.'

But was a girl ever going to look at – or at any rate not stare at – a gawk with no hair, and who couldn't even read, and kept wanting to write from right to left? One day, just ten years ago, he walked into the common room wearing his blonde wig with the middle parting. 'A fellow pupil was in there, one of the most marvellous people I have ever met. He had polio, he had a club foot and a hook for a hand, and he just looked up at me and smiled, "What's your problem, Dunc?" That question was a crucial turning point.'

He was 16 then. It was the year his father died of a stroke. Those second generation eyelashes momentarily moisten. 'It's not that I miss him, for his presence is always with me. Yes, he'd occasionally turn up for my early competitive swims. I think he was a bit embarrassed at my devotion for him. He didn't talk much but once, in the very trough of my despair and torments, he said to me, "My boy, just remember your name is Goodhew and be proud of it." That was another momentous moment.'

Six years later he was swimming in the European Championships. 'The night before the race I dreamed Dad was there in the crowd watching me win. And he was smiling. When I woke up there on the chair by my bed was Dad's old cloth cap. It was the only thing I ever had of his. I put it on. My Dad was a God to me.'

He wore the cap at the Moscow Olympics two years later. I was there in the crowd. The place was seething for the breast-stroke final. The Russian or East German would surely win. The swimmers paraded round the pool like brooding boxers in their dressing gowns. Duncan wore his Dad's old cloth cap. The tension eased as the throng laughed. The gladiators disrobed. Duncan reverently placed the cap behind his block.

'In the heats I had brainwashed myself to pile on the pressure; to go for a psychological advantage; to make the Russians watch me and worry. For the final I decided on a new tactic. I decided to relax because this time I was going for the world record too, wasn't I?'

Silence, a bang, six splashes sound as one. Shrill screams pierce the hall. 'Twenty five metres out I realised my plan wasn't working. I forced my will to concentrate as it had in the heats. I had an unbelievable turn. Even the Russians said it was unbelievable. But that was a big mistake.

'I thought the turn had won it for me. Out of it, the water suddenly ripped; you must never "tear" the water: I did: it left bubbles behind my fingers and made me spin terribly, like an outboard motor just out of the water; it could have been fatal. For 20 metres I couldn't get it under control. I screamed at myself, "Duncan, if you're not going to get it under control you're not going to win!"'

He climbed out of the pool and, gilded at the breast, refused to doff his Dad's old cloth cap even for a victorious happy and glorious national anthem. Then, mysteriously, he lost the hat. It is still somewhere in Moscow. But it had done its stuff.

Three years on he is at Leeds not only as a bald, beaming beacon, a totem for the new tyros in the tank to emulate, but as

British swimming's most remarkable young professional entrepreneur. The dyslexic is putting his university degree in business studies to good use with charm, appeal and originality. He still stammers and stumbles if he has to read a speech in public: 'but without notes I can rabbit on for hours.'

Competitive swimming, he says, receives a lot of stick because it's such a 'young' sport. Children are so good at it, although he concedes, some parents and coaches drive them too hard. 'Youngsters take it up, work tremendously hard, but then finish by the time they are 20.

'There are three basic ways of succeeding – an unquestionable belief in your own ability, an unquestionable belief in your coach's ability, and an understanding of the whole philosophy of the drive and motivation of competition. In swimming, most wholly trust in the second method, a few in the first but most of them are too young to go for the third.

'Up to a point it is the same in other sports. Like that amazing man Wilkie. Ask him why he's great and he'll just say, "I suppose I was blessed with some talent." Seb Coe will say the same. I don't know what someone like Steve Ovett would answer, but it would certainly be something different. There has to be a philosophy behind what he does and has achieved. It might be so personal he won't let it go to anyone.'

There is no doubt about it, he says, that everyone, 'even the dumbest of dyslexic dropouts', has to be good at something. 'I must be statistically right. Well, just think of all the possible things there are in the world that someone could be good at. A billion billion things. The luck is discovering what you're good at. Then the most crucial thing is recognising that you've found it. Me? Sure I was just lucky.' For my part, I'll be looking differently at moving froth in future.

3 December, 1983   **Frank Keating**

Zola dances a soft-shoe shuffle

Zola Budd has signed a new and lucrative deal with Brooks Shoes—leaving the men from Nike cursing—but says she may still run barefoot in the 3,000 metres. 'Perhaps I might try out the shoes in the heats,' she concedes in her tremulous, almost inaudible, heavily accented squeak. It leaves the shoe salesmen still sweating on their commission. 'Jeez, how d'ya deal with this kid?'

Americans loop the loop at that sort of cool business talk from an 18-year-old. A phenomenon that they did not create, for once, is one heck of a novelty here and when Miss Budd arrived last Thursday the airport howdy'a do in the press lounge was, as someone remarked, like the first couple of scrums in a Bristol v. Gloucester midweek rugger match.

She has now been, reluctantly I fancy, delivered by the *Daily Mail* to the British Olympic team. Her newspaper minders still lurk but they seem to have even bigger problems than Miss Budd to attend to—not only the editor himself but the chairman, Viscount Rothermere, is coming to see what makes Zola run and get their money's worth—and it would be a calamity if their tickets were to go astray.

The Mailmen had a last, narrow squeak on the plane coming over. Zola was invited up front to see the captain flying the machine. 'Why me?' said the shrewd Little Red Riding Hood. 'Because,' said the steward innocently, 'there's a freelance photographer with good contacts at the *Daily Express* waiting up there to take your picture.' Nice try.

While the *Mail* and their scoop were fair game—and, to be sure, the righteous desperation in the eyes of previously sane men in defending the chequebook journalism has enhanced the gaiety of an English summer—they have handed over their small and delicately formed treasure into an even more impenetrable vault—the British Amateur Athletics Board. Nigel Cooper, the general secretary, turned the key.

215

In San Diego yesterday the former South African student of political science at the University of the Orange Free State was wheeled in to meet the American press. As you can imagine, the shutters were clicking like a million crickets at sundown on the Veldt.

'Come on,' pleaded Cooper like a nervous school-master. 'Let the dog see the rabbit!' It would have been a good phrase if he had predetermined it. Then he laid out ground rules: 'Miss Budd has graciously consented to meet you . . . anyone who wants to talk politics can leave now . . . we do not want any embarrassing questions.'

Embarrassing? Well, he said it.

The next 20 minutes were punctuated by such loaded inquiries as: 'When you line up to run will you think of other South African runners unable to make the trip?' Or: 'Win or lose, will you be going back to live next week in South Africa?' Or: 'Deep down, would you rather win the gold for England or for South Africa?' And so on.

At each Cooper leapt in—'We will not accept that question.' Zola, gold granny spectacles glinting, tiny pearl ear rings in her lobes, above her brand new Brooks Shoes T-shirt, awaited, wide-eyed, the next anodyne, allowable query.

'Yes, I think Mary Decker a very, very good athlete and I admire her very much. After I saw her on TV at home in Bloemfontein . . . but I'll be running against many other runners . . . and, yes, I'll decide my strategy as I go along . . . and whether I run barefoot or not . . . and certainly I have been homesick. Isn't it natural for people to miss home? Don't you?'

It was touching when she said, so softly to have the whole American media corps cupping one great hairy hand to their ear and scribbling like mad with the other: 'I just want to run. Running has allowed me to see the world and meet all these people. Running had helped me discover myself. When I run I feel so good. It is so difficult for me to describe the pleasure I get. It has made me discover what I can do and what I can't do.'

It doesn't hold up well in the re-telling, but it was a very moving passage.

I thought of the last time I saw Zola—barefoot in the park at Birmingham a few weeks ago. That press conference, permission *Daily Mail*, was run by Marea Hartman, secretary of women's amateur athletics.

When someone asked Miss Budd if she missed her animals back home on the farm, Miss Hartman looked at us and sneeringly muttered: 'She's surrounded by enough animals here at this moment.' Yet even then Miss Hartman must have been planning her story that has run for two weeks now in the *News of the World*—'Secrets of the dorm in the Olympic village' and 'Not many of my girls are virgins' . . . It's a funny old life.

So it was that some of the British team from here went on a bus trip across the Mexican border on Saturday. On the way back, Zola's coach and Svengali, Pieter Labuschagne, was apparently a little worried that his South African passport might upset the US border guards who are very strict there. He sailed through. So did Zola. But the journey was nevertheless held up.

The border officials were giving the fifth degree to one of Zola's new team colleagues, who was born with a British passport. Why did she want to enter the US? etc, etc. All the usual hateful rigmarole. You've guessed it. She was a black girl from Birmingham.

31 July, 1984   **Frank Keating**

Panic stations

Having flirted with floods from Typhoon Herbert in Thailand, it was with a sense of persecution that I learned in Hong Kong that Typhoon Joe was on the way.

Joe did not at first seem booked for Hong Kong, but dithered lethargically out in the South China Sea. It would take a few steps, towards China, then chassé west towards Hainan, then go back on the China tack. The result of this indecisive behaviour, however, was a Hong Kongish drift, so they hoisted Typhoon Signal One.

'What does it go up to?' I asked a Chinese person. 'What's the scale for typhoons?'

'Ten,' he replied. 'Ten, typhoon is here.'

Plainly, One was nothing to worry about. I went off to the Tiger Balm Gardens, named after the panacea that made $20 million for a couple of Chinese brothers, and thought the gardens equally useless. Then up to the Peak, where the rich have a permanent view of the 'world's second most beautiful harbour'.

Marred by haze, it came second to the view of the clusters of Mercs and Rolls-Royces adjacent to the pools of the tycoons. But several hundred hopefuls photographed the ships riding sedately at anchor, through steamed-up lenses.

The rain fell straight. Our 14-seater bus was held up for a stream of ambulances carrying casualties from another bus that had turned over on the slippery hill.

At Happy Hour in the Yum Sing Bar, the resident foxfaces mingled with the visiting kind and there was more talk of water – this time the needs of six million people. It has always been an acute problem – see Bruce Shepherd's account of the Imperial sanitation initiatives in the (first) *Hong Kong Guide* of 1893. The population had swelled to 200,000 and tourists were coming through in torrents. Now China provides 30 per cent of the water supply. They have only to turn it off . . .

The only mention of Typhoon Joe was dismissive. 'It's out of season. It'll blow itself out. We had Ellen in September; that was nasty, but it filled our quota.'

So perhaps it was the 1997 prognosis and the plight of the Hong Kong dollar that lent the talk a baleful flavour.

'Six months ago I'd have signed for another contract without hesitation, but now I'm not sure. I've started noticing how they spit all the time.' – English lawyer in government service.

'If I want to make Major I have to sign on for *eleven years!* But I'm not selling my ovaries to the Corps.' – Irish Captain of Midwives.

'I signed up for *life* when I married. As of now I've served 28 years. The marriage lasts because I'm travelling all the time.' – American Singer salesman.

'You better not go out with Chinese girls, unless you give

a false name. To go out with them is a commitment. You rat on it and their relatives come beating at the door.' – Irish Captain.

Some were only talking about next day: 'They say optics are the best bargain and I'd be tempted to get a pair of specs but unfortunately my eyesight's perfect.'

'I hate all this bargaining. I wish they'd come out with the price and be done with it.'

And some only stared down into their drinks and said nothing until the Happy Hour was up.

I padded out into the night, with the neon Chinese characters shimmering in the drizzle, and the hawkers grimly cooking in stalls rigged in the lee of bamboo scaffolding. I walked through Wan Chai and Happy Valley, which takes its name from the horse race track, to Food Street.

In London if you go to Bread Street or Milk Street or Pudding Lane, you can't buy these commodities, but in Hong Kong Food Street is nothing but food. They say you could eat out for several years without using the same restaurant twice, and Food Street would anyway take care of the first month. A watery moon sulked over Hung Hom and the harbour as I opted for a Szechuen establishment. It was a mistake. To eat Chinese one should go in a mob. As it was, I sat alone at a great round table laid for eight, like King Arthur when the Knights were all away on assignment.

By next morning, Joe had stopped going round in circles and they had hoisted Typhoon Signal Three. But they had also hoisted fresh laundry, and I set off across the water with seven in hand to haggle Kowloon-side, try the rural delights of the New Territories and take the pulse at the Chinese border.

The State Ferries are nice little green-painted vessels, 50 cents downstairs, 70 cents up. For the extra you get a windowed cabin, while those below have merely lashed tarpaulins to keep out the blown spume. The trip is over in eight minutes, but in that time the passengers achieve catatonic immobility, to be jolted back to frenzied life only by impact with the further shore.

It was a bit windy, Kowloon-side, and the fitful sun had yielded to squadrons of cloud. Looking back from the famous Peninsula Hotel, I could see hurrying figures on the quay silhouetted against the storm froth with their umbrellas blown sideways to make star shapes.

It is a common tactic when bargaining to say you'll come back another time. But my vendor trumped this by saying he was closing his shop and would not reopen that afternoon. Why not?

He replied pityingly, 'You do not know? Typhoon Signal Eight has been hoisted.' The shutters of his shop crashed down.

Eight! How could it be Eight already? What had happened to Four, Five, Six and Seven? 'Is no Four, Five, Six, Seven. Typhoon signals only One, Three, Eight, Ten. Eight, everything must close.'

Like tennis, then: 15, 30, 40, Game. I was outraged at being deprived of China. But anything that compelled a Hong Kong shopkeeper to curtail his selling in normal hours had to be taken seriously. Everything was shutting down. People were running.

Out on the gunmetal sea, boats were sliding away to the typhoon shelters. Six weeks before, when Ellen struck, many had dragged their anchors and a dozen wrecks littered rocks of nearby islands. At the ferry port a notice was chalked on a blackboard: 'Typhoon Signal Eight has been hoisted. Ferries will stop running any moment.'

But not, presumably, in mid-harbour, and one was ready to go – I glimpsed stragglers scrambling aboard. But the long passage beyond the turnstiles was ominously empty. I trotted forward – and found I had no coins but some Thai bahts.

Gearing myself to vault, I felt a tap on my shoulder – an official. Perhaps I should now wait out the typhoon in gaol. I recalled that the only survivor of the Mont Pelée eruption in Martinique had been a convict. But he wordlessly plied the machine and it sprang open. (The 50 cent entry, but this was no time to negotiate an upgrading.)

Standing to windward, where there was more room, I was approached by a youngish man with two dabs of moustache that exactly matched his eyebrows. He came close and said, 'Want to meet a girl?' 'What girl?' I asked, bemused. 'Nice girl,' he said.

The late Kenneth Tynan, who proudly wrote of having goosed a girl in a plane over Gander, might have thought it a good way of mitigating a typhoon. I could only reply lamely, 'No thanks, I have a rather tight schedule.' 'Typhoon a long time coming,' he said. (No one else knew this, but he was right.) Disembarking, I noticed him wheeling a bike and wondered if he would have borne me off to the girl on the handlebars.

Back on the Island, Central was seething. Taxi drivers were locking their cars and squeezing aboard trams and buses. These were not only stuffed with people, but their indicators read 'Depot'. Furthermore as the whole town had apparently left for home at once, they were all motionless. Everybody I spoke to in the long queues replied in Cantonese.

The great empty buildings were shut, but I found a basement bar still open, and a friendly resident foxface with a whisky. He advised me to go straight home. How, I asked. 'You could walk to the Lee Garden Hotel in an hour.' How long had I got, I asked. 'I don't know,' he said, and grinned. 'Half an hour, perhaps.'

He started out nonchalant, but as he warmed to his theme of previous typhoons, splitting trees at 160 mph, and tossing cars and ships about, he frightened himself. He recalled that his own house was on the exposed west of the island, and his plants would need bringing in. Abruptly he scuttled from the bar.

So I walked in eerie solitude, meeting nobody at first but four schoolgirls huddled under a flyover. The wind was gusting about 50 mph and my umbrella was mangled within minutes. The rain thrashed through my cagoule, filled my shoes and shoulder bag. Disaster books suggest you take refuge from typhoons in a ditch, but even in construction-mad Hong Kong ditches never come by when you need them. Sometimes I passed empty taxis. The first had raised the fare to $30, the second to $50. By the end I was saving $100 by not taking them. *Tout comprendre c'est tout pardonner:* Typhoon Signal Eight cancels their insurance.

I lost my way several times, imagining myself whirled sky-wards like Judy Garland in *The Wizard of Oz*, but at last squelched into my room on the 20th floor (would it sway?) as the phone rang. It was a Hong Kong Radio reporter wanting an interview on my feelings about the place as a tourist spot. He'd be with me in an hour. He never came.

Neither did Joe. Like all the frustrated guests, I had to eat in the hotel, and fell asleep soon after, watching television. I woke to hear a newscaster say Joe had veered off and 'petered out in a tropical storm over China'. I hoped 'petered out' said it for the people in China too.

28 November, 1983   **Alex Hamilton**

On dog-watch in the dictionary

Anyone can do any amount of work provided it isn't the work they are supposed to be doing. That wise remark was made by someone like Robert Benchley, and since there never was anyone like Robert Benchley it must have been made by him. At any rate, I have just proved to myself the truth of those words, yet again.

I have a thousand and one pressing things to do – changing the light bulb in the bathroom, finding good homes for the kittens, writing the best novel since *Anna Karenina*, that sort of thing. Instead, I have frittered away more hours than I care to admit in investigating the subject of dog's dinners.

It all started when someone asked what was the difference between a dog's dinner and a dog's breakfast. Off the top of my head I said that I thought that if someone had made a complete mess of something then they had made a dog's breakfast of it, or a pig's ear. On the other hand, if they personally looked a complete mess, then they looked like a dog's dinner. Like an unmade bed. Like something the cat brought in.

This answer served the immediate purpose, but I wasn't fully satisfied. It kept niggling at me, this dog's dinner, so after closing time, instead of changing the bulb in the bathroom, I started reading dictionaries. Dogs everywhere. Dog-collar (clergyman's) 1860s; dog Latin; enough to make a dog laugh, Pepys; a hair of the dog that bit you (a drink taken to counteract drunkenness) 1546; every dog has his day 1561; a dog's nose and a maid's knees are always cold 1639; dog in the manger 1573; and so on.

The *Shorter Oxford* didn't have dog's dinner, but the *Collins English Dictionary* very rarely lets you down. There it was, dog's dinner, meaning dressed smartly or ostentatiously. Exactly the opposite of what I thought it meant. Not at all like something the cat brought in. More like the cat's whiskers, or the cat's pyjamas, or the bee's knees.

It's annoying as hell to find you've been using a word wrong all your life. It makes you feel like goddam Mrs Malaprop, if you want to know the truth. (I've been reading *The Catcher in the Rye* again, and the style is sort of infectious. It really is.) So what I did was suddenly remember that word that old General de Gaulle used in the May events of 1968. Reform yes, he said, the *chienlit* no. Since by *chienlit* he clearly meant a state of terrible confusion, it was important to know whether *chien* (dog) *lit* (bed) was translated as dog's dinner or breakfast. The idea seemed promising.

Standard French dictionaries were no help, which was no surprise since they are no good on slang and anyway nobody had heard of a *chienlit* before De Gaulle used the word. At the time, *Le Monde* even had a long and learned discussion of the subject. So I sallied forth and acquired a copy of the new *Harrap's English–French, French–English Slang Dictionary*.

The cover of the book says it contains 50,000 modern words and expressions from the colloquial to the very vulgar. You can say that again. Practically every word you can think of in either language has a dirty meaning of some kind. Did you know that in French marmite is a prostitute? There are 81 synonyms for penis in English, and 87 in French, including *andouille à col roulé* (roll-necked sausage), cyclops, chipolata, cigar with a moustache, macaroni, zizi, and zob.

Anyone can spend any amount of time reading a dictionary provided they are not reading about the word they are supposed to be looking up. If you don't believe me, try *Harrap's Slang Dictionary*. Everyone knows that the French are frogs and the English are *rosbifs*, but did you know that we are also *homards* (lobsters) because of the colour we go when we are exposed to the sun? And to have a period is *avoir les anglais?*

Not only are there masses of extraordinary expressions for everything to do with all bodily functions, but a great many words which seem calculated to lead to embarrassing misunderstandings. In French slang, a WC can be a telephone, and a telephone can be a gherkin or a snail. And be careful if you ask for parsley in France. It can mean pubic hair. In France, feet are penguins, and in English they are among other things beetle-crushers, hoofs, plates of meat, tootsies, trotters, and dogs.

Ah yes, dogs. I turned to *chienlit* and what did I find? *Sapristi!* It's nothing to do with a dog's bed. This should have been obvious because the word is feminine and *chien* is masculine. What De Gaulle actually said was *chie-en-lit:* shit in bed. French friends I have discussed this with have all been amazed by this explanation of the word, partly because they all get it confused with *chiendent* which is a weed. However a phone call to a learned gentleman in the Auvergne (there's no limit to the research one can undertake on a subject like this) confirmed that the mighty Robert dictionary says that the word was used in this sense in 1534.

The next thing was to look up dog's dinner, which was a matter of a few hours since I was constantly distracted by such expressions as 'a bit of how's your father' (*une partie de jambes en l'air*) and words like guesstimate (*calculer au pifomètre*). Finally I got to dog. A gay dog, a lucky dog, a sly dog, my dogs are killing me, dog-end, a dog's life, to go to the dogs, top dog, let sleeping dogs lie (in French it's the cat that you don't wake up), to see a man about a dog (*aller aux WC, uriner, arroser les fleurs*). In the middle of these was 'dressed up/got up like a dog's dinner' which in French is *en grand tralala/sur son trente-et-un/sapé comme un milord*. So it's not a mess at all. In big tralala. On his thirty-one. Dressed up like a milord.

This only raises more problems. Why do we dress up to the nines in England when the French are on their thirty-one? What is so smart about a dog's dinner? And what is a dog's breakfast? It will be some time before there's a new bulb in the bathroom.

26 April, 1984   **Richard Boston**

The great age of John Gielgud

Here he comes, with that quick, lightfooted cat's walk, his back still as straight as a dancer's, domed head carried theatrically high, sharp eyes without glasses, and dressed with all the imposing sombreness of a Harley Street specialist. On the verge

224

of his eightieth birthday, John Gielgud looks and sounds remarkably undamaged by time.

He stands posing for our photographer on a stairway of the Garrick Club, moaning gently about the gathering fuss which attends his octogenarian celebrations. He would much rather be looking at the new exhibition at the Tate, he would sooner be at home in the country where he lives with his friend of many years, Martin Hensler. And yes, he dreads saying too much to journalists, and dropping sufficient bricks to ruin even a sliver of his famous reputation.

And, of course, there is birthday dinner at the Garrick, attended by the club's unlikely patron the Duke of Edinburgh. Should he write his speech or say a few impromptu words, he wonders. And then there is the danger he will weep some of those famous, easy Terry tears if he's not fully prepared.

'Why not cry,' I suggested. 'It would be wonderful to see you crying.' He gives one of his inscrutable, withering looks, like a judge noticing something indecorous in the well of his court, 'Oh, no that wouldn't do at all.'

Now he sits in an empty retiring room at the Garrick and sets out on a quick voyage over and through his brilliant career. This, and the fact of his birthday, is being marked by two books, one, *The Ages of Gielgud*, with a collection of essays by friends, colleagues and critics, is a 'tribute': the other, by Gyles Brandreth, described as a celebration, is chiefly notable for its feast of photographs: like a moving picture show of Gielgud's life.

The Gielgud of the famous early stages in the 1920s and 1930s seems worlds away from the mellow Indian summer actor of today. There he is, unrecognisable in a photograph in Gyles Brandreth's book as The Poet Butterfly in *The Insect Play* – soulful in huge wings, pumps, a green laurel wreath on his fair hair, and hands outstretched.

That was 1923, his second professional appearance and his first flop. But just over ten years on, according to Alec Guinness's beautiful evocation in *The Ages of Gielgud*, there is Gielgud strutting in the stalls, the perfect martinet director, striking terror into the hearts of those young actors he was directing in *Hamlet*, with Gielgud his own and perfect Prince:

'Oh don't fidget, Frith Banbury! Alec Guinness, you are

gabbling. Banbury, your spear is crooked. Now turn upstage. No, not you. You, turn the other way. Oh, why can't you all act. Get someone to teach you to act.' So Guinness, the terrified prentice boy, remembers it in affectionate horror.

Gielgud remembers himself then too as well. 'I had no idea how I terrified the small people,' he says, referring of course to the fact that the likes of Alec Guinness loomed very tiny in those days. 'I think I was very ruthless with them, even though I believed I was very cosy and thought everybody was on good terms with me. But I think I did work well with a lot of people. Harry Andrews, for example, who became such a splendid actor was very shy of me and terrified of me. And I used to give him a terrible time at rehearsals. And I even gave Alec a bad time without noticing it really. I was so busy with the whole production.'

That sort of alert but distracted vagueness, the butterfly quicksilver intelligence passing from the vital to the trivial and back again, rather typifies Gielgud then and now. So too does a nostalgic but clear-eyed relish for old theatrical ways. It was 'an old school tie' period, with the men wearing suits for rehearsal and no question of any actor calling him John.

'Marie Tempest,' he recalls in amused enthusiasm, 'used to make the actors come down to rehearse in dinner jackets and she used to put on evening dress to come to the theatre. She loved all that and insisted on it; that sort of martinet discipline was a wonderful thing in its way. People don't have it now. But you'll find it in all people of my generation: Peggy, Wendy or Olivier and Richardson – I've never known any of them to be unpunctual or lacking in polite manners and courtesy.'

But if this remembering makes Gielgud sound like a splendid antique in a roomful of Conran furniture, then the impression is wrong. Michael Billington in his useful essay in *The Ages of Gielgud*, is one of the only contributors to interpret the actor's career freshly and point to his willingness to take risks and experiment, right from the 1957 Prospero, girded unexpectedly in towering rage – and he might also have mentioned his 1955 King Lear in its Japanese space age designs, overwhelmingly reviled for its modern strangeness.

Strange would also be the least impolite adjective to describe an extraordinary essay by Harold Hobson in *The Ages of Gielgud*. It is a triumph of sustained innuendo; willing to wound and yet afraid to strike, breathing sweet niceness as well as stooping to below-the-belt blows. Hobson admits with something close to pride that the central idea in his contribution is 'perverse, brash, impertinent, and reckless.' As a self-criticism this is flattering. Hobson suggests that 'many problems' in the actor's career would have been 'eased' if Gielgud had had a wife and children, and some 'sickening depths' would have been avoided. Sir Harold is, of course, entitled to his surmises, even if they are factually incorrect, but his long obsession with Gielgud's marital state and his fantasies of the actor's lack of 'abiding domestic love' are surely matters best left out of an eightieth birthday tribute, and wrestled with in the privacy of the critic's own home.

However great Gielgud's willingness to experiment within classic moulds, his foray into the new dramatic territory came comparatively late. He concedes that theatrically speaking the 1950s was not always very happy. 'I had an unlucky streak. The plays were not very well chosen.' He may have been impressed and excited by *Look Back in Anger* – 'I felt this a new generation. I don't know how they live, but I see from their despair how they must be,' – but he was still to be found popping up inscrutably in Noel Coward's *Nude with a Violin*. 'I loathed it and I was very unhappy. It was a great success but nobody came round to see me afterwards or wrote good notices.'

But after the call came from the new generation, the chances were duly seized. When he and Ralph Richardson went to the Royal Court for David Storey's *Home* they were both very anxious. 'We expected to find very tough treatment from these young people – you, know students and very young people. But they were very nice and I think it amused them to find the difference between two generations, and if you bridge that you get on very well.'

It is this diffidence which is also true to Gielgud: 'One's confidence is rather apt to go down.' Without Peter Hall or Lindsay Anderson he rather doubts whether he would have had the courage to take the leap into the unknown new waves. Whereas in the old days he would merely say to Binkie

Beaumont, the powerful impresario, I want to do this play, and it was virtually cast and arranged within a weekend.

And it was in those days too that he had complete theatrical certainty; it was, after all, Gielgud who persuaded Ralph Richardson and Alec Guinness not to take part in *Waiting for Godot*; 'Somebody asked me to do *Godot* again the other day. And I said, having persuaded Ralph and Alec not to do it I really couldn't do it myself now. It would be betraying their trust.'

Now he thinks perhaps it was wrong to keep away from the theatre of the absurd. And now too he is beginning to think about returning to the stage. It is seven years since he was last seen on the boards – in Julian Mitchell's half-baked *Half Life*. But he is being very careful.

First he admits that he might return if 'the right thing comes along.' Then he suggests it is the unexpectedness of theatre which makes it exciting and rehearsals which he misses. Finally he says there has been an 'intriguing' offer, of a classical role, at the National. 'I'm being very cagey. I don't want to play eight times a week or twice a day, and I don't want to tour. I'm being very difficult.' He also, and rightly, requires a great deal of money. I urge him on. But he says he wants only to play a part now if he is convinced that he can do it better than anyone else, and he takes much convincing.

He broods about his own character in reaction to all this and concluded that in the 1920s he and his friends were inclined to send themselves up before anyone else could. 'It was a very clever move, but it also made one very self-conscious. And I think perhaps I kept it on too long.' He hardly seems self-conscious to me, but there it is. 'I think I am. That's why I like acting, covering up, sort of escapist. I always took a very escapist view of the whole business. I still do. I like imaginary worlds. I'm still, secretly, really rather an old romantic.'

30 March, 1984   **Nicholas de Jongh**

Flying: a joystick to be held

The Schneider Trophy is not up for grabs again. It sits in its permanent home in the Royal Aero Club with its winged figure, symbol of speed, lightly kissing a waveborne zephyr with a sensuality that is eternally French. Britain, as every schoolboy used to know, won the French armaments millionaire's trophy outright in 1931 with a third successive victory in a Supermarine seaplane from which the Spitfire metamorphosed.

Its designer, Reginald 'R.J.' Mitchell, legendary fighter against reactionary elements in the Ministries and undoubted genius, put everything he knew into the Supermarine S.5 and S.6B which beat the oposition into a cocked hat. Mind you, the first version, the S.4, crashed during practice at Baltimore through wing flutter and, thereafter, everyone agreed that maybe the pilots needed special training.

And when it came to 1931, the crucial year in which Britain could achieve outright victory, the British Government withdrew its support for the Supermarine project and success ultimately rested on a donation of £100,000 from Lady Houston. In the end, Britain flew the course alone.

There is, in any case, a slight tarnish on the trophy or rather on the jingoism it tends to generate, because the United States should have won it back in the twenties when the Curtiss CR-3 and the Wright racers dominated the field. Had the US chosen to fly over the course in 1924 when all the opposition pulled out, the trophy would now be sitting in a Washington museum. As it happened, this gesture of sportsmanship—putting the race off for a year—let the Europeans in.

When the nations clashed again in Baltimore in 1925 the US —with the Curtiss biplane—won again, a second successive victory that would have been the third had all the races been run. By 1926, things had changed. Mario Castoldi had designed the brilliant Macchi M.33 which, had its engineering detail been as good as its aerodynamics, would probably have carried the trophy off to Italy. It won in 1926 and the US Government promptly withdrew its support from the race. But the Macchi never won again.

From then on it was all Mitchell, Supermarine and Napier Lion engines and finally, in 1931, the masterly SN.6B powered by the incredible Rolls-Royce 'R' engine that was rated at 2,350 horsepower. This, of course, was what the old Schneider Trophy was about. It was intended to compress development times, to push forward the belief, held very strongly by Jacques Schneider, that the real future of aviation lay in seaplanes, perhaps in giant amphibians, bringing a warring world closer together.

Psychiatrists can probably explain why Schneider, like Nobel, had visions of technology for peace from a high perch in the structure of technology for war. But Mitchell, Supermarine and Rolls-Royce, having convinced the men at the Ministry that high power and high performance went together, set about producing the elliptical wing Spitfire which US aircraft manufacturers still regard as a production nightmare, and for which all who flew them thanked God.

Those who delve into aviation history might like to take a look in at the Mitchell Museum this summer, for the British Hovercraft Corporation has just completed the rebuilding of the last remaining SN.6 (N248), which was built for the 1929 contest, originally fitted with the Napier Lion engine and then refurbished as a 6A in 1931 with the new Rolls-Royce engine. It never flew in the Schneider race in its enlarged form but it might have been third in the 1929 race had not its pilot, Flying Officer 'Batchy' Atcherley, lost his goggles, got smothered in oil, and inadvertently turned inside one of the course pylons. ('Ever been lost,' said Pilot Officer Prune, 'why, only the other day . . .')

Prune is a little esoteric for the uninitiated, and it may not be enough to say that his was a well-known figure in the early forties, flying upwind to cool his engine down and generally having finger trouble. He too is somehow part of the legend and, if he's still actually alive (through incredibly good luck) then we should apologise and retire quietly. But neither Prune, nor Mitchell, nor the Schneider Trophy will ever go away; they are spirits in the aviation cupboard which, from time to time, must be released for a day, lest the world withers without them.

That is why, three years ago, with the unacknowledged backing of Rolls-Royce and Vickers, there was something like a Schneider Trophy Race held over the old Solent Schneider course to mark the 50th anniversary of the founding of the trophy. Historians might puzzle a little over this half century since most records suggest that the trophy was introduced after the Gordon Bennet Cup race banquet in Paris in 1912. But who wants to quibble about a year of two, especially as there is to be something like a Schneider Trophy Race again.

This one, again over the Solent course (three laps, round pylons, with a total distance of 135 miles), is to be known as the Digital Schneider Trophy Race. This has nothing whatever to do with the Einstein Clock Paradox, nor with time even, in the sense that the old Schneider races went to the fastest. It is to do with home computers, a grand day out and Rollo Swaveley, whose activities continue to make the world of sport possible. For Digital are putting up the prizes, the Royal Aero Club's racing arm is doing the organising, and the Pipers, Cessnas and others (will Spencer Flack be there in his hybrid Spit?), will set off on their handicapped way on June 24.

It will be a kind of mini-King's Cup race, with everyone crossing the line together for the benefit of the TV cameras and the waiting crowds. Over the sea the aircraft will be down at mast height, pulling up to 500 feet wherever they cross over the coast to make a turn. The turns are less than 100 degrees to keep G-forces down—you are hardly on your wing-tip before you come out again, bang on line and at full bore—and nobody will get oil on their goggles.

But there will be some, assailed by the thin engine notes, who will hear the deep, sonorous, unmistakable note of the Rolls-Royce 'R' and its offspring, Merlin and Griffon, booming over the course and over the Channel. It you never sat behind one, you never lived. Old men have their memories and the young must have their toys. But this race is something else.

8 May, 1984 **Anthony Tucker**

Playing the game

I played cricket again last Saturday. I had not previously lifted a bat in anger for almost thirty years, but some weeks ago—against the advice of family and friends—I agreed to take part in an invitation match between the St Paul's All Stars and Councillor Richard Knowles's XI. Dick Knowles is the Leader of the Birmingham City Council, a representative of the constituency which I have the honour to serve at Westminster, and was, when I most recently contested that seat in the Labour interest, my election agent. St Paul's is an area which voted particularly heavily for me at the conclusion of the victorious campaign. In fact, what with one thing and another, I had to play—despite my apprehensions.

Some of my anxieties are best not publicly mentioned—and were more or less dispelled by the purchase of a batting box at a local sports shop. The three concerns to which it is decent to admit in print were clothes, muscles and—most agonising of all—the probability that I would make an idiot of myself. Years ago, when I sometimes got my foot to the pitch of the ball and always whitened my pads on a Friday night, I swore never to become a pot-bellied ancient who waddled across village greens as a caricature of a real cricketer. But I decided that invitation match had been organised in order that the likes of me could appear ridiculous. Humiliation would be a triumph.

The decision to treat it all as a joke ended my sartorial dilemma. I possess a pair of cream canvas trousers which have been bleached from fawn by a series of Tuscan summers. Together with an old white shirt they made a fair copy of proper cricketing gear. Indeed, they were *too* like the real thing for a man who treated the game as a joke. I toyed with the idea of pinstripes and braces. But in the end compromised on light blue all over.

I knew that the muscles were beyond help. At the pre-match throw-about I could not lob a return to the wicketkeeper without causing an agonising pain in my shoulder. I had a despairing suspicion that younger fielders had joined a conspiracy to protect me from bending down. One youth, instead of tossing the ball in my direction, carried it across the pitch and pressed it into my hand. I recalled the mixture of compassion and contempt which I felt for my father during a game between parents and youth clubs when he was six years younger than I am now. Then I remembered that I was only playing for fun.

Councillor Knowles's team had, naturally enough, a municipal flavour. Barney Downey, sometime chairman of the county council, was in the side. And the corporation's staffs were represented by John Williams, the senior caretaker of Nine Stiles Comprehensive; Mr Huge, the headmaster of Ladypool Primary School, and a fireman who—for reasons which I assumed to be associated with a desire to popularise his service —insisted on playing in rubber thigh boots, flame-proof overalls and a traditional helmet. It was when the fireman offered to open the bowling that Councillor Knowles suggested that since I claimed such knowledge of cricket I ought to assume the effective captaincy. I readily agreed, tossed up, won, and put our opponents in to bat.

It then became clear that although I was treating the game with a carefully contrived frivolity, the St Paul's opening batsmen were playing to win. Both wore immaculate white flannels and shirts with badges in the corner of their collars. And they walked out to the wicket with the air of men who owned their bats. They took 23 off the fireman's first six balls. And I decided that every volunteer bowler would have two self-sacrificial overs. By the time that my turn came round each of the open pair had mysteriously stood on his wicket immediately after scoring 50. My fourth ball turned sharply—after the second bounce. The bewildered new batsman dollied up a catch to mid-on. It was my first wicket since Bridlington beach in 1948. Although we were only playing for fun I felt very pleased with myself.

The All Stars scored 174 by the end of their 15 allotted overs, a total within which they were contained largely because John Williams insisted on bowling as if he had played cricket before.

Unfortunately, he retired hurt after turning his ankle on the edge of the matting wicket and we were left with only nineteen of the twenty batsmen who made up our eleven. I decided that councillors Knowles and Downey should open, followed by two young men who claimed to be accomplished batsmen. Knowles made a particularly brave sight in a borrowed scarlet cap which reminded me (for several reasons) of the one which Steerforth waved at the point of death. He survived both Downey, B. and the two self-confident young men.

I then realised that the fate of the game hung on me. The first ball which I received was pitched a foot outside my leg stump. I swept it expertly off my pads. But unfortunately Dick Knowles was not ready for my call. As well as being run out, he sustained a painful muscle injury and limped off, struggling to maintain the socialist fraternity which had previously typified our relationship. My second ball flew even wider down the leg side. I swept again and missed. Long-off appealed. The wicketkeeper drew my attention to the umpire's raised finger. I walked proudly back to the tea-tent attempting to stifle a temptation to warn the errant official that he need never waste his time visiting my Friday-night advice bureau. I tried to recall that as we were only playing for fun my duck did not matter.

But it did matter to me. After thirty years all the old emotions were renewed—hatred of the bowler, contempt for the umpire, envy of Mr Huge batting away as I could have batted, the desperate knowledge that the mistake having been made the error cannot be redeemed. Not until next year that is: Councillor Knowles' XI versus the St Paul's All Stars is to become a regular fixture. I shall return; only playing for fun, of course.

14 July, 1984   **Roy Hattersley**

Patient merit

Limbo is a lovely land. I clung to it as long as I could, I have lived there, sort of, for nearly three months, hitched to an electrical machine that claimed to be, at least for a while, better than a body. And so indeed it was. Now it is returning to the real thing that is unnerving. Who wants life when there is limbo?

No one who ever had the choice.

I am told it was a pleasant sunny summer. I saw it, occasionally and indifferently, through a hospital window in south London. I could have asked no more, nor did I. Apparently they thought it was worth spending our money on the huge ray apparatus. It was flattering, but time-wasting, since the end is the same anyhow.

Perhaps it worked. In this context one doesn't talk of Cure, but of Arrest. The paradox is that Arrest means Liberation. So they sent me home, where if you want a prison you must make your own. This is not simple when you also have to make a living. Much easier to make a dying.

The huge advantage of a tolerant newspaper is the privilege of using it, once in a lifetime, not to entertain others but to discover oneself. Time, as they say, will tell. In the meantime one scribbles at random, grateful when even a sentence comes out right.

I am trying desperately to remember the thing I used to do. I use this space and your time to practise my lines again, groping to recall what I am supposed to be all about, because, until I discover that, there is no point in doing, or being, anything. Maybe there will be, maybe not.

In three short months, though they were long for me, I changed a lot, but the world changed more. In hospital it is not only difficult to keep abreast of what goes on outside, but the need to do so fades. More immediate things intervene. The Threat to Democracy means a lot less than what is, quite literally, a Pain in the Neck.

Anyhow, newspapers were all I ever knew. They have no meaning without context. Context now is the occasional reference to something before last spring. I study them now as a sort of practice-ground for memory, an attempt to make a context of my own.

The friendly schoolboy who distributes our ward's newspapers tell me that he sells 20 *Suns* and one *Guardian*: mine. He looks at me curiously. 'Were you a reporter?' I say: yes, used to be. 'Could I be one?' Sure, if you hurry up. And then

235

by and by you'll be in this bed and I'll be selling papers to you, and we'll all be out of work but Robert Maxwell.

Newspapers must be therapeutic; I am beginning, though only just, to feel better.

All those weeks ago, the more I groused and complained about the government the stronger I got; it needed my big mouth to be shut for a month or two for Thatcherism to start its collapse. Should I perhaps retire?

When I went to bed, Mrs Thatcher was invulnerable and her arrogance proclaimed it. Surrounded by her coterie of nervous nobodies, she had only to mention 'Falklands' to cue in the inane applause. Now three months have reduced her from sermons to squeaks. derided even by the pop-press which only yesterday was a crew of crawling yes-men. Her day is done and perhaps theirs too.

'Mrs Thatcher's post-Falklands halo has finally worn thin. She is seen as a callous authoritarian. In fact she was widely hated. . . .' In what paper was that? The *Daily Telegraph*, if you can believe me. There must be a creeping plague of sanity infecting the press. Even the *Economist* joined in gibes though putting its fingers before its lips.

Mrs Thatcher apart, there must be public figures other than Arthur Scargill, but from the papers and the TV news one would never know it. The miners' case seems to me just and proper; I feel just occasionally regretful that the whole debate, or non-debate, must be symbolised by two gentlemen as resolutely unattractive as Mr Scargill and Mr MacGregor, so wholly obsessed with their personal considerations that I realise (perhaps for the first time) how easy it is to become disenchanted with public men, of any kind.

One retreats, erratically, to reading. Someone gave me a book by Francis Pym that said nothing while claiming to be 'forthright'. The day Mr Pym becomes forthright will be the day when Lord Whitelaw becomes dynamic, or Michael Foot becomes unkind.

Apropos—three times Michael Foot has come all the way to the South Bank briefly to redeem my loneliness. Even for Michael Foot, this is a singular kindness. I am only regretful that in his new political solitude he has the time to spare on mine. Why is the Labour Party so sinfully ungrateful to its most honourable men?

For the rest, one cultivates one's own introspections. The face I see in the mirror—rarely now, since I no longer shave —is not what I remember, but more and more resembles an amateur Dracula. No wonder how totally unimportant one has always been to one's closest people. After the motions of regret (poor James, but he had it coming), absence becomes the norm and reappearance a chore.

Anyhow—hello world; remember me?

24 July, 1984   **James Cameron**

Index